I CROSSED THE LINE

THE LIAM DUNNE STORY

To John,

I always likened you to
this boy,

Happy Christmas,

Mark

with Damian Lawlor

Sliabh Bán Productions
P.O. Box No. 6369,
Fortfield, Dublin 6W.

Softback ISBN 0-9545829-2-6
Hardback ISBN 0-9545829-3-4

A CIP record of this book is available from the British Library.

Photography: Ray MacManus, Brendan Moran, Sportsfile
Additional photographs: Daily Telegraph, Syl Ivors
Layout and design: Mary Guinan, Temple of Design
Printed in Ireland by Future Print

Special thanks to Pat Duffy in Readymix for all his help and support.

ACKNOWLEDGEMENTS
(Liam Dunne)

Once my mind was made up to go ahead with this book, I decided to be straight down the line all the way. This is just the way I see things, it doesn't have to be right or wrong. I hope it's a good GAA book but I also hope it's a lot more than that.

There are many people I want to thank. My sisters Gráinne, Siobhán, Fiona and Ailish. My brothers, Kieran, Tomás and Seán. Through all the bad times we have stayed very close together, something that has been special to me. We were lucky to grow up together and have the craic, which is not a problem for the Dunnes.

To Tom, Willie, Mick and Jimmy and the Oulart-The-Ballagh boys of 1994 who made history by winning the club's first county title. To Liam, Rory, Seamus and the Wexford boys of 1996 – we got to the top of the world together lads and it was an honour to share the voyage with you. I want to say a special thanks to Andy and Patsy Roche, two people that played a big part in my life.

When times were bad and I sometimes felt there was no way out, my good friend Brendan O'Connor was always there. So too were Sport and Foxten. Liam Griffin was the same; a man who never put me wrong in life.

Three great hurling men rowed in behind me for this venture. John Doyle of the Cleary-Doyle Group was one of the main men who set up the Wexford Supporters Group, a great help to hurling and football in the county over the years.

Wexford Park would not be what it is today only for the work of Pat Neville, even if the man himself would not want to take the credit for any of it.

Anthony Darcy has been a friend of mine for a long time. He comes from Tinahely but has always held Wexford close to his heart. We had a few good days on the golf course together, although Anthony seems to spend a lot of his time in the bunkers.

Brian Carthy was the man who put the idea for a book in my head and his company, Sliabh Bán Productions Ltd, were a pleasure to deal with. Thanks Brian for your honesty, time and professionalism. It was a pleasure to work with you.

Mary Guinan put in some hard work and showed great patience in designing the book. I enjoyed your company, Mary, thanks for all your help.

Many hours were spent writing this book in the company of Damian Lawlor. I had never met or spoke to him before but over the months we were together working on this venture in Oulart and the Ashdown Park Hotel in Gorey, a friendship was made.

I feel now as if I have known Damian all my life. Having read the book it's only now that I realise how many ups and downs and twists and turns I have faced in my life. Damian put them together in a fantastic fashion. Thank you for your time and dedication. I have a new friend for life.

To the people of Wexford. All I ever wanted was to do my best for you. Thanks for all the support over the years.

ACKNOWLEDGEMENTS
(Damian Lawlor)

Life gets easier when you surround yourself with decent, genuine people. And I'm extremely lucky in that regard.

At the start, this was an exciting, daunting project to undertake but it quickly became more than just an assignment. After months of research I started writing in May. By June I was on a mission: To bring Liam Dunne's story to life and do it justice.

I had admired his hurling skills for several years from the terraces and reported on his many controversies from the press box but somehow, we had never met before February 2004. Suffice to say that we are great friends now. Thanks Liam, Eithne, Billy and Aoife for everything and to Liam's mother, Eileen who is a great character.

My hope is that the book will do Liam's life and career justice, his story is one of the most fascinating, honest and enthralling in the GAA. With the endless support and belief of those close to me and with the strength of the story, we now have his tale chronicled forever.

I want to thank those people now. Since we first met, my girlfriend Ruth has encouraged me to the last, she is very supportive and I am lucky to have her in my life.

My colleague and friend Jackie Hennessy is one of the most positive people you could ever meet and she helped me immensely, not only by sub-editing the book but by being a great pal as well.

Richard Gallagher is also one of the most respected sub-editors in Irish journalism. I now know why. Thanks to you and Evelyn for all your help, confidence and advice along the way.

Christy O'Connor is a top GAA writer, a mine of hurling information and a rock solid man. This is one of the few occasions that a Tipp man could possibly join forces with a Clare man! I appreciate everything Christy.

Cian Murphy has been a colleague and friend for the past six years. I learned a lot from his first book with Mike McNamara and he was never short of a word or two of support on this journey. Garry Doyle, my old mate and sparring partner, is also a man you would want in your corner.

Kieran Shannon was always there. 'Shak' helped start me off with the *Star* newspaper almost six years ago and was the first person I told about the book.

Jackie Cahill and Paul Collins were on the other end of the phone all year long. We threw ideas around and helped each other get by in a busy GAA season.

Brian Carthy is a man apart. He would stand on his head for you and at times he did just that. I never looked on him as a publisher, always a friend.

Seán Boylan is an amazing person. His herbal remedies tasted worse than sour milk but they got me through the busiest year of my life. Liam Griffin is of the same ilk and was a huge help. Alan Aherne was most gracious with his time all year.

Sportsfile's Ray McManus and Brendan Moran provided the inspiration for the book's front cover; Mary Guinan from the Temple of Design did fantastic work on the lay-out; while Sharon Murphy and Maire Scully were invaluable in promoting and marketing the book.

I haven't seen much of the lads in Kilruane lately but friends stay friends. Cheers for all the crack over the years, Shane, Chalky, Cronan, Mark, Sleepy and the rest of the lads.

I want to record my thanks to the *Star* newspaper editor Ger Colleran, MD Paul Cooke and sports editor Eoin Brannigan for giving me a chance in this business.

The final word goes to my family. My father, John and mother, Mary are both top class people who have put others first throughout their lives. I'm proud of them. Thanks for everything. I hope that success follows my brothers, Seán and David and sister Colette wherever they go.

I dedicate my part in this book to my late grandmother, Margaret Glennon, Cloughjordan and Kilruane.

Much has happened in my 16 year hurling career and more still in my life which vanishes under your eyes. One minute you are centre stage in Croke Park, a purple and gold shirt on your back and the next it's all over. But life still goes on. I made mistakes and plenty of them during my years in hurling but above all I enjoyed my time. I hope you enjoy reading about it.

As I flick back over the years, there are constant reminders of those who have helped me. My greatest supporter in life has been my mother, Eileen, never too far from my mind whether playing in Croke Park or just doing my daily work. With her down-to-earth attitude to life, I gratefully acknowledge her role in any success I have had on and off the field. Thanks mother.

My wife, Eithne, has carried the burden of a lot of my downfalls over the last few years. She always stays in the background but now it's time to take some of the limelight. Eithne is a brilliant partner and a great mother to Billy and Aoife, two fantastic little people that are the shining lights in our lives.

Dad passed away in July 2004. It was a great pity that he never got to see the new house at Kyle Cross and to get a chance to read my book but deep down he never left Oulart. And our hearts.

I had been consumed by my first addiction, football. And as soon as that was taken away from me, I just knew what would happen. It was as if I had no choice
Tony Adams, Addicted, 1999

– CHAPTER ONE –
Down and dirty

Kilmuckridge, Wexford, November 1, 2002, 2 am

It's a story that needs to be told.

I want to give you a look beyond the tunnel, an insight into what 16 turbulent years as an intercounty hurler were like, how you can isolate those close to you and instead build a life to revolve around sport. The game has thrown everything at me, good, bad and ugly. Most of it has been my own doing too. But not all of it. It's time to get some stuff off my chest.

At first it was an obsession to win something for Wexford, who had not lifted a cup of any sort since 1968. When I first started out, one of my team-mates, George O'Connor, had played in 16 major finals and lost 15 of them. That was what we were up against. Wexford were perennial losers and I grew to be one as well.

When I look back on it, we had so much talent but used to shit ourselves at the thoughts of winning a trophy. It took me eight years to help shed the tag and when I finally did it was like a walk on air. I drank to toast our All-Ireland win in 1996, drank some more when I won my third All Star that Christmas and went on the beer all over again the following year when we retained our Leinster title. Then I broke my leg and this time decided to drink to ease the boredom. It was brilliant, I could take alcohol for almost any reason. Like when I was at home like a spare tool in crutches and out of the game for 16 months or like when, six years later, I became the first intercounty player to be sent off in three successive championships. Any excuse for the booze.

Many stories are often built around the theme of success but you don't always read tales of the price of it or the pitfalls involved. The most powerful part of my tale lies in what happened after the summer of 1996 when the backslapping died down, the cheers faded and the streets emptied. Maybe that's what makes it different.

I have tried to be straight down the line about everything that went on. Most GAA fans think of me as a dirty little bastard that broke fingers for a living. Christ, I was out of line on several occasions but I don't think I was the criminal they made me out to be, not when you see some of the stuff that goes on at the moment, lads spitting at opponents and hitting each other on the head.

I was never like that. As a 5ft 8in squirt who was usually deployed at either centre or wing back, I was much smaller than guys I marked and sometimes a good bit slower; so I played on the edge to survive. Mothers winced when they saw me mark little Johnny for fear I would take his hand off but they didn't realise that at the same time I was dreading being taken to the cleaners by their sons.

It's hard to stay at the top, or anywhere near it. I'm playing against young lads whose fathers I found a handful about 16 years ago. One roasting will signal the end. I'm on the team since 1988 and I would love to call it a day but quite simply, I can't go out like this, not after a five-month slump on the beer, not after getting the red card for the third summer in a row.

I want to walk away with a bit of class, with my reputation intact, but it won't be easy because over the years controversy dogged me the way verbal bloopers follow George Bush and tribunals haunt politicians. It's time for a clean slate; give it one more go and get the bad stuff off my chest as well. So here goes.

I have been a boil on the arse of the GAA for the past few years and have not been much better for my family to deal with. But how could anyone else like me when I almost hated myself? You don't become a heavy drinker if you are at ease with yourself. But I did.

My name is Liam Dunne and I am 35. I'm still in love with hurling, even though the only thing left is to fail a drugs test. And as sure as Jesus, I'll overdose on a cough bottle next or take two Lemsips and the Irish Sports Council will come and test me. Then I'll have the clean sweep. Hurling was always my first addiction and once that looked like going down the tubes, I turned to my second hobby, drink.

It's my own fault that after almost 16 years of intercounty hurling, I still have a point to prove. It's the last thing I need at my age. Jesus, I should be sitting down with my slippers on, looking back at the scrapbooks and telling my young lad, Billy, about the good times. Instead, I have to run myself into the ground for one more season just so I can retire with a bit of dignity. And for someone who was once described as the best hurler in the country, that's a long fall.

It's never healthy to be addicted to anything, I suppose, not even sport. And I finally lost control of the wheel and went into freefall when I hit Martin Comerford on the shoulder in the 2002 Leinster final. It wasn't Martin's fault, it was mine, and so I walked the line yet again. The same happened in 2000 and 2001 and I was the first player to get red cards in three consecutive years. Not quite the piece of history I was looking for. I turned to booze for a few months then, forgot about everything else in my life and went haywire for a while. They say that alcohol is like love. The first kiss is magic, the second is intimate and the third is routine.

It just became a habit and you join me at the start of November, the first night in five months I haven't taken a drink. I know my body clock well enough. We have ticked together for over three decades and it tells me something is missing. It's crying out for what it has lived on for almost half a year, the taste of Bulmers or Heineken.

A look at the alarm clock tells me it's 2 am. I must be off my head. The normal Joe Soap might go down for a quick cup of tea or hot milk so I decide to give that a shot, only it's not tea I want.

I draw the duvet back softly, conscious not to wake my wife, Eithne. She has it hard enough as it is, looking after our two little children, Billy and Aoife, and needs her rest.

I move toward the fridge and I'm not going to say no. On a frosty night, this is a warm and friendly greeting, as cosy as I am going to get. Opening the door, I reach in and take out a couple of cans of Heineken.

Something inside says 'Stop! Cop on and leave it back!' But my head is boss right now so I slug back the first one and move out of the kitchen, passing the mirror in the living-room. A mirror, it's as good a place as any to go soul-searching because there is no place to hide and sure enough I'm exposed.

Jesus, is that really me? I look like shit. A sad bastard who thinks he has the weight of the world on his shoulders. Roy Keane looks in the mirror every morning so he can see the truth; he cannot tolerate fooling himself. But I am fine with the self-delusion. I turn away and head for the couch. A few beers won't kill me.

I ask the same question every morning of myself: 'Have I got something to offer Manchester United?' At this moment in time the answer, always, is yes.
Roy Keane, July 25, 2004

– CHAPTER TWO –
Look back in anger

As I sit down with the Heineken in my hand, the reminder that I used to be someone sits on the mantlepiece: the first All Star award I won, 12 years ago.

Two more followed, in 1993 and 1996. Life was good then; my career was even better. They say these awards separate you from the rest, that an All Star possesses something extra, boundaries that few others can find. Go out and play your game, everything else will look after itself. But I am no hero now.

While I used to push my body to extraordinary limits as an athlete, running up mountains for stamina and down them for speed, I have already failed the first small test on my comeback by not staying off the drink for even one night.

I'm not quite a frumpy, middle-aged man but I'm well out of shape. Casper boasts a better colour. A few weeks ago my skin started to sag. Frown lines and ageing lines. All my own fault.

I first slipped down the slope in 2000 when I was sent off against Offaly. It was my first time getting the line for Wexford but it happened again the year after, and the year after that again. Mud stuck and soon I became known in the game as a poisonous little hoor. Liam Dunne: back page news for all the wrong reasons.

If you know the GAA and understand hurling, then you may get where I'm coming from. If you don't know the game, you might struggle to comprehend why a grown man chose to go on the beer and neglect his family just because of problems on the sportsfield.

And sure, it's only a sport. But it's a parochial one and a national one. It gives you a chance to make your name or leave a mark on life, a chance that would not be there otherwise. So I gave hurling life status and as I got older, pushed my wife and kids to the side so I could feed my habit.

At first, the love wasn't reciprocated. When I was a young lad, managers and selectors said I was too small to make it. Others ignored me because of where I came from and what school I went to. But I think I proved them wrong.

My brother Tomás had to deal with the same sort of treatment. He was one of the best players in the county but had to wait seven years between his first and second game with the Wexford senior team. Eventually he proved them wrong too.

I held my place on the Wexford senior team for 16 years and played 126 intercounty games as well as countless tournament and challenge matches.

Respect was something I valued, but three red cards over all of those games and that respect wasn't long disappearing. You do the maths, though. One red card every 42 games. Jesus, I'm no Osama Bin Laden.

Sitting here nursing a can of beer in the winter of 2002, I know I could have one more year with Wexford but must be extra careful because a referee will send me off if I even look like doing something dirty, no questions asked.

Pick a game of hurling, any game. Say it's Wexford against Offaly. If Brian Whelahan pulls a stroke like I did, he won't be sent off. He wouldn't do it anyway but I'm just saying that's the way it is with me now; if I step an inch over the line I'm gone. Disciplinary officials from a hurling hotbed like Cavan or somewhere will gladly throw the book at me too, if they can stay awake long enough during the hearings.

Since the first red card, managers have encouraged their teams to go down injured when I'm around. It's some craic. If I pull, they hit the deck. I've seen lads rolling around in agony and then once play moves on, I ask them if they're okay and they're fine. Some lads will try anything to get an edge.

I don't mind supporters having a go either; they pay their money and are entitled to scream what they like in my direction. But I do mind what they say in front of my mother and wife. I'm not getting paid for hurling for the county. If I was they could say whatever they wished.

The TV pundits are getting a good few bob, though. I've taken a right old lash from them in recent years; it's their job. A few of them reckon I'm finished and while they could be right, I'm not going to listen to someone like Pete Finnerty from the *Sunday Game* telling me where I stand. I'm not listening to a waffler like him giving the country his opinion.

Finnerty was my captain on the 1991 All Star trip to Toronto and I never met a guy with a bigger head or a finer opinion of himself. Everything revolved around Peter the Great out there. It was 'me this' and 'me that'. We all had to listen to what he won and what he should have won over the years and although I was only a greenhorn starting out and should have been in awe, five minutes was enough in his company.

Now I have to listen to him having the craic at my expense on TV and I wonder why, if he was such an expert, he never did any wonders for Galway after he hung up his sliotar but instead is happy to sit back in a studio armchair, laughing and joking at the likes of me. Whatever about Finnerty, the rest of them can hardly all be wrong, I suppose.

The John Troy clash was my first red card for Wexford. I did clip him but although I promise you I got the ball first, he went down on the ground, screaming like a baby.

My next walk to the line was an absolute joke for all concerned, when we played Tipperary in the 2001 All-Ireland semi-final replay. Their wing forward Brian O'Meara missed out on his last chance of appearing in an All-Ireland final and that was down to me as well because I started it. There were public campaigns waged to try and get Brian freed for the final and rightly so; I couldn't believe we had been sent off in the first place.

It was handbags at paces; you would see more aggression in a convent. No other hurler would have walked for that incident bar Liam Dunne. But because there were two of us involved, Brian had to go as well.

The last red mist arrived just a few months ago, July 2002, and has had the worst effect on me of the lot. I was accused of splitting Martin Comerford's head in the last few minutes of the Leinster final against Kilkenny, despite the fact my hurley only made contact with his shoulder. I did hit him a silly blow and the referee had little choice but to send me off. And yet, while it was senseless, it was not as vicious as people made out. Some members of the Kilkenny backroom staff told him to stay down, make it look bad.

'Don't get up Martin, don't get up, keep the head down, he'll get the line.'

It was only Martin's first year. He's a grand chap but was new to the scene, so of course he was going to follow orders, do what he was told. But there's more. After that game, people started to harp back to the 1996 All-Ireland final when Limerick blamed me for breaking Gary Kirby's fingers early in the match and putting their danger-man and free-taker out of the game. That outstanding charge enjoyed a new lease of life when Gary appeared on a TG4 documentary and had a right old go, questioning my attitude and suggesting I had it all pre-planned.

Jesus, you don't approach an All-Ireland final in that frame of mind. I didn't go out to do him. I actually held him scoreless and got man of the match in that final. The Wexford defence didn't give a free away in the entire second half so he could hardly have been a match-winner from placed balls.

While we both contested a dropping ball early in the game and we did make contact, he pulled the same time as I did and the ball broke loose. Moments later he pointed a huge free; there was no talk of a broken finger then.

His body language however was not that of a hurler in an All-Ireland final. I think he knew as the game wore on that Limerick were about to lose their second final in three years.

But I was a handy scapegoat in defeat.

So there you have it. After 16 years of top-class hurling, this is what I have come to, a bitter man with time almost up.

Those in the Kirby, Troy, O'Meara and Comerford camps may believe they were right, but though I have always played the game hard I have played it fair.

Put your hand up and I will pull if the ball is there to be won. I will try and win the clash but I won't compromise the situation by trying to avoid your hands or fingers in the process.

From time to time, I will also tap a lad in the chest or the ribs just to see how he reacts, to see if he wants to be on the field or not. Call it childish but most hurlers do it all the time. Look at the Clare hurlers when they take the field. They are like men possessed. They will do anything to put you off your game. It's not just them; there are loads of lads out there who are no angels but I'm the clown that's known for it and gets caught.

'Don't put your hand up around that lad, he'll take your fingers off.'

'Pity to see him finishing his career like that, he used to be good.'

'Remember 1993 and 1996, he played some stuff.'

Nice tags to be labelled with for the rest of your life. No mention of the All Stars, the All-Ireland, the two Leinster medals, the two Railway Cups and the three county titles with Oulart-The-Ballagh.

At first I thought the drink would help me get through the close season. I was never a stranger to it, enjoyed the session as much as the rest, but this time the depression and alcohol have blended into a lethal cocktail. Silly, isn't it? But what the hell? We live in a drink culture anyway. No-one will notice.

And they didn't. But while I kept my habit quiet enough, I soon started to feel the same after 10 pints as I used to after five or six.

More worrying was the fact I did not need the company to go for a few pints. I was as happy on my own as I was with friends. I would talk to Mick the Shilling if I had to but could just as easily slink into a corner by myself.

And it wasn't just one pub that I would go to; there were a few handpicked all over the county and if they opened late, well it was good enough for me.

The couch, however, became my most dangerous refuge. Going to the pub and drinking is one thing but this was a lot more sinister. I dread to think what Liam Griffin, my old manager and friend, would say if he could see me. Or what my former team-mates would think, guys who used to respect me and sometimes look my way for a bit of guidance. They would be sympathetic, I'm sure, but I never needed pity before; I was one of their leaders.

After another two cans, I rose from the couch, walked to the mantelpiece, and spotted my All-Ireland medal. I remembered the day well. How I would have loved to bottle that feeling in September 96! But Griffin knew the pitfalls of victory. He called the entire panel into a room the morning after that win over Limerick and seriously dampened the mood by warning that one of us, one of the men who won Wexford's first All-Ireland title since 1968, would become an alcoholic.

'Some member of this group will be in trouble,' he said, in deadly earnest, and his words really caught us.

Half of the team were already contemplating where to go drinking for the rest of the week. The other half were arranging the social schedule as far as Christmas.

But he was not finished: 'And enjoy this moment because after today you will never be together as a squad or a group again.'

Jesus, take back our medals altogether, will you.

I can tell you now that he was right on the second count. We were never together as a group again, which seems unbelievable for a party of 30 men who almost lived with each other for a year.

And on the first count, was he right? Was I 'the one' he was talking about?

I will be straight. I don't know what the actual definition of an alcoholic is or how close I am to being one. But right now, in November 2002, I am fairly close.

I think I can stop drinking but I'm not sure if I want to. It's kind of confusing. Sometimes I think I can get on top of the problem at the drop of a hat and just stay in but when I ended up on a tear until 7 am a couple of days ago, I wasn't so sure.

My memories of most of that night are vague but I recall fumbling in my pocket, gathering some loose change for the taxi fare and handing it to the driver. Luckily, he chose not to ask what I was doing out at that time on a midweek night.

As I arrived in home, the wake-up call I had been desperately looking for hit me smack in the face. Thank God for it. My two little children were in the hall, five-year-old Billy and little Aoife, who is only three. They said nothing but their innocent stares were like a thousand piercing daggers.

'What was Daddy doing out all night? Where was he?' their eyes seemed to ask.

Feeling lower than I had ever done, I rubbed their heads and tucked them into bed.

Eithne said nothing when I got to our room. I quickly fell asleep and eventually woke up at 11.30 am to the realisation there was no-one in the house, which suited me.

I didn't really want to talk to anyone. I knew I had been an absolute prick to live with but it was finally time to do something about it.

I made a cup of tea, sat down and thought about how I could drag myself out of this mess. Some people have no-one to turn to but I was lucky in this regard. The solution was pretty obvious.

After sipping my tea, I picked up the phone. Liam Griffin, the man who got me my first sales job without even knowing me, would have the answer because he always did.

Griffin had got that job because, as he said, while he didn't know me, he believed in me.

'Liam, it's me,' I said. 'I need to talk to you for 10 minutes. Friday will do fine. See you then.'

This guy knows me inside out. He had made me captain of Wexford for the first time. He reversed the decision a few weeks later but he did it for the county and the team and it was his call. We had become close friends and I felt I could tell him anything, which was just as well because things had gone way too far. I had crossed the line.

Tomorrow, it was time to go back.

*Liam Dunne was no Mother Teresa. But he was not the Hannibal Lector
that people make him out to be either.*
Liam Griffin, former Wexford manager, March 2004

– CHAPTER THREE –
The three-in-a-row

I take the blame for my downfall squarely on the chin but every stream
has a source and you can trace the start of my troubles back to 2000.

After three years of stalling, it was supposed to be the year
Wexford hurling got back on a high again.

The county board formed a committee to find a new manager in
the wake of the departure of Rory Kinsella, and we were excited about
the new man and what he could bring to the job, how he could shape
or mould us back into Championship contenders.

Rory had been brilliant to the team. He was a players' man to the
last and showed huge loyalty by playing me even though I was not fully
right after breaking my ankle and losing almost 18 months of hurling.

Anyway, this committee shortened their list down to two
candidates: Pat Herbert from Limerick and Joachim Kelly, the former
Offaly hurler.

Unfortunately, at the end of the day expense became an issue and
the county board opted for Joachim because they thought they could
save a few pounds in mileage.

I am full sure that when Joachim took over he meant to do his
best for us and it's possible someone from a different province would
have worked better but not a guy from a county who were among our
fiercest rivals.

Frankly, it's not an era I remember with great fondness. We reverted to the state of chaos in which we had been back in 1995.

The Wexford Supporters Club ensured Joachim was looked after like all intercounty managers these days. He was supplied with a Citroen car that had 'JJ Byrne's Garage' plastered all over the side so he had no complaints.

He was a decent bloke but not a good manager. For example, we could get away with murder and lads just did what they wanted. Before the Championship, we were supposed to have given up the beer but one player had to be pulled out of the Centenary Rooms not long before a big game after telling us the week before he was giving up the booze like the rest of the squad.

The end result was that we approached the Offaly match, our first game in Leinster that year, in poorer shape than any team I'd been involved with. The League campaign was poor and the week before that first Championship match, Joachim and his selectors, Brendan O'Connor and Mick Butler, brought us down to New Ross for a Chinese with the aim of bonding as a team.

Some of the boys were used only to bacon and cabbage and had hardly ever seen fried rice or noodles so they ate all around them. A few days later, when the burping and farting finally left our systems, we were sent out to play Offaly at Croke Park.

It's an awful thing to say but I took to the field that day suspecting we were going to get a right hiding, and after five minutes my worst suspicions were confirmed. We had no answer for Offaly, who came out at 100 miles per hour. Usually, after 10 or 15 minutes, a guy can start to get his second wind but it never came that day.

With 10 minutes gone I could feel the pressure, and as a ball came down from the sky, I pulled wildly on Paudie Mulhare and hit him on the back of the head. I didn't mean it but I should have got the line. Paudie put his hand to his head: 'Jesus Christ, Liam, what did you do that for?'

'Paudie,' I replied, going over and tapping him on the chest, 'whether you believe me or not, I didn't mean to hit you on the back of the head.'

Referee Willie Barrett gave me a yellow card and there were no further problems between the two of us for the rest of the game. No, the only difficulties were in the Wexford dressing-room, where lads knew in their hearts and souls we were a beaten team.

I tried to lift it in the second half. 'Fuck it, Declan, just pull on the next ball,' I roared to Declan Ruth, who was finding big Gary Hanniffy almost impossible to manage. Again, Willie shot me a look, clearly not too happy with my attitude.

Next thing, Offaly brought on John Troy as a sub. There had been a history between us going back to 1994 when he pulled wildly on me and nearly took my head off, and 1996 when, still bearing a grudge, I did the same to him.

As bad as I felt on the pitch, huffing and puffing, he looked much worse. He was coming back from a hand injury, and a blind man could see he was seriously overweight.

Soon, the ball bounced toward our goal and I went to flick it away. I got the ball but also caught Troy on the hand and down he went like a bag of spuds, roaring on the ground.

Willie Barrett was 40 yards away but I could already see him going for his pocket and knew I was gone.

'Willie,' I pleaded, 'when you watch this on TV tonight, you'll realise the mistake you made.'

Hardly able to hear me above the howls of pain coming from Troy, he said nothing but gave me a second yellow and then a red card. For the first time in my intercounty career, which started all the way back in 1988, I had been sent off.

The Offaly crowd cheered and Troy got up straightaway, a miraculous recovery. As I walked off the pitch, the abuse became more vocal and insulting. I was told later that the Kilkenny manager, Brian Cody, who was in the stand, went over to my 'friends' and told them to sit down, which they quickly did. It wasn't to be Cody's last time standing up for me and that's something strange for a lad from Wexford to say about a Kilkenny man.

In the dressing-room, I cursed Troy but I was the fool now. I sat in the dressing-room thinking of my mother and how hurt she would be, never mind my team-mates after our hammering, 3-15 to 1-8. I also thought of Liam Griffin and what he would say to me, how I had let the side down after everything he drilled into us in 1996.

Larry O'Gorman, the best hurler I ever played with and one of the greatest characters as well, was someone I soldiered with during most of my career but had been dropped by Joachim. Rather than watch the rest of the game unfold, he joined me in the dressing-room.

'It's bad out there and it's getting worse,' Larry moaned, and when you see The Brother, as he is known, in a bad mood, you know things cannot be good.

We were drubbed by 13 points and after the game, Joachim came over and told me not to make any rash decisions. He was talking about me walking away from the game but I had no intention of retiring and, as it turned out, I was back hurling a week after the Troy incident.

I went straight back playing with Oulart-The-Ballagh and soon began to look forward to 2001, a chance to get back on track. I felt there was little chance Joachim would stay on as manager. His selectors, Brendan O'Connor and Mick Butler, tried to arrange a meeting with him to find out what his plans were and eventually they met halfway between Wexford and Offaly. Joachim told them he hadn't his mind made up. A few days later, they learned that Kelly was not staying on, but as far as I know they never heard it from the man himself.

We were hardly filled with hope, then, when word circulated that another committee was being set up to find another new manager, but this time they did better. Tony Dempsey, now a Fianna Fáil TD, took over and brought Ger Cushe, one of my main friends and a former team-mate, and Davy Morris in as selectors.

Early in their reign I, as one of the elder berries of the bunch, was asked to make a speech. I begged the squad to pull in the one direction. We had been fighting everyone, it seemed, since Rory Kinsella left, but with Tony we had a real players' man and there were just no excuses left.

That year, though Kilkenny smashed us 2-19 to 0-12 in the Leinster final, we reached an All-Ireland semi-final with Tipperary. They looked to have us well beaten in Croke Park but we showed remarkable spirit to claw our way back with three incredible goals in the second half, two from Larry O'Gorman, who wound the clock back with a sensational display. In the end Tipp were the ones hanging on for their lives. But with 45 seconds left and Tipp on the rack, referee Pat O'Connor blew his whistle and declared a draw: Wexford 3-10, Tipperary 1-16. We had prepared well but maybe deep down we knew we had lost our chance of reaching another All-Ireland final.

Still, Liam Griffin was in the back-room at this stage and one of my old sparring partners, Martin Storey, had been called back into the panel after his retirement and so we felt there was a decent chance of causing another shock.

Pat Horan was the man in the middle for the replay, which was staged in a downpour at Croke Park, and it wasn't long before he lost all control of the game.

In one corner Rory Mallon and Eoin Kelly were taking lumps out of one another, while down at the other end Mitch Jordan and Tomás Costello had also started flaking each other. I looked across the pitch, where Darren Stamp was delivering on his earlier promise to smack Tipp's wing forward Mark O'Leary, who we had found a handful in the drawn game, when he scored four points from play.

At this stage, I poked my marker, Brian O'Meara, a few digs to see how he would react. Now Brian had never hit a man in his life but all the same I reckoned I'd see how he would handle it.

I tipped the end of the hurl into his ribs and straightaway he tapped me back with the bos of his hurl. It's macho stuff but it happens in hurling games all the time. I walked backwards but hit him another little tip whereupon he turned around, drove his hurl up where it really hurts and left me winded.

But I wouldn't let it go and so I drove the hurl into his ribs again. This went on and on until we had hit each other a fourth time and the linesman Pat Aherne had his flag up. It was silly stuff and I presumed all we were going to get was a dressing down and maybe a booking.

How wrong I was! By now Horan had lost what little control he'd started with, his face was bright red and you could see he was under serious pressure. Before the game, his umpires had arrived late, which hadn't helped, but it seemed rows had broken out in every area of the field and he was all at sea; the occasion was too big for him. He sought Pat Aherne's advice and the linesman pointed out the two players he'd seen digging each other. I went over to Horan: 'Jesus Pat, it's not that bad.' But he was about to lose the rag and the next thing he produced the red card and flashed it at both of us. I could not believe what was happening. Brian O'Meara looked at me in disgust.

'Look what you're after doing now,' he said.

'Ah Jesus,' I replied.

As I walked off the pitch for the second year in a row, I felt as low as I had ever done. The crowd didn't really jeer this time; they were pretty much concentrating on another row being waged down the other end of the field between Mitch and Tomás.

I put my head down in despair and trotted along to the sideline with my hurl in my hand. I looked up briefly to see Jordan arriving alongside me. He too had been sent off.

In the dressing-room, I was disconsolate. Tom Dempsey, another close friend and former team-mate, came down from the TV studios to console me. Tony Dempsey brought the team into the warm-up room. Alone, I put on my tracksuit as he tried to rouse them one last time.

'Lads, we can still do this,' he roared. And then he went around to the lads one by one. He came to Mitch Jordan.

'Mitch. I want you to get in front of your man for the second half. Get in front and win that ball for us. What do you say to that?'

'Jaysus, Tony, I was sent off 10 minutes ago.'

That put the apple in Tony's throat and ended his speech fairly quickly.

Things had happened so fast. Very few had seen Mitch get the line and I nearly cracked a smile when I saw Tony's face, but quickly remembering my own troubles I just dropped the head again. The lads went out on the field and tried their best but we never had a hope and were well beaten, 3-12 to 0-10.

After the game, I walked out of Croke Park a broken man. I can only imagine how Brian felt, but I couldn't believe we had been sent off. The first people I saw were my wife and two kids and it was a huge relief, to be honest. Little Aoife was only two then and all she wanted was to get up in Daddy's arms; she didn't care about hurling. Here I was, leaving Croke Park as a man, after playing a man's game, and going back into my private life, where a little girl is waiting just to be picked up and hugged. She was so innocent but I was delighted with the hug; to tell the truth, there weren't too many others who wanted one from me.

A few days later, Mitch and I were called to a Games Administration Committee disciplinary meeting in Dublin. Séamus Howlin, the Wexford chairman at the time, collected us and on the way told me I would get a month's suspension but warned Mitch he would get three.

We approached Jack White's pub and decided there was little or no point going to Dublin if that was the case, so we asked Séamus to let us off there but he refused and reminded us that we still had a chance of getting Brian O'Meara off the hook so he could play in the All-Ireland final against Galway.

We stayed going but it was the biggest waste of a night and the worst decision I ever made, going to HQ that night. Pat Horan had sent his report into Croke Park on the evening of the replay and not even Nelson Mandela, Bono and John Hume together could have changed it.

We met Brian O'Meara, Nicky English and Tipp secretary Michael O'Brien up there and, players being players, Mitch and I went up to chat to Brian. The Dublin football manager at the time, Tommy Carr, came out of the room. He had been in hot water for his verbal roasting of referee Michael Curley but didn't seem too troubled by his experience inside the corridors of power.

'Cheer up, lads, it could be worse,' he quipped. But Brian O'Meara didn't seem too confident as he went in first to explain the situation. Mitch went in next and finally I was called before the committee.

I have never seen such a crowd in my life.. There were definitely two who were half asleep and another who had his hand under his ear to prop his chin up and looked like he was dozing off as well. Another guy from Cavan or somewhere, a great hurling man I'd say, was also on his way for 40 winks and wasn't even listening to what I was saying. All we were short of was Waldorf and Statler, the two boys on the balcony from the *Muppet Show*.

'If you saw what happened in the Kilkenny-Galway semi-final the day after our match, you will understand that Brian O'Meara and I were harshly treated,' I insisted. 'The stuff that went on between those two teams at the start of the game was X-rated. There were some awful tackles and hits that were let go. And if Brian is to miss an All-Ireland final over something silly like what we were involved in, there is something seriously wrong with the GAA.'

Yawns all round. They didn't even look up. I knew it was a waste of time and it was no surprise to me when O'Meara's ban was upheld along with my own for striking with the hurley. I was very upset that Brian missed the final and it overshadowed everything in the run-up to the game against Galway. *The Star* newspaper ran a 'Save Brian O'Meara' campaign and the whole country was talking about it. But let's just say I was not getting as much sympathy as Brian and rightly so, I suppose.

I was portrayed as the bad boy but I really felt that if Brian had got off with the suspension I should have as well. I thought the GAA and Horan had made a huge mistake in the first place but there was no-one else called to account except O'Meara and I and it sickened me. You only have to take the 2003 All-Ireland football final as an example, when Armagh's Diarmaid Marsden got sent off. The Tyrone guy Philip Jordan went running straight into him and referee Brian White put the Armagh corner forward off. It was a horrendous decision and I sat in front of the TV screaming at the injustice of it. And then, later in the year, they handed out a Vodafone All Star Referees award to White, another joke of a decision.

But while the sending-off really upset Brian, it had an adverse effect on me too. All of a sudden, I was being demonised and it wasn't long before an earlier incident, the Gary Kirby one, was dragged up as proof of my criminal tendencies.

If the GAA was a wild-west town, my face would have been on 'Wanted' posters on every saloon bar and every dusty street. It even got to the stage where letters were arriving in the post, lovely pieces of prose and poetry accusing me of being a dirty little bastard, good for nothing only mayhem.

Back home, I got plenty of support, but even still, the lads, my friends, were only half joking when they asked me if I was going to do the decent thing and call it a day. I didn't mind the ribbing but other things were starting to worry me. There was never much abuse from players or opponents on the field but my private life took the brunt of it instead. I now had a reputation; the name Liam Dunne was being mentioned for all the wrong reasons.

When I went off on holidays to Lanzarote with the Wexford team, my mind was still a little uneasy. I couldn't help thinking of the hurt my mother and wife must have felt, Griffin too, when I got the line, people who had done more for me than anyone else. When my brother Seán enquired if I had considered going for three red cards in a row, I just laughed and told him to watch his back at training but not for one moment did I dream it would come true.

In the 2002 Championship, we ended up playing Kilkenny in the Leinster final and although they were dominant in every hurling showdown in the province since about 1997, Wexford trained to win this game and really believed we would. Griffin popped in and out of the camp and was a huge help. Tony, Ger and Davy had also worked well with us and I was in no doubt we would beat them and cause a shock.

Big John Hoyne came over to mark me and didn't hold back. Our exchanges reminded me of the shuddering tussles his predecessor and my old friend John Power and I used to enjoy. With five minutes to go, Wexford were right in there, only a point down.

Declan Ruth had held their danger-man, Henry Shefflin, exceptionally well but all over the field, Wexford men had done their job and there was never more than two points in it. With time almost up, I looked at Hoyne and asked: 'Have ye not got enough Leinster medals?'

He tipped me with the hurley in the chest and replied: 'It's not Leinster medals we want at all.'

He was not being arrogant; they had more provincial medals than they knew what to do with and another one would be no big deal, but there was no way they were going to let us have a title either.

With just a point in it, their manager, Brian Cody, switched Martin Comerford out to mark me and almost immediately, James McGarry floated a puck-out down on top of the two of us. I stayed where I was and pulled. Martin Comerford moved forward and I hit him on the back of the shoulder. It was a stupid blow, especially when I knew I was already a marked man with referees. He went down and the medics came racing onto the field like it was a lifesaving operation and started to pour water on his head. What about his shoulder? Where I actually hit him.

I had pulled 10 times harder on John Hoyne and nothing had happened. But now Henry Shefflin came running at me and a few of the Wexford lads made a go for him. There were a few right shots exchanged. I stood there and braced myself for what was to come. That's when some Kilkenny man urged Comerford to stay on the deck. As I said, it was his first Championship so of course he was going to stay down but I felt like hitting the guy who had told him to do so. That made my blood boil.

By now Ger Harrington, the referee, had little choice. 'You're off,' he said calmly, as he flashed the red card.

'Ah, fucking hell!' I whispered, the wind taken out of my sails. I wanted the ground to open up and take me there and then. I was mortified, disgusted, devastated, embarrassed and crushed. At the same time, I was mystified as to why I had pulled on Comerford like that in the first place and raging with the fuss his camp had made over it. I like Martin, he's a good lad, but there he was holding his head and yet I had only made contact with his shoulder. Of course I knew what I was doing when I pulled on him and I knew the referee, who had a great game in fairness, didn't have much choice given the circumstances. But this was the worst I had ever felt on a field, worse than when I had broken my leg or lost the 1997 All-Ireland semi-final.

I walked off the pitch. Tony Dempsey called me over and although I looked at him, I just went straight by him and into the dressing-room for my third early shower in as many years. Fittingly, the water was cold this time.

On the way into the dressing-room, I met the same steward I had met after being sent off after the incident with Brian O'Meara the year before. He told me to sit down and have a cup of water. I told him he wouldn't be seeing me here again, peeled off my gear and headed for the shower, absolutely dazed at what had just happened. I turned the water on and, as I said, it was freezing but I stepped straight under it, felt nothing. As the drips poured down on me, I really felt like ending it all there and then, which is stupid because it's only a game. Wexford could have scored a winning goal outside but I wouldn't have noticed.

As it turned out, we lost by two points, 0-19 to 0-17, and almost immediately, our goalkeeper, Damien Fitzhenry, came into the dressing-room, saw me and came over to where I was sitting. Throwing a comforting arm around me, Fitzy said: 'I don't know what to say to you.'

I didn't know what to say either. All the usual faces flashed through my mind. Eithne, my mother, my aunt Ann: they were all up in the stand again. Groundhog Day. We had all been here before but this was the worst.

After that game, I did something I never usually did and travelled home with the team. In my mind, this was my last journey with the Wexford senior hurling squad and I was going back home with them. Before we hopped on the bus, I met Eithne and she was in a far worse state than me. All the lads in the family crowded around and sympathised but I couldn't shake the empty feeling inside. This was just humiliating. All down the years, I had my toughest battles against Kilkenny and had saved my best hurling for those games but now they were laughing at me. I looked around at the lads on the bus. Many of them were just in the squad for the first time and I knew they would have many good days ahead of them, but for me it was the end, and no harm either.

I went home and drowned my sorrows with a mixture of vodka, Baileys and Heineken. It was no time to be thinking straight.

The day after that game, the realisation that I would be gone for two months hit me. The GAC would ban me for 'ungentlemanly conduct', which warranted a four-week suspension, but because it was my second dismissal within a year, it was automatically doubled.

I knew I had to get away from town, so Eithne, the kids and I decided to head off to Dungarvan for a couple of days. But we soon found there was no getting away from it there either. I met Dan Shanahan, Fergal Hartley and Paul Flynn, all Waterford hurlers, and they were talking about the whole affair again. My head dropped even lower.

Word had it that Griffin was furious with me so I avoided him, and also stayed away from my mother's house, until the week after the Leinster final. Mam had held onto all the papers and, reading them, I found little solace or comfort in any, except for a few words of comfort from Brian Cody, who argued that I was unlucky to have walked.

A couple of days later, I travelled to Portlaoise to see Wexford get cleaned out by Clare in the qualifiers. That defeat ended our campaign.

Afterwards, I brought my young lad, Billy, into our dressing-room to see the lads, thinking it would be his last chance to meet his heroes. As we walked out, Clare's Colin Lynch came over and shook hands with Billy and me. Lynch had been the original bad boy of the GAA in 1998, when the Association seemed to be hunting for his blood. This was a guy who had the entire country on his back after the 1998 Munster final with Waterford, when he was subjected to a witch-hunt after pulling hard right from the throw-in.

Colin didn't say much to me but what he did say struck a chord: 'Don't let them get to you, Liam.'

It was a small gesture and I appreciated it, but in a sense it came too late. By now I scarcely had the stomach for anything and was feeling worse with each passing day. I didn't want to do anything, had little interest in work and never wanted to see a hurling field or play a match again.

On the Tuesday after the Clare defeat, one of my friends, Ray Keogh, asked me to go and see his Dad, Christy, who was sick. Christy had handed me my first ever Wexford senior jersey and was a man I had an awful lot of time for so I told Ray, who was also on the squad for years, there was no problem.

We went to see him in a nursing home the following day and I brought my Leinster final jersey with me.

'What's that?' Ray enquired.

'It's the last jersey I will wear for Wexford and your Dad gave me my first so I want him to have it,' I replied.

'Well, if that's your last jersey, I'll frame it,' Ray said.

We went up to the nursing home and poor Christy was looking frail. Lying back in his chair, he opened his eyes and saw me.

'Are you having a hard time of it, Liam?' he asked.

'I am, Christy,' I sighed. 'Some lads won't even look at me.'

'Well,' he whispered, 'when a lad won't even look at you, that's the biggest sort of a bollix you can get. At least if a lad looks at you and faces you, there's something in him.'

They were words I didn't forget. We went back to Ray's house and Christy passed away on the Friday of that week. I went to the removal that night and they put my Wexford jersey on his coffin.

After that, hurling was the last thing on my mind, and in fact there was little or nothing occupying any space in my head. I went on an excursion of alcohol. Officially, the binge started on July 13 and I drank every night until the first weekend in November. If there was beer in a glass, I had to get it down and on to the next one.

It continued right until the morning that I saw my two little kids on the doorstep and arranged that meeting with Griffin.

That Friday could not come quick enough; I wanted to pour all this out to the man that I would give up everything for, the man who got me my first job when he hardly even knew me.

Thankfully, the day came and, Griffin being Griffin, the 10 minutes he promised turned into three and a half hours.

'You look terrible,' was his opening greeting, and I spent the next hour telling him just why. For once, I did most of the talking and spelt it out.

I told him about the binge and how the sending-off against

Kilkenny had almost destroyed me. He said it was easy to see how bad I felt because I had no shape and just looked terrible.

'I can see by your physical condition that you have let yourself go,' he said, straight out. 'Your wife and family are suffering but there is a way out. If you are prepared to start work now, I think you can dig yourself out of this hole.

'Stop drinking now and start training. You have one more year to offer Wexford and salvage everything. One more year, but only if you start now,' he warned.

Feeling relieved, I went home and thought about what he had said. I decided to do as he had advised and try to dig myself out of the hole. It was like a weight off my mind so what did I do? I went straight to the pub and had a right few pints. It was a dreadful thing to do. But I didn't go out on Saturday night. For only the second time in nearly six months, I stayed in.

It was no surprise, though, that I couldn't sleep and I hankered for a taste of alcohol in the middle of the night so I got up and went down to the kitchen. This time, I ignored the fridge and instead drank cups of tea. At 6.40 am, I got up a third time and again turned a blind eye to the temptations that lay inside the fridge. Instead, I looked in the mirror and forced myself to see a different person.

'There's only one way to dig myself out of this fucking mess,' I said, teeth gritted. I put on a pair of togs and socks. Over the togs, I put on tracksuit bottoms and threw on a T-shirt. Over the T-shirt went a black plastic bag, a jersey and a tracksuit top. That was the heavy stuff but there were a couple of final touches: a wet suit and cap.

We lived two minutes from Morriscastle beach and at 7 am on November 3, 2002, my bender officially stopped. The wind howled mercilessly as I jogged down to the beach. It was an unfriendly place and I got no sympathy whatsoever from Mother Nature as I was blown along in the pitch dark, half afraid someone was running up behind me. Way back, there was one light, a lone lamppost that shone like a beacon beyond on the roadway that I kept looking to for reassurance. My first run only lasted a few minutes but I stopped, walked on and ran again. Once more, my legs gave way but I continued running after another few minutes.

I stayed at the beach for an hour and came home with my gear absolutely drowned. Later that day, at 4 pm, I was down there again and that night I scored another big plus by staying home for the second night in a row.

On Monday morning, I was down at Morriscastle beach at 7 am once more and again that evening. When I returned home, I went looking for my diary, looked up that day's date and in large, clear print wrote:

> *My goal for 2003 is to be the Wexford Hurler of the Year.*
> *Honour and Respect. Liam Dunne, November 5, 2002.*

Two little words that meant so much: honour and respect. It was a long time since I had either and it would require something extraordinary to get them back. Maybe I never would.

*I can get up in the morning and look myself in the mirror
and my family can look at me too and that's all that matters.*
Lance Armstrong, US cyclist

– CHAPTER FOUR –
The wonder years

Someone once told me life wasn't about the size of the dog in the fight, more the size of the fight in the dog. It was good advice.

All through my childhood, I was quiet and easygoing but deep down I was a fiery little hoor and not to be messed with. In sport, I seemed to be smaller than most other lads my age and it took me a long time to find my feet but when I did, I quickly learned to compensate for those two or three missing inches and found out there were other ways to make do.

I arrived into the world, destination Gorey, on June 12 1968 after giving Mam a relatively trouble-free birth. Five siblings had come before me, so there were no trumpet blasts or anything like that. The Dunnes had seen it all before, you see, so apart from a few strange heads of black hair looking into the cot at me when I came home, I am told it was soon back to your stations. We grew up in that sort of an unfazed environment.

And it was just as well because there were eight of us in our family. I had two sisters on each side of me and three brothers older so it was a fight for your own corner.

Home was Kyle Cross, a cottage at Kyle-Oulart in the Oulart-The-Ballagh parish, about 12 miles from Gorey. Over the years, there were three or four extensions added to the house. I got a chance to buy the house at 34 years of age, decided to make a new start and sat munching a choc-ice on the wall as builder John Kennedy and his men bulldozed it to make way for the next generation, my own lot.

We were close enough as a family without being painful or over the top about it. While we would look out for one another, there was a nice age difference from the oldest to the youngest so we all had different agendas. At the end of the day, we can still look each other in the face and do one another a favour. Isn't that what it's all about?

It wasn't always simple, though. By the time that my father, Tom, had finally left home in the early 1990s, I had kind of grown up without him being around. All in all, we turned out okay but it was tough.

An engineer with Irishenco, Dad was based in Dublin in my early years and that still allowed him to hurl for the parish until the call to go to London came and then he was even farther away. The nearest job Dad got to Oulart when I was a kid was in Rosslare. After that it could be Cork, Turlough Hill, Limerick or Britain, where he was based up to the time of his death in July 2004.

When he ended up working in St Helena, off the coast of Africa, it was really the end of his close involvement with the family and we knew things were not going to change when he started missing birthdays and holidays.

I do remember my father making hurleys for me when I was too small for any of the normal sizes. I also know he brought us to matches when we were kids and he was the one who started us hurling, but that's about it, they are the memories.

He took a decision to work away and gradually made the choice to stay away. He was gone for most of my life afterwards although he did come home for my wedding in 1996. He rang me from Dublin Airport the following morning and we chatted for a few minutes. He said he had to go to catch his flight and I never suspected I would see and speak to him only once after that.

That was early in July 2004, when I went to see him in a Southampton hospital, where he was terminally ill with leukaemia. The rest of my brothers and sisters had been over to see him weeks beforehand; I said I would go when I was ready.

But you can never be ready for something like that and when I finally got it together and visited him, it was difficult. We chatted for a while and I would say that both of us found it hard to deal with; there were plenty of questions I wanted to ask him, like why did he have to lose touch and why didn't he come home a bit more. I wanted to point out how tough it was growing up with no father around and how hard it was for my mother and the rest of them. But what was the point?

He was very sick and didn't need the hassle. Instead, we talked about how things were in Oulart and we talked about Wexford hurling, two things we would always have in common.

At the end, we shook hands and I knew that was the last time I would see my father. His absence didn't stop me thinking about him over the years but thoughts can go only so far.

My mother, Eileen, however, has always been there. She was and still is Ground Control for the eight of us. When she was a child, her own family moved from Wexford to Cork and back again when her Dad, Patrick, was made Garda sergeant in Oulart village. Mam loved GAA as well. She played camogie in Cork with Grenagh and when Oulart started a club in 1984, she always stayed involved. She met my Dad in the village years back; they got married and we soon started to arrive on the scene. Her brother, Seán Woulfe, used to spend his summers between Wexford and Cork, where he hurled with all sorts of clubs, illegally, I might add. Seán was a strong swimmer but at just 24 he was swept off a pier with two friends and while they survived, he didn't. They found his body seven days later.

Another of my mother's brothers, Borgie, a good hurler, also suffered a tragic death. His home went on fire one Easter weekend and while he and his wife got out, he heard his children screaming and went back into the house. Borgie never came back out and only two of the children, Damien and Willie, made it out.

A few years later, when Willie grew up, he went out on his motorbike one Saturday evening to get a bag of chips and was killed. That's tough in anyone's language.

There were happier times, however. It was like *The Waltons* at times in Kyle-Oulart; four boys used to sleep in one room and the girls in another but there were no sweet goodnight calls from one to the other as we dozed off. You were more likely if you were yapping to get a shoe in the face to send you to sleep.

I don't really remember many of my early days but I suppose that in itself suggests we were happy enough. I do recall that later, when things moved on a bit, two of us transferred into another room, which was an absolute luxury.

As for the rest of the place, well the only heating we had in that house was the summertime. We had a great big oil cooker alright but there was never a whole lot of oil put in it and little wonder that we looked forward to spring, summer and the warm weather so much. Although Dad had a good number, there were that many of us he would have needed a job in rocket science or brain surgery to keep it all going.

We had plenty of hobbies and stuff to keep us active. Our interests were well varied but they mainly centred on sports and music; we were always hitting a sliotar or playing some instrument or other.

Kieran, the eldest, played underage hurling until he was forced to pack it in because of poor eyesight. That's what he told us anyway. From what I recall, he was no Christy Ring. He used to play in goal and there are just some things that even glasses cannot help you with. He went on to qualify as a secondary school teacher but could not get a job in his chosen field back then and turned to the South Eastern Health Board, where he still works.

Tomás works as a roofer and has always been the 'chancer' of the family. That lad had a go at everything and got blamed for most of what went wrong anywhere within a 10-mile radius of the house. He was a great hurler who played senior for Wexford on and off for 10 seasons until 1994 but didn't get half the credit he deserved.

Over the following years as I hit the town, I would encounter selectors and county board officials who slated Tomás for his wildness. I would agree it was scandalous behaviour even though I was probably a much bigger culprit.

Tomás always got caught but he has always been a success at what he put his hand to.

Seán works for Munster Joinery, who are based in Ballydesmond, Co Cork. Growing up, he tried all types of sport from squash to table tennis and was good at most of them. Later on, he won junior football and hurling All-Ireland titles with the county. Although he was the fastest thing on two legs at the time, he used to play in goal, which I always felt was such a waste.

My multitalented sister Siobhán was the first superstar in the Dunne family. She had two Gaelic football All Star awards by the time she was 24 and also played for Wexford in an All-Ireland camogie final, which they lost.

My mother always reminds us that Siobhán was the first All Star in the family and she's right. Siobhán was a great player and was always on the go. After winning the two awards, she went to Dublin for international soccer trials.

We had a great laugh all the way up along over our little sibling rivalry, and I got huge pleasure years later, the morning after my third All Star, ringing her to gloat that my days of trailing in her shadow were over. Siobhán works as a horticulturist now.

Fiona was another graduate of the Dunne sports academy; she had little choice but to play. Like our youngest sister, Ailish, she played camogie for most of her youth. She now runs O'Brien's pub in Killenagh. Gráinne, a devoted housewife these days, was the only one of the family not to compete and instead opted for music when we were kids. My mother maintained she was the only one with sense but she also succumbed to the hurling bug and married Pat Dooley who won an All-Ireland 'B' medal with Kildare.

There was always a lot of competition when we were kids because no matter what one member of the family achieved, there was always another to do something better a few days later. When I won my first All Star, a local reporter, David Medcalf, came to the house, but not to talk to me at all; he wanted to grill my mother on the sporting achievements of the family in general.

'Eileen's famous sporting family have done it all,' his article read and, one by one, it detailed the honours we had collected. Mam was fairly proud when she saw that hitting the newsagents.

There is no doubt that knowing the lads at home were just as good as me in their chosen fields kept me on my toes but while we were always into something competitive, there was a fairly relaxed feeling about my early days in Oulart.

As with many families, there were times during my childhood when our family or one of the neighbours needed a dig-out and certain people were always quick to offer the helping hand. Fintan Cooney was one such Good Samaritan.

Times were hard enough around our area because the economy was often in tatters but we were lucky we had this man. He was the ultimate believer in community spirit, owned a bit of land, a pub and a grocery shop. To say Fintan Cooney was good to the Dunnes, and many others in Oulart, would be an understatement. I'd say a lot of locals might not have got through the hard times only for him. He thought nothing of putting his hand into his own pocket and asked nothing in return.

A former chairman of Oulart-The-Ballagh GAA club, he died after a heart attack and was buried on the day we beat Offaly in the 1997 Leinster semi-final. I ran out first on the bench for the team picture that afternoon and offered up a few seconds' private thought for him. At the funeral the following day, Fintan's wife, Clare, who is also my godmother, singled me out to thank me for scoring a goal to his memory.

Now, I don't really know if he did guide the ball into the net for me – it probably owed more to a mistake by the goalkeeper, David Hughes – but I thought of Fintan when I hit the back of the net from a 65-metre free and remembered him after the game again. He was great to us, my mother especially. Some people come straight into your mind when you cast it back. Fintan Cooney was one of them.

At various stages, the eight of us streamed into Oulart National School, where the principal, Michael Bracken, performed an incision on my first day by separating me from my minder, Kieran, who was in fifth class. Michael carried me down to junior infants as the tears streamed out of my eyes. I did not want to be there.

'What's your name?' he asked.

'Liam Dunne,' I stammered.

'Are you Kieran's brother?'

'Yes.'

'Well, listen to him and not to Tomás and you'll be okay.' Despite the fact he was a lovely man, I was afraid of Michael for the rest of my time at Oulart NS. I suppose from day one I knew that school and I were never going to be close friends.

It was there, however, that I began to realise there was a lot of history in the parish. And Irish history doesn't boast many finer moments than the 1798 rebellion. You talk about battles but one of the few we won in that era was at Oulart Hill, where rebels led by Fr John Murphy, Edward Roche and Morgan Byrne defeated the North Cork Militia. It was a great win for the United Irishmen, though they lost nearly every other skirmish.

And I have more than education to thank school for. The friends I made there: Bartle Sinnott, Bartle Redmond, Martin Dempsey, Henry Cleary and Gay Cooney are still my best. I tasted my first drop of alcohol with those lads, they laughed at my first car, I got involved in my first scrap trying to stand up for them while they ran away, and we've ended up bailing each other out ever since.

They were the wonder years. The village never seemed too small for us by the way. Oulart has developed now but back then it had the usual layout: church, school, shop, monument to 1798 and, not surprisingly, two pubs, Cooney's and the Sportsman's Inn. That was it, straightforward and simple, but it had everything I wanted.

Top of the list was hurling and when I was eight and about three foot tall, I played my first game for Oulart-The-Ballagh under-10s. We came up against Shelmaliers/Castlebridge and because of my size I was tucked into corner forward, where I prayed to the Man Above I wouldn't get hit. Two things I remember about that game: we got bottles of 7-up afterwards and Anthony Stamp was our captain. Anthony would later die in a freak accident in what turned out to be one of the worst years in the parish's history, 1987.

But in the actual game, I can't even remember hitting a ball. They had put me out of the way but with Dad over the team, there was no chance I would be substituted. That sort of nepotism still exists in Wexford to this day and it gets under my skin. If my chance in management ever comes, we'll see what can be done about it.

So an undistinguished debut but Dad kept making little hurleys for me because I was shorter than others and needed a special stick. I remember getting my very first hurley from a local man called Frank Randall, who had been making them for years. Of course, the one Frank gave me was way too big so my father spliced it for me, basically trimmed the handle of the hurley down and put a little v into it.

Over the next few years, I was coming thick and fast to Dad asking for sticks to be shortened until I caught him on a bad night and he told me to go down to the shed and do it myself. Innocent as I was, I started on my good hurleys, wielding the jigsaw and glue in the shed like a seasoned professional, or so I fancied, but of course making shit of all my sticks.

By the time I got the hang of the whole routine, I was left with a fair few duds.

Still, I kept practising hard and often with them. I also started watching games on TV. For some reason, I really latched onto the Galway team of 1979 and 1980. When they played, I was glued to the box watching classy players like Iggy Clarke, Seán Silke and the

Connolly brothers in action.

My memories of watching Wexford in the late 1970s are vague. For me it was all Galway and my main man, Cork's Jimmy Barry Murphy. Looking back at my scrapbooks from 1977, it's interesting to see that I drew a picture of the Liam MacCarthy Cup on the last page of my first ever collection. I suppose every young lad in hurling territory does it at some stage but it's good to see the ambition was there from day one.

My aspirations in the classroom, however, took longer to develop. The only reason I began to find school tolerable in the first place was because we were guaranteed game time between 2 and 3 o'clock. I would hurl my heart out during the day and pray it wouldn't rain so I could play an under-12 game that night. I never won very much at underage level and that was usually because we came up against town teams like Enniscorthy, who were a lot stronger. And while that was disheartening, the notion of stopping never occurred to me.

Eventually, things took a turn for the better: when I was in fourth class, Breda Jacob joined the school as a teacher. She was married to the legendary Wexford hurler Mick, and together with Joe Hyland and Liam Keogh, she took over our under-10 team.

Breda, whose sons Rory and Mick are on the current Wexford senior team, was my first proper hurling coach and she brought me to a different level by simply holding skills competitions and teaching the class to jab-lift, roll-lift, solo, hand-pass and tackle. If some lad got 20 roll-lifts in a competition, I would be green with envy and would speed home to train that night and make sure I got 21 the next day.

Around 1980, Mick Jacob senior took a special interest in me and asked me to go up to the local field and hit back the sliotar as he practised his free-taking. This was the big time now. I was Mick's Mini-Me and delighted to be, thank you very much. Although I was only 13 at the time, the truth is I idolised the man and was thrilled to be asked to bang a few balls with him.

We used to go to Mass every Sunday but my reasons for attending were far from religious. Mick would always go to first Mass and I wouldn't even look at the priest. Instead, I would wait for Communion and try to walk past him while he went to the altar, just hoping for some sort of acknowledgement from him. Some went to pray to God but I was sitting only two seats away from the real one and didn't need prayers.

It was a dream to even hit the balls back. Fair enough, I was under massive pressure to get the ball back to the 70-yard line, where he was lofting them over. I was like Sonic the Hedgehog, buzzing all over the place, driving balls out to him with all my might, running back to collect them and striking another one out the field.

Mick would say a few words when he sensed I was flagging and it was like putting petrol in a car because I would just lift my game one more time to keep clearing the balls out the field for as long as I could. Another local hero of mine was Ned Buggy. I used to idolise him.

I tried to copy his style of free-taking, where he had the left hand off the hurl and put it back on again just as he was about to strike, but I could never do it and soon abandoned my efforts. Ned won an All Star in 1979 and presented me with the only real medal I won at underage, the 1981 Rackard Cup, and I was chuffed.

We later went on to play handball together and I actually marked him in a hurling match later again, when he pulled a foot over the ball and pulverised me with a smack. I looked at him in disbelief. Imagine Ned Buggy hitting me! Still, it was great to play against him.

Maybe hanging with the heroes started to pay off. At 13, I was brought into county under-14 trials as a corner forward and they left me in the panel until the Leinster final, when I was dropped.

The managers, Pat Murphy and Bill Hayden, never actually told me I was chopped but I was so small and miserable they probably forgot. Instead, they asked me to carry the hurls for the final and I told them to get stuffed, that I wanted to go to the stands and watch Wexford, who were in three finals that day. We lost all of them, something I was to get fairly used to in the years to come.

I wasn't really that upset about getting the heave-ho. To tell you the truth, I was afraid of a good few lads that we came up against around then and as a small corner forward I was getting a lot of smacks and wasn't too brave about it either.

There was some compensation for me when the club went on to win the Wexford under-14 Féile na nGael competition. In the All-Ireland series, we were hammered by Galway and, interestingly, only three of that team went on to play senior for Oulart-The-Ballagh. The following year, I made the county under-14 team again and was brought on after 10 minutes of the Leinster final against Kilkenny, and once more we were thrashed.

But while hurling was a night-and-day job, there was more on my mind as well. I had also been playing a lot of soccer at the time and had been going very well for nearby Kilmuckridge Vocational School, where I studied, or at least attended, after national school.

At 14, I was playing about four years above my level and my efforts started to catch the attention of a few local scouts. To tell the truth, I was big into it and absolutely loved playing in the middle of the field, the department where one of my future heroes, Roy Keane, was to make his name.

There was a fair danger that hurling could have gone by the wayside, especially when I came home from school one day to discover that big news awaited me.

I was just 14 years of age and already my sporting career was coming to its first crossroads. It would be the first of many difficult junctions along the way.

All animals are equal but some are more equal than others.
George Orwell, *Animal Farm*

– CHAPTER FIVE –
The wizard of OZY

As a kid, my main ambition was to play hurling for Wexford but I was also willing to see how far I could take my soccer career. The idea appealed to me mainly because it looked like my hurling ambitions had stalled, especially after my graduation from Oulart NS to Kilmuckridge Vocational School, which was not one bit fashionable in the GAA world. You really had to be attending St Peter's to break into intercounty hurling at that stage.

That sort of shit was rife in Wexford at the time but thank God, we have moved on, though not fully. We still have selectors trying to get their own favourites on teams, despite the fact they are plainly not good enough.

Back then, Oulart was not a fashionable club and the likes of Tomás and I would lose out to some other lad who was on the county team because his father knew someone. The prejudice was a lot worse back then than it is now so it was no bad thing to throw myself into soccer as it was the main game at Kilmuckridge VS anyway.

I played each day as hurling went on the back burner for a while and my friend Pat Rossitter and I developed into decent players. We were two of the main figures in the team that won the Wexford Schools Cup in 1981 and I really enjoyed my central-midfield role.

One evening early in that same season, word filtered through to the school that I was picked for Ireland under-15 trials. This was a big surprise because firstly it had never crossed my mind and secondly I was underage again the following year, 1982, when a trial was much more likely. But Pat got the call as well and we travelled to Dublin to play the Waterford Youth team, who were about three years above our fighting weight.

I got a right land when I walked into the AUL sports complex, because it seemed we had the Ritz for changing-rooms, a five-star job. There was gear laid out and folded for me and not a ditch in sight to tog out in. Everyone had his own designated area and we were introduced to two of the team's 'star' players; one was on Luton Town's books and the other had just signed with Leeds United. They definitely had a bit of time for themselves alright but it seems no-one else did because the pair of them never got anywhere in the end.

I could have got used to that way of life. I remember my mouth was still wide open as I tried to figure how to sneak home the trendy playing gear in front of me. Our teacher, Michael Enright, brought us up to the capital for the trials but his influence wasn't enough to see us onto the first 11 and so we were handed substitutes' jerseys.

Still, that was fine. Better to come in and make the impression. And we looked on in amusement as our team-mates got the runaround from these gigantic poles from Waterford, some of them sporting the beginnings of a dodgy moustache on their upper lips.

At half time, though, the grins were wiped from our faces when Pat and I were plucked from the comfort zone and thrown into midfield. We got stuck in and held our own, and looking back, I thought the game went well for both of us.

We were instructed to go back to our clubs and wait for word from the FAI. The prospect of making a career across the water had never occupied my mind but I was ready to give it a shot if the call arrived. In the end, I didn't have to worry. The advice from the Irish management was to keep the game up but I hadn't made the cut this time. Never mind, I did keep soccer going with the school and my two teams, The Ballagh FC and St Joseph's, and we went on to win a lot of trophies, but by the time the next year's trials came along, I already had my hands stuck in another pie, handball, and had lost most of my interest in the beautiful game.

Where I got time for school in between my sporting pursuits I don't know but the fact that I was never one for the books was no great surprise to Mam and when my 1983 Group Cert exams came around she held out little hope for me.

Nevertheless, I slowly took to the books. When I would go into a room to swot, my family presumed I was just reading comics in between a text book. They had about as much faith in me as Michael Moore has in George Bush.

Still, when the results came, I surprised them all with six honours, two passes and just one fail, not the seven or so predicted for me by my loving family.

For the record, here are my 1983 Group Cert results. Irish NG (I had decided at that stage one language was enough for me); Woodwork B; English C; Maths C; Geography C; History C; Mechanical Drawing C; Metalwork C; Science B.

Now, I was hardly Dr Liam Dunne PhD yet and even after these fine results I still couldn't see a career in Trinity or UCD beckoning. But by no means was I ready to leave school either even though, at the time, it was the done thing to push off after the Inter Cert. Instead, I was keen to give it a good old go for another year and maybe then wave goodbye to the education system.

For days my mother remained in a state of mild and pleasant shock over my results but I knew I had sacrificed a bit of hurling and soccer to study and was aware that if I put more work in I could keep going in school. For example, I knew as much about science at the start of second year as I did of the Irish language but had applied myself to it during the second and third terms and actually ended up liking it. So I pondered my short-term future and, to pass the long summer away, got a job with Andy Roche in Blackwater, only a few miles down the road. I was 15, had a Group Cert behind me and was only waiting for the voice to break before finally gaining my membership card to the Men's Club.

Andy ran a joinery business and I thought I could give him a hand, but after my first day I'm sure he thought otherwise. The first task I was handed was to put two panes of glass into a window, a job that would usually take maybe 20 minutes. Andy left me on my own and told me to head back to the workshop when I was finished.

That was in the morning. When he returned later that evening, I was still scratching my head. It took me most of the day to install them.

'I thought you were able to make your own hurleys, Liam,' Andy scowled.

'I am Andy, but I never claimed to be able to put glass in a window.'

A look of despair spread across his face and I'd say he wondered what he had let himself in for. Little wonder, then, that I was confined to the workshop for the rest of the summer, which I actually loved. After a while, I even got the hang of the job.

Shortly before the end of that summer, my brother Kieran qualified from UCC as a secondary schoolteacher. But even though he had worked very hard to get the results he just could not get a job. It made me think that if someone like him couldn't land a full-time position, what hope had I? I decided to leave school.

In the end, it was no tough choice. I had never fully intended doing the Leaving Cert anyway, so Andy and I agreed terms and he paid me my first permanent wage packet: a princely 35 punts per week. It was a lot for me and much more than Kieran got in his first job. In fact, I had to subsidise him with a few loans despite the fact he was eight years older.

The job was fairly relaxed and you could talk hurling, which suited me. Andy's Dad, Jim, had been on the 1940 Wexford junior team that won the Leinster final, the county's first big win in 30 years, so there was no getting away from the game in work.

It helped even more that two of my best mates, Martin Dempsey and Bartle Sinnott, also took time out of school after they had struggled with the Group Cert. It took their parents that much longer

than my Mam to realise the boys were wasting their time with
academic pursuits.

I had a bit of sense by now and was saving a few quid, and as my
hurling career still hadn't taken off, I devoted most of my spare time to
handball. There was something about handball I liked; it was not hugely
popular but it was fast and tricky and suited someone my size.

I won a bronze medal at the Community Games in Mosney in
1981 and kept it up. Of course the fact I was a teenager meant once I
found a new passion, every other sport and interest went out the
window. I went on to win under-14 singles and doubles, with Pat
Rossitter, at the Wexford Championships. By the time I was 17, I was
winning under-21 titles and significantly adding to my trophy cabinet all
the time. The local newspapers said many of my wins were inevitable
but, in fairness, while I was good at the game, there was a very small
pool of players around the circuit and that didn't help my progress. But
Nicky O'Toole drove me the length and breadth of the country to help
improve me all the same.

I continued the game at a pretty high standard for as long as I
could and in my last year at under-18 played Peter McAuley from
Louth, who had won numerous world titles. Everyone in the game saw
it as a huge test and while he beat me 21-17, 21-4, it was great to be
even in the same alley as someone of that quality.

Although my love of handball never waned, matches were
increasingly hard to come by as there was just no-one to play. And so I
rarely played once I hit 18, which was a shame, but in hindsight I can at
least say handball later helped my hand-to-eye co-ordination for
hurling. While I was sorry to eventually call it a day, the lack of
handball competition allowed me to devote more time to my new
vices: women and nightlife. At 16 I started 'tipping around', as the lads
at home would say.

It was now that I sampled my first drink, when I strolled down the
village to Linda's Nightclub a boy and staggered home thinking I was a

man. I ordered a large bottle of Harp. The lads, Martin Dempsey and Bartle Sinnott, were nearby so I had to make it look good but it was tough because the bottle was almost bigger than myself.

One pint later and I really was twisted, the floor coming up to meet me, but I just kept a stupid grin on my face, snuck into the corner and hoped the dizziness would go away.

As a further demonstration of my new-found manhood, I also invested around this time in a lovely set of wheels. Well, it was lovely if you were a big girl's blouse or a 78-year-old granny. For some bizarre reason, my first purchase was a bright yellow Ford Fiesta, price 2,500 punts, with the licence plate OZY 678. If a lad ever wanted to remain discreet in Oulart, he had no chance driving this screaming-yellow heap of junk around the place and looking like Big Bird.

It cost me another £700 to insure it, but having being brought up very independent, I wanted my own car and this rotten yellow machine was what I ended up with.

My first crash duly came in the OZY. Luckily it wasn't fatal, and the following morning, as I had little recollection of the night before, I found it strange to see so many briars tangled up in the wipers and hanging out the window.

There were times, I honestly think, when that car drove itself home. It was like Herbie from the movies, or so we liked to think.

Like Herbie, when he was angry, OZY had a habit of getting his own back on you. One night, trembling with hope, I brought some girl out of a disco and we headed to the car. Trying to act cool, I went to open the door, whereupon the handle snapped off. I strolled around to the passenger side; that handle snapped as well. But like any red-blooded young lad about to get lucky, I wasn't going to give up so I crawled into the boot and up through the car, eventually unlocking it and opening it for the two of us. I can now tell you that it wasn't worth all the effort.

Apart from doing ourselves harm, we never really caused much grief to others during our teenage years, though I clearly remember our first real serious altercation.

Most teenagers get into hassles with bikers at a late-night disco or outside a chipper, but we stooped to an all-time low when we were run out of an old folks' party.

After a trip down to the local nightclub, Linda's, we decided there wasn't much happening, but one of the lads got a tip-off that there was a party in nearby Curracloe. It was a wind-up, though. Our mole neglected to say it was a senior citizens' function. Undeterred, we went in and donned the party hats and started blowing all sorts of whistles and singing with the grannies. We thought it was some crack but one chap really took exception to our presence and even though a local man, Larry Donohue, stood up for us, we were told to clear off.

With a few pints down me, I left and hopped into a car that still looked bright yellow even in the pitch dark. I had my party hat on and was about to drive home with the lads when I turned on the radio and quickly copped that my car didn't actually have one.

'We might as well clean out what's in it,' Bartle Sinnott laughed, sticking a few golf balls and tapes in his pocket.

'Might as well, now that we're here,' I agreed. We fleeced the car before withdrawing and eventually finding OZY.

Days later, we met Larry again and he looked upset. I asked him was there anything wrong and he said he was raging because his car had been broken into and his stereo and other belongings had been stolen. My face dropped.

We had mistakenly and drunkenly gone into his car but all we took were golf balls and tapes of The Drifters. Someone had come along and fleeced the car after us.

'Jesus, Larry,' I sympathised, 'some people would take the eye out of the back of your head.' And I made my excuses and left.

Between the messing, I kept my hurling going and was called up to the county under-16 team in 1984 but was once more dropped as they went on to win the Leinster blitz.

A year later, I was in no doubt that I would make the minor panel when the time came to go to trials. So I played away with the club and tried to prepare for what was to come. I need not have bothered; word got back to me that I wasn't hurling well enough to merit even a trial.

At that stage I was playing at centre back, having told the club selectors I was finished in the forwards, and when I later saw some of the lads who had made the squad, I was just disgusted.

In fact, I still feel raw about not making that team. Some of the players were absolutely putrid and I've never heard tell of a lot of them since, yet I was deemed not good enough to even get a chance. The real reason, of course, was that I was not a student at St Peter's College. Had I been studying there, my chances of making the Wexford minor team were so much better. But I had been at Kilmuckridge VS and proud of it and my own club would not have been the most fashionable either so I had to bite my tongue and wait for the season to drift by. Let no-one tell you we are all equals in Wexford because this who-you-are shit still goes on here today. Some are more equal than others.

At least motivation was not in short supply for my last year as a minor, and in the 1986 Leinster Championship I was finally selected to play on the team and lined out at right-half forward against Carlow. We beat them well, I played fine and we had another good win over Laois in the semi-final.

Lying in wait for us in the final, however, were Offaly. They annihilated us. It hadn't helped that our management opted to make 13 changes from the semi-final but in truth, Daithí Regan, Michael Duignan, Declan Pilkington and company simply destroyed us. And right through the next eight years or so, they were well on top of us.

That day, though, I played my own game: sidesteps, swerves, ball control, running up and down the field, striking off both sides, and what I didn't score that day, I set up for the rest of the team.

As I walked off the field, crushed and disheartened, Fr Butler approached me.

'Young Dunne,' he said, as he clasped his two hands on my shoulders, 'you're going to have many days back in Croke Park, many days.'

I looked at him, silently asking forgiveness for thinking this holy man was talking nonsense. But maybe I began to believe a few weeks later when I was called up to the county under-21 team. Imagine, I couldn't make the minor team a year before and now here I was on the under-21 team. Someone else can try to figure it out.

Anyway, the under-21s met Offaly again, this time in the Leinster final, and we drew. I was brought on as a sub for the replay, which we won. But I looked on from the bench as we beat Derry in the All-Ireland semi-final before Galway won the Championship with the likes of Joe Cooney and Gerry McInerney.

People think I had a great old time of it but that was the sum of my career up to minor level: a Rackard Cup medal; a Féile medal and a sub's place on the county under-21 team that won the Leinster title; 18 county handball and three Wexford soccer championships.

That's pretty miserable in my language, but even then I didn't realise the extent of the famine that lay ahead.

But to tell the truth, after what happened to the village of Oulart in 1987, winning trophies was about the last thing we were concerned with.

Life is what happens to you when you're busy making other plans.
John Lennon

– CHAPTER SIX –
Tragedy visits Oulart

There is a moment in everyone's childhood or teenage years when innocence is swiped away and replaced with a harsh slap of reality. The people of Oulart-The-Ballagh got much more than a slap of it in 1987; we got a full-force blow in the face.

There is nothing like a death of someone you know well to knock the stuffing out of you, but when you are young and it happens twice, well, it just leaves you on your knees. When I turned on the radio early on March 2, 2004, and heard on the news that the Tyrone footballer Cormac McAnallen had died the night before, I was dumbfounded. The first thing that came into my head was what a lovely chap he was and how in the name of Jesus could this have happened. It's sometimes a cliché when people pass away, but Cormac really was top-class, an honest and friendly guy. I had the pleasure of knowing him. We sat together at the 2003 All Stars and although he seemed a quiet lad at first, he soon chatted away and we had a great conversation, mainly because he was such an interesting bloke.

At one stage, Cormac said I must have been sick of the All Stars and asked me how many functions I had been at. He was genuinely surprised to hear it was actually my first since 1997.

His death just left a trail of disbelief around the country and I never saw so many from different corners of Ireland express their sympathy. I suppose Tyrone people will never get over it, especially after one of his former team-mates, Paul McGirr, had also passed away during an Ulster minor football clash in 1997.

Like a lot of the Oulart people, I felt our tragic memories were rammed home again when I heard of Cormac's death; 1987 is a year seldom mentioned around these parts but it's never too far from our minds either.

After strolling through my teenage years without too many worries or cares, I had just started to concentrate on breaking into the club senior team. Anthony Stamp and Richard Ormond, two guys slightly older than me, were also busy making a name for themselves. Anthony was only about 21 and was part of the team that had just beaten our arch-rivals Buffers Alley in a tournament game. To us, it felt like the All-Ireland final because you didn't get the satisfaction of beating those lads too often.

But shortly after, word ran through the village like wildfire of Anthony's death in an accident near The Ballagh. We really didn't know how to take it.

I didn't anyway. It shook everyone in the village. We're a close lot and while you might have one or two families not talking to each other, there would be a strong sense of unity.

But seeing grown men hurt and looking at how long it took people to get back on their feet left us all vulnerable for a long time afterwards. For once, hurling just seemed like a meaningless little hobby, no more than that. Country people are great at rallying behind a family in times of need and that was exactly what happened as people supported the Stamp family. Locals undertook all sorts of acts of kindness that would genuinely leave you in admiration of them.

They say time is the best healer of all and maybe it is and maybe it isn't. But just as things were starting to get back to normal for the rest of the village, we heard more tragic news, this time of Richard Ormond's sudden death.

Once more, the area was grief-stricken. Two young men with it all in front of them had been taken from their families. No-one had expected it and no-one around knew what to say.

In a way, Richard's death was worse because the whole county sympathised with us now and the outpouring of grief was even bigger than when Anthony had died.

Richard was only 22 and made me captain of a team for the first time at under-10 level. He was driving a juggernaut and it jackknifed about two miles outside Gorey, at a spot only 500 yards from where my uncle Billy was killed.

Like Cormac McAnallen, Richard was the role model of the village and you could tell that by looking at the sleeves on his scout's badge; he was so decorated there was barely any more room left on them. You had to achieve many different things to earn a badge but Richard had dozens of them and was a real leader. With Anthony, he had played on the team that won the 1985 under-21 Championship. Both of them were set for good, solid senior careers and yet, here they were, taken away from us in their prime.

How do you react? The first instinct was to turn their deaths into a cause and try to win the club Championship in their memory. Playing for your county is supposed to be an honour but when Christy Keogh selected me at wing back on the Wexford under-21 team that year, I cared little for it after what had happened to us in the village. Most of the lads on the Oulart-The-Ballagh senior team felt the same. The tragedies had brought us closer and we made a pledge to try and win the club Championship for the two lads. But in hindsight, a trophy seemed so insignificant at the end of it all. Maybe such passionate resolutions, like 'winning it for the lads' are inevitable after a sudden death but in a way I feel it's not a healthy exercise; nor was it a good idea to be showing us, before games, the jerseys the two lads used to wear.

I think we were shown them once too often because while we went out that year and trained ourselves into the ground, we came a cropper in the county semi-final. I lost the cool in that game and was sent off for the first time – I wish it had been the last – in my career.

Cloughbawn were the opponents on the day. They had the game won but my direct marker, John Fleming, was absolutely sewing it into me. He kept tipping me on the top of the head, pulling my helmet down and taunting me.

'You're only a little chap, Dunne. Go home.'

It wasn't a lad having a bit of banter; there was needle and what sounded like a bit of malice in his taunts. I managed to ignore him but made a silent vow that John Fleming would get what was owed to him some day.

But despite my self-control toward Fleming, I was sent off for an altercation with another of their players, Tom Byrne, and for that I got six months. Although I was intending to attend the county Games Administration Committee hearing, I was told beforehand that even if I brought Mother Teresa as a character witness it would be to no avail, so I gave it a miss.

It was the end to a horrible year but I suppose there was some compensation seven years later when I went on to win the club's first senior county title with Anthony Stamp's brother, Declan, and Richard Ormond's brother James. And I suppose my mood lightened a little when I was called into the Wexford senior panel for the first time and just smiled when I thought of the trouble I had making the minor team just a couple of years previous.

While I had been out enjoying myself on the town as a young man, I was also putting more into hurling than many other lads in the county at that time and it felt brilliant to get the call-up, but at the same time it was a big surprise. It took me so long to get out of the traps but I had always felt there was prejudice against my club. The fact Tomás had never played minor for the county was seen as an absolute scandal in the village at the time, but as I say, to make the team it was often a case of who you knew.

My friend and clubmate Martin Storey hadn't played minor for Wexford either so I entertained no great hopes of getting any sort of a senior call-up after my past experiences with the county. But I got the nod. First though, I had to wait for my six-month club ban to end. Meanwhile, the Wexford manager, Christy Keogh, was forever asking me when I was free to play. I was only 19 but was playing some stuff and the management wanted me quickly on board. Because I couldn't play League games, they arranged challenge matches against Waterford so they could take a look at me for when the suspension did end.

My first taste of intercounty hurling was fiery. Welcoming me to the intercounty stage, Decies midfielder Shane Ahearne told me it was 'the only fucking time' I'd wear the county colours. Nice one, Shane. I played against him twice in a few weeks though and held my own. I knew there was a lot more to come if I got the chance. Christy's other selectors, by the way, were Robbie Jacob, Tom Mooney, Bernie Rathford and Hopper McGrath.

I did fine in the two challenge games and was duly handed my League debut at wing back against Tipperary in 1988. Over the next few weeks, I kept my head down and tried to make no silly mistakes and it was absolute fantasy land when I learned I was picked for our senior Championship match against Laois a few weeks later.

There was little or no fuss at home at the news of my Championship debut. My mother had in a sense seen it all before and anyway she had no car at the time so she found it hard to get to games; she didn't even make it to my debut in the end.

Dad was away as usual and the brothers weren't that interested, to be honest. And as for the girls, well they had their own things going on and they hardly batted an eyelid either. But it was a dream come true for me and naturally I was dead nervous; I never slept a wink in the lead-up to that game.

There was little or no advice for me from my peers; it was a case of 'look after your own patch' and I didn't really feel comfortable asking my new team-mates for tips because, well to be truthful, they weren't exactly the most welcoming bunch.

There are certain guys I went on to win an All-Ireland senior medal with that wouldn't even look me in the face or give me a word or two when I first joined the squad. As my own career developed, I always remembered that ignorance and would try to have a quiet chat with a new guy coming into the squad.

Anyway, I didn't get the red carpet, but that didn't affect me as much as it backfired on some of those lads who ignored me; they were dropped within a year or two.

Along came my big moment, the day I had waited for since I was a kid, when I drew pictures of the Liam MacCarthy Cup and kept cuttings of Mick Jacob, Jimmy Barry Murphy, the Connollys and Noel Skehan in scrapbooks. Around the village, people had kept the build-up at a low key and no-one treated me any differently. That all helped but still, minutes before the game I was a nervous wreck, going to the toilet every five minutes. I sat in the cubicle and wished my father was there to see me. I felt angry and sad at the same time that he wasn't.

Along with John Conran, who guided Wexford to the 2004 Leinster title, I was picked at midfield. He was coming to an end and I was starting out; maybe both of us had a point to prove.

Eventually, the game got underway. All was going well until Pat Critchley, who was selected at corner forward, dropped back as a third midfielder for Laois, and while it was a tactic that was hardly ever used back then, it worked wonders for our rivals and had the opposite effect on us. We didn't know how to handle the situation and they ran rings around us at the start. As I was the young gun, it was the easy call to put the blame on me and, sure enough, five minutes before the break, I was moved to wing forward. I knew what was coming at half-time and barely looked up as they told me I was being taken off.

Wexford went on to win that game but I was very disappointed myself. A few days later, I picked up a copy of the *Irish Independent* to learn that Martin Quigley had been recalled for the Kilkenny match and there was no L Dunne either in the starting team or on the subs' bench.

'Here we go again,' I thought.

When people asked me about being dropped, I shrugged my

shoulders as though I couldn't give a toss either way, but in truth I was devastated. I couldn't believe I had been taken right off the panel.

Then fate intervened. Larry O'Gorman broke a bone in his hand days before the semi-final and when I came back from playing pitch-and-putt, I got a call from Bro John Cahill, who did all the dirty work for the management team by telling players they were dropped. Bro Cahill asked me to return to the squad and I agreed. Even though I wouldn't see a sniff of action that day, I was handed Larry O's number seven jersey for the occasion.

We beat Kilkenny, but once more I was axed from the panel for the Leinster final with Offaly. They asked me to carry the hurls for that game but I looked on from the stands with my father, who had come home for the game, and my mother while we got beaten by the Faithful County, 3-12 to 1-14.

The barren times continued with the club and the county under-21s, and when the 1989 senior season started, Martin Storey and I were left out in the cold while other guys from my club were brought into the panel. Although we get on fine now, I held my own clubman and Wexford selector Robbie Jacob responsible for my omission; I felt he should have known what I was capable of. Storey felt likewise.

In the end, I was hurling so well for Oulart they just had to call me back in, and that's not being big-headed. My face didn't fit Wexford hurling at the time but I was determined to slot in somewhere.

The relationship between Liam Dunne and Wexford hurling was brittle. I was in and out, musical chairs. Six weeks before they met Kilkenny, I was drafted in again but with no League games behind me and no signs of any chance to prove myself, I had the feeling I would be surplus to requirements soon after.

No shock then when I read in the paper a week ahead of the Kilkenny match I had yet again been scratched from the official squad. They didn't even have the guts to tell me I was gone; let a newspaper do the job instead.

There was nothing more I wanted than to hurl for Wexford but I didn't even bother having words with the management, and they never even gave me a ticket for that game. I was by now built up with fury but just decided to prove them wrong, though admittedly I thought I had been doing that all along.

I'm not going to harp on about results and personal performances; I don't want my story to be like that. But just to see how off the ball the senior selectors were, take a look at my displays in the 1988 under-21 Championship. I scored 0-12 from wing back against Laois, about half of which were from frees. In the same competition a year later, I got the same against Carlow before Kilkenny took us in the next round. I had been voted Man of the Match in the 1989 under-21 Wexford final, but once more we lost to Buffers Alley.

My days of underage hurling were now over and here I was, finally in the real world but, for all my huffing and puffing, with zilch to show for it. It wasn't a great return for almost 15 years of competitive sport but although I held no personal animosity towards Christy Keogh, who at least wanted me in the camp, there was one motivation in relation to the rest of the Wexford management, and that was to prove them wrong. Top of the list was my own clubman Robbie Jacob. For a long time I didn't see eye to eye with him. Those selectors got the boot anyway after the loss to Kilkenny and by the time Martin Quigley, Dave Bernie and Jimmy Furlong took over for the 1989/1990 League, it was a foregone conclusion that not only would I be in the panel but I would be on the team as well.

In the lead-up to the new season, I gave everything I had at club level and was a certainty to make the Wexford team. We had been beaten in yet another county final by Buffers Alley; it was our fourth defeat at the final hurdle and we had yet to reach the Holy Grail. But out of the campaign I got a call-up.

A few other guys joined the squad as well but like dominoes they were dropped one by one. This time, when the official list of 25 was drawn up, I was still in.

Finally, I felt comfortable in the same group as the likes of George and John O'Connor, Billy Byrne, Martin Storey, Eamon Cleary and Tom Dempsey and didn't look to the sideline after making one mistake, fearing a substitution.

Guys were a bit nicer to me when they saw me making progress, which I suppose shows how fickle is human nature, and I played most of the League vying for a wing-back slot with Larry O'Gorman, Seánie Flood and John O'Connor.

It was all the same to me who I was up against for the position because I was going to make it regardless; my mind was made up. Behind the scenes, Dave Bernie was another with plenty on his mind. Deep down, he knew we were light years behind other counties so he brought a more professional approach with him, which resulted in the Wexford Supporters Club being founded, under the guidance of John Doyle. Dave contacted the successful racehorse trainer Jim Bolger and got him involved, and through his contacts, the 'Club' expanded. We were much better looked after once that was established and had tracksuits, proper gear and all the basics we wouldn't have enjoyed in the past.

I enjoyed playing in the League games and really felt like we were at something when we reached the 'home final' against Kilkenny, who won well, 3-12 to 1-10, leaving us facing Laois in the Championship. We were not in the best shape after losing the League, but whatever we had was enough to easily get us past the poor bastards, who we always seemed to meet and beat in those years.

There is no doubt, in hindsight, that we went into the Dublin game taking them for granted and we were duly caught on the hop in one of the worst ever results for our county. They beat us 2-16 to 1-17 and we were left on the scrapheap. Call it sour grapes if you like, but Pat Delaney of Laois, not the best referee I have ever seen, was in charge of that game and he seemed oblivious to the fact they wanted to take our centre forward, Martin Storey, out of the game as soon as possible.

Now Dublin had a decent team, with the likes of Brian McMahon (their second All Star), Shay Boland, MJ Ryan and John Twomey, but their manager, Lar Foley, had them wound up like psychopaths and hurling was not top of their agenda.

Early on, Storey nearly had his nose taken off by their resident hard-man, Tommy McKeown, and as the game developed, we got the feeling we were sitting ducks. At the end, I felt as bad as I had ever done on a hurling field, slumped deep in the doldrums. Being part of the team almost seemed an embarrassment, which was hard to take.

I will never forget the dressing-room afterwards; it was like Beirut in the bad times. Lads were black and blue and had lumps taken out of them. It's all very well to say we learned from that game and they never beat us after that but what a backlash there was at home. The local press went nuts and rightly so.

It had been a dire year. The League final defeat had been one thing. Although I had done well marking DJ Carey, we had lost the game after all, and then the Dubs mugged us. The club scene was a total washout as well and we blew like a timid breeze out of the Wexford Championship.

At this stage, we were too used to accepting defeat with both the club and county. We were underachievers with no tangible hope of shedding that tag. It was small consolation that I was one of the few to come out of it all with a bit of reputation intact. You don't celebrate getting the right numbers for the Lotto if you haven't bought a ticket. But it had been my first year getting a fair crack at the whip and that was the only reason I got away without much criticism.

The likes of John Conran called for club teams in Wexford to be less 'physical' and concentrate on the skills of the game. He urged the county board not to respond to supporter pressure but to keep faith in management.

Another man involved with the underage scene at the time, Liam Griffin, said the root of Wexford's problems was at national-school level, where children were no longer hurling. Griffin maintained the county was in a crisis and he was right. So you can imagine my amazement when I heard I had received an All Star nomination for the season just gone by. We had been beaten by Dublin in the first round of the Championship and yet I was on the short list. I didn't know how in the name of God I was there.

Little did I realise that the next few weeks would see my career turned on its head for good and that a lad from a small, country village, who had struggled to make the county team for so long, was going to become big business. I certainly wasn't prepared for what was about to happen.

Youth will come here and beat on my door and force its way in.
Henrik Ibsen

– CHAPTER SEVEN –
The silver lining

From being a small-town hero with an underachieving club and a county going nowhere, I suddenly stood out from all the rest. It's amazing what two little words can do for you. All Star. It has a nice ring to it and even though I was never one to sing from the rooftops about my own game, this was a fair achievement, considering we had done nothing as a county.

I don't think I changed after the award. I mean after two years and just two and a half Championship games, I still couldn't fathom how I had even got a nomination for the 1990 short-list in the first place. Wexford hadn't seen fit to hand me a regular place on the panel in the previous three seasons, for God's sake, so how could this happen?

But the journalists picked the team and they obviously saw something worthwhile so along with Kieran McGuckian from Cork and Galway's Gerry McInerney I was nominated for the left half-back position, while my old buddy Tom Dempsey was in with a chance of a place on the full-forward line.

The two of us headed up from Wexford to the All Star banquet in the Burlington Hotel, not having a clue what to expect. Whatever about Tom, this was all new to me anyway.

We were told to gather in a room, where I ordered a pint of Guinness. When I went to pay for it, the barman told me it was a free bar. This development seemed to me almost as good as the All Star nomination itself. I could get used to this way of life and the attention that went with it.

A few reporters gathered around but apart from Tom O'Riordan, to whom I had spoken a few times, I hadn't had many dealings with journalists from the national papers and knew very few of them.

In fairness, I had gained a decent profile out of that year's National League but can say in all honesty I felt I had no chance of winning an All Star. Cork won the Championship so surely they would dominate the list.

After losing the League, they faced Tipperary in the Munster final, whose manager, Babs Keating, still claims he was taken out of context when he stated that 'Donkeys don't win Derbys.' They don't, but as sure as there won't be snow at Christmas, Babs's comments backfired on him and Cork went all the way.

Back at the Burlington, we were finally called together for the naming of the team of 1990. The tension was worse than in the dressing-room before a Leinster final. I remember getting a shake in my leg as the MC announced another new player had been selected: Liam Dunne from Wexford had made the left-half-back slot his own.

Not for the first time, but for an entirely new reason, I nearly choked on my pint of Guinness and almost felt queasy. Surely this couldn't be right.

But Cork's Tomás Mulcahy, one of the game's superstars, came over straightaway and congratulated me. I wasn't on magic mushrooms after all – I had actually won an All Star.

'Congrats, Liam! It's well deserved,' he said, grasping my hand.

'Erm, thanks, Tomás. Well done yourself!' I replied, still dazed.

'I didn't actually get one,' he laughed.

After that, the first thing I did was look for Dempsey and I didn't have to try too hard to find him. We spent the night together and you couldn't ask for better company. I toasted the journalists and had a great laugh with Johnny Leahy from Tipperary. It was my first time getting to know him and I found him to be great company, but we didn't do each other any good because it was well into the early hours when we called it a day.

Leahy was one of the game's characters. He was loved, hated and misunderstood all at once but what a genius he was on the field! Of course he might have been a bit of a pup, but most of us are at some stage.

The next morning, I was the last hurler down to get my picture taken for the official All Star 1990 poster. Without doubt, I'm the sickest-looking GAA player you'll ever see in one of those pictures. My eyes are so far back in my head that I look more like a rock star than an All Star.

Paul Curran, the Dublin footballer, was the only player who turned up after me but at least he had some bit of colour left in his cheeks. I was white as a sheet.

As I hit the road for home, the realisation struck me that things would never be the same again. I tried to make it seem like no big deal but deep inside I was burning a fire of pride. On arriving back in Oulart, I deliberately played the whole thing down, even putting my All Star out of sight in a plastic bag, but Mam and Dad were waiting at the door for me and you could see they were proud.

With Dad gone away so much, it was rare to see the two of them together. I suppose that made it even lovelier to find them waiting at the door and I won't forget it. It was one of the moments I will treasure, a chance to show the old man what I had achieved; after all, he put me on the road in the first place.

The All Star was soon extracted from me and given pride of place in the Dunne residence, on top of the TV. There had been little fuss around home when I made my Wexford debut but all of a sudden it was Mardi Gras in Oulart. And this was also a real big thing for Mam.

The local press made a fuss. They came to interview Mam and compare the achievements of Siobhán and I. Of course my multitalented sister kept reminding me she had twice as many All Stars as myself, so my bragging rights were severely dented at home.

I tried to keep out of the limelight that evening and repaired instead to the quiet and friendly confines of Fintan Cooney's pub, where no man's reputation is safe, no matter who he is.

The man himself was waiting for me inside with a bottle of champagne. Not for me, thanks, I told him, I'd rather have a pint of Guinness.

The ever-faithful Tom Dempsey took his life in his hands by coming down to the village and joining me. Buffers Alley men were usually about as welcome in Oulart as Ian Paisley at a Celtic match but Tom got away with it that night.

The celebrations continued well into the night and for several days, until it was crystal clear to me that my days of just being an ordinary fellow were over. I was suddenly recognised a lot more and was asked by several clubs to make presentations.

This is how a lad can get sucked in by drink. It's the first step towards losing the run of yourself. Hurlers generally don't refuse invites to these functions because they know they will be slated if they do. The problem is it's not long before people are buying you pints and more pints. Soon the trap is sprung.

People mean well but if you turn down an invite, word spreads rapidly and you get a bad reputation, especially if the request is to present medals to kids. But when you do turn up, you are under pressure to stay until the end of the night and drink the pints they put before you. As I said, it can become an alarming way of life.

When one club learns you are on the circuit, expect at least five other calls; you can imagine the scene. Wexford have the best fans in the land but they were starved of success and finding an All Star among them was the closest thing they had to a bit of glory. I didn't mind obliging clubs and I didn't mind having a few pints along the way, but others might feel uncomfortable in that role.

One evening Duffry Rovers requested I come down and present medals to their juvenile team and I told them there would be no problem. I handed over the goods to their team captain, Damien Fitzhenry, and two years later he was playing behind me in the Wexford goal. That shows you what can happen in the game in a short space of time – not that I needed any reminders, having struggled to even make the county squad in 1988 and 1989.

The celebrity lifestyle continued with an interview with South East Radio, which for me at the time was like the BBC World Service, apart from the accents. All the national journalists seemed to have my number by now and I didn't mind chatting away with them, which is all part and parcel of the GAA.

There is no point in saying otherwise, the All Star really changed people's perception of me. It opened doors wherever I went and in many ways made up for being stuck in the doldrums so long.

The real bonus was our trip to Toronto late that year, where the 1990 hurling and football All-Ireland champions went out to play the new All Star teams. I had barely been past Tinahely but here I was heading to Canada.

Tom Dempsey made the trip too and we flew from Dublin to Shannon to collect the Munster lads.

Apart from the Cork guys, who just refused to mix with us, there was good interaction on that trip. I also remember looking on in awe of the Kerry footballer Jack O'Shea and thinking of how much this guy had won in the game.

Offaly's Johnny Pilkington and Brian Whelahan were both there as well, as was their goalkeeper Jim Troy, who roomed with me. Dempsey was next door with Noel Sheehy.

Dempsey was the chief entertainer on that trip. He set the fire alarm off one night and within seconds big Jack O'Shea was sprinting down the corridor towards the exit door in his boxer shorts. I was strolling up the corridor with a sliotar in my hand and, fully aware the alarm was a hoax, stopped Jacko in mid-sprint and asked him to sign the ball. Semi-naked, but obliging as ever, he scrawled his name and then tore on out the door.

The trip was great. I had been to Scotland in 1988 with the Ireland under-21s but this was the big time. Most of us got on well, though the Cork lads, as I said, didn't want to know about the rest of the entourage. They spent most of their time in a bar called The Cellar so one evening Dempsey and I went down there to see what was so great about the place. We were quite ready to mix with them but they more or less ignored us, so we left.

The match itself was very competitive. I remember Tomás Mulcahy and Declan Carr having serious words with each other during the exhibition game. There were some heavy shots taken between the two. Teddy McCarthy was all the rage back then and there was a big fuss over which All Star team he would play for. Teddy won All-Ireland medals in both codes with Cork that season but as it turned out he was actually sent off in the football exhibition so he couldn't play the hurling anyway.

The trip was a real eye-opener. You found yourself mixing with the likes of Nicky English, a genuine superstar, and it was easy to take the eye off the ball and start thinking this will always be the way. But being a hero is about one of the shortest-lived professions around.

Despite the All Star, my ambitions were only starting. I felt there was still a point to prove in Wexford so when we got back to business in February of 91 I knew I was up there to be shot down.

We got to the League final that year and lost again, this time by 2-6 to 0-10 against Offaly. We had beaten Kilkenny after a semi-final replay and fell at the final hurdle again. It was sickening to lose two finals in a row because, no matter what way it's perceived now, the League was big business back then.

Along the way, we met our Dublin friends again and though the most recent encounter had been saucy, this was a game like nothing I have ever played in. It was a bloodbath from start to finish. Lar Foley probably thought he would get away with the tactics he had inflicted on us the year before, but there was no chance. 'Remember 1990,' was our war cry.

Minutes into the game, John O'Connor nearly lost an eye when one of the Dublin players pulled high on a ball. The eye injury was so bad certain newspapers apologised for printing a photograph of it the next day.

After that, without being too macho, it was stand and deliver from us. We beat them by two points and this time they were the ones that arrived butchered into the dressing-rooms at the finish.

If such a game took place now, six lads could easily have gone to jail for offences and I'm deadly serious. Besides almost taking the eye out of John O they had also targeted Martin Storey, who was battered all over. If you had a queasy stomach out there you were in trouble.

But the win meant nothing when we eventually lost the final and there was now an underlying fear in the team – we seemed to lose every final we played right down to the Oireachtas and the Walsh Cup.

I remember one of our first losses to Offaly some years before in the Walsh Cup. They were all back in the pub as if no game had taken place at all; the cup meant nothing to them. Wexford would have loved to win it, though, but like the rest it went by the wayside.

Things didn't get much better for the Championship that year either and the underachievers tag was stuck firmly on us. It was Groundhog Day again, we beat Laois in the first round of the Leinster campaign and then faced Kilkenny, which fuelled my personal firefight with John Power, their rugged but classic centre forward.

Power and I delivered some heavy blows in that game and there was a mark on my leg for three weeks afterwards. I actually hated him over our first few encounters but gradually grew to admire him for what he is and would now consider him a real gentleman off the field and a fine hurler on it.

John always played me well. He was never going to do much scoring but he was always creating, and years later he was still making the likes of DJ look good. For this game, however, his creative streak was nullified because we just spent the hour flaking each other, which I could live with. Over the years we might have let go a few fecks here and there, but there was no real mouthing between us.

We should have won the game and although we led at the break from an Eamon Sinnott goal, they won by 2-9 to 0-13. It was typical Kilkenny.

Of course, every serious hurling fan will remember that as the match where DJ took his famous steps on the way to clinching a crucial goal. The result hung on a knife edge until that incident changed the game. DJ came tearing after a high ball. Kilkenny's Liam McCarthy nudged me in the back and out of the way and the ball almost merged with DJ like a hand to a glove.

Photos show five of us chasing after him and by my reckoning he took eight steps with the ball and then hit it. People still discuss it and some claim he took many more but in my book he was only three steps over the legal limit, and sure what is that in the GAA?

Fair play to him, I suppose, if he'd taken 20 steps on the day he'd have got away with it. I still maintain that our keeper, Ted Morrissey, should have saved it anyway. It certainly was stoppable. Ted should have been ready for it. DJ had no option but to go for goal because they needed it and it wasn't the hardest shot to stop.

Still, everyone had to shoulder the blame. I mean, we badly needed scores at the other end too but there was no chance because we had two players who couldn't play there, John O'Connor in one corner and John Conran in the other.

They couldn't hold their places out the field but were shoved into the corner and so we never looked like hauling it back and lost by just two points. Another hard-luck story.

Disgusted, I shook hands with Power and I said: 'See you again, sonny.' And that was it, we were out.

I never recovered from the defeat that year. I barely hit a ball for my club and it really took the sting out of my game. Larry O'Gorman scored 2-4 off me in the Wexford Championship soon after for Faythe

Harriers, although he claims it was more like 3-11. Something was wrong with our club too; I recall us scoring 4-12 in one Championship game and still losing.

Still, everyone expected I would pick up my second All Star at the end of that year and I was foolish enough to listen to them. Things hadn't gone well but I had done pretty well in the season. To be truthful, I had hurled 10 times better in 91 than I had the year before and had coped well with John Power so I bought into the publicity and actually believed I would make the All Stars. Silly me.

There were 13 Munster men picked. DJ Carey and Michael Walsh were the only two from anywhere else. The years were ticking away and the clock shows no mercy.

But I just looked to 1992 and was heartened when it began full of promise. Tomás, at 30, was the new prodigal son of Wexford and had regained his place in the county squad after seven years out in the cold. He held his place with George O'Connor for the season. But where had he been for seven years?

He had always hurled well for Oulart-The-Ballagh and had been ignored, probably because he had a huge reputation for doing what hurlers shouldn't be doing and that was going out on the tear. I reckon if you are good enough for the job and are willing to go training that should be enough. But Tomás wasn't a politician, you see. We are back to the old chestnut of who you know and where you come from.

Anyway, my other brother Seán had just won his second All-Ireland medal, in junior football this time, and Siobhán had just won two camogie medals with Wexford, so overall it was a good time for the family.

April arrived with an air of hope and optimism. I like that month; the slate is clean, winter is over and it's the time when you can sense the hard work starting to pay off, and in those days it signalled the start of the real business in the GAA world.

The club played a tournament game to kick the season off and unlike now when club players normally just turn up for the Championship, the county players had to show their faces.

We played St Martin's on this occasion and near the end of the game I felt something snap. I took off my boot and, just to illustrate the highly scientific approach to sports injuries we had back then, I went over to a tap and poured cold water on it before heading for the pub. I found it too sore to move so I sat down, handed people money to buy me a pint and later went home to bed.

The next morning it had swollen like a balloon and turned yellow and blue, not unlike the Wexford colours. Our club chairman, Joe O'Shaughnessy, brought me to see Dr Pat O'Neill in Dublin and I underwent surgery by Dr Ray Moran, brother of the former soccer international Kevin. Five pins and a plate were put in and I was told to take 12 weeks off. Lovely.

I was strictly confined to Beaumount Hospital, where the nurses had a great laugh at my expense, or more specifically, at the expense of the dodgy bunch coming to visit me.

The nurses were mostly from Dublin and found it hugely entertaining to see these rough country lads with their inscrutable accents arriving in groups of six and seven. Some of the old reliables, the two Bartles, Tom Sinnott, Mike O'Dowd and Martin Dempsey, visited me for the sole purpose of eating everything I had in the locker. One night, it was pretty late when the boys arrived and munched all my provisions apart from a box of Maltesers, which I refused to let go. They suggested an escape down to the local pub for a pint and, bored off my tree, I agreed, threw on a tracksuit and headed off to the Beaumount House, where we slaked our thirst.

Now two days after a serious operation, a pub is the last place you should be, but I just had to get out. Two security guards stopped us on the way back into the hospital and threatened to report me for a breach of hospital regulations. To make matters worse, one of the lads, Mike O'Dowd, had part of a hurley stuck in his shin bone, which had become so badly infected he could barely walk, and when the security guard saw both of us limping, he thought we were taking the piss.

We managed to defuse the standoff by telling him how desperate I had been for a pint and explaining that Mick had half a camán lodged in his leg. The guard just sat there scratching his head but in the end let us through, and Mick even succeeded in getting that bit of a hurl seen to.

Cyril Farrell from Galway had taken over the county team and although the League was dismal, he had a few weeks to work with us and brought Wexford to a Leinster final.

Cyril had introduced a lot of hurling into the set-up and he knew what he was at. He started getting lads to train at 7.30 in the morning and got a good response. I missed out on the lads beating Laois and Dublin and sat in the dressing-rooms, deeply frustrated, as we got past the first-round and semi-final games. So I was more than delighted when we qualified to meet the Cats again in the final, because by the time that game came around I was fit enough to come into contention.

Cyril and Martin Quigley called the shots equally and it was decided not to start me, which I was okay with. We got hammered 3-16 to 2-9 in the final and while I was brought on for Diarmuid McDonald in the second half, I didn't enjoy a moment of it. McDonald was doing fine on John Power at centre back but he was young and the selectors took the easy option of calling him ashore.

The truth is that we were beaten in a lot of sectors that day and, unfortunately, that was the end of Cyril. Like Michael O'Grady in 1987, he wasn't given enough time at all.

Afterwards, I tried to stand back and analyse what was going wrong. In five years of intercounty hurling, I had played the equivalent of only five Championship games: 1988, a half hour versus Laois; 1989, dropped; 1990, one game, versus Dublin; 1991, two games, versus Laois and Kilkenny; 1992, a half hour versus Kilkenny. That was only three full games, not good enough for a 24-year-old with aspirations to go to the top.

Aware that my career was not going to go back in time, I put everything I had into my club for the rest of the year and we reached the county final. Robbie Jacob was our manager at the time and after beating Cloughbawn in the semi-final, we had two weeks off before the big one.

Robbie trained us four nights in the first week and three in the second. I told him we had done way too much but he told me where to get off and when we went out against Buffers Alley once more in the final we couldn't walk. They cleaned us off the field and we didn't even manage a score from play. We had left everything on the training pitch and lost our fifth county final. At the time, Buffers Alley sewed it into us.

We were a club, a county going nowhere. And for once, we were damn sure of reaching our destination.

Players wanted to get the jersey but they had no real commitment to it.
They blamed referees, drinking, pitches and anything else they could think of.
It all came down to self-belief
Ger Loughnane, Raising the Banner, 2001

– C H A P T E R   E I G H T –
Doing the Hucklebuck

No other team or county has ever celebrated failure quite like Wexford.
We are glorious in victory and even more splendid in defeat.

Look back at the Clare teams that Ger Loughnane guided to All-
Ireland titles in 1995 and 1997 – everyone loved them at the start but
they were the most hated team in the land by the time they won their
second title. But all through the years, Wexford have remained a firm
favourite; many would see us as their second team and will get behind
us when their own side gets knocked out.

'Poor old Wexford, sure they'll give it a lash anyway.'

Even though the boys won a Leinster title in 2004, it remains the
mentality. But it's no wonder because flick back through the annals and
you will see that we became so used to losing we just accepted it.

I will never forget 1993 for two reasons: I played some of the best
hurling of my career and we got to League and Leinster finals and lost
both of them. Despite the fact we were beaten in two finals, Wexford
people still saw the year as a success. God help them, they were so
starved of success, it probably was.

Under Christy Keogh, we went unbeaten in the League and beat
Limerick to reach the final, breaking in new players like Damien
Fitzhenry, Eamon Scallan and Larry Murphy.

At last, it looked like we were moving up a gear but we had been
here before. This was our third League final in four years and we had yet

to win one and it would be tough against a Cork side with gala names like Teddy McCarthy, Tomás Mulcahy, Jim Cashman, Denis Walsh, Ger Cunningham and Kevin Hennessy.

Unlike now, the League was big business back then and we would have loved to win it for the fans. I will never forget those days in Thurles, running out in front of crowds of nearly 30,000 and the whole of Wexford looking for that elusive slice of success.

I suppose the real find of the season was Fitzhenry. Just two years before, I presented him with medals at the Duffry Rovers presentation night but here he was now making his name in the Wexford goal, an example to everyone. Fitzy came from a huge sporting family of 10 boys and five girls but soon made his own name.

Before the first game, my brother Tomás got a well-deserved start when Dave Guiney, late for the game, had a minor crash and that let Tomás into the team and I was thrilled; he should have been there anyway.

Although there were six years between Tomás and me, that season would bring us much closer and it probably had the same effect on the rest of the family. My mother was in her element now and really enjoyed that year, although my father was still in the Isle of Wight and Luton and only got home every two months or so then.

We enlisted the help of all my cousins from Cork, the Woulfes, with whom we used to play out our own Cork-Wexford sagas all those years ago. They came down to see the final, wearing the red but not begrudging Tomás or I a bit of success at the same time.

The first encounter was close throughout and at the end, Martin Storey was tripped by John Hartnett. The referee, Willie Barrett, awarded a free and we missed a golden chance to win it when John O'Connor drove it wide with only 45 seconds left.

It ended 2-11 apiece but I really enjoyed the game and played some good stuff. The newspapers said I was the finest hurler in the country at that stage and while I wasn't too sure about that I did feel really comfortable in Thurles.

Delighted with ourselves after drawing with the likes of Brian Corcoran, who was fast becoming a legend, Tomás Mulcahy, Kevin Hennessy, Teddy McCarthy and Jim Cashman, we went back to Hayes's Hotel after the game to a reception hosted by Royal Liver, sponsors of the competition. There, you could see the contrast; the Cork lads sat down drinking minerals while the Wexford lads absolutely hopped off the free beer. You could already tell who the winners would be.

Our lot set a fine example by slugging off a few bottles of wine but at the other side the Cork manager, Canon Michael O'Brien, had his troops well in order – they were on 7-Up.

One evening before the replay Christy Keogh went through the team, player by player, to discuss tactics and encourage us by identifying weaknesses in the opposition. He was animated as he went around the dressing room.

'Niall McDonald, you will be on Ger Manley. Stop him from getting to the ball first and the job is done.

'George O'Connor, you'll be on Seánie O'Leary. You're quicker than him so use your pace and he will be helpless.

'Tom Dempsey, go straight for goals and no messing – take your scores.'

He then turned to Eamon Scallan and placed his hand on the shoulder of our new corner forward.

'Eamon, you're on Brian Corcoran on Sunday. God help you, son!'

What could you do but laugh? Brian was the Young Hurler of the Year in 1992 and truly one of the best I have ever seen but Eamon didn't exactly need to be told that two men wouldn't have stopped Corcoran back then.

The replay arrived and we gathered in Thurles again. I felt we were relaxed enough to do the job, land the League title and get ready for the Championship, and the rest of the lads were even more confident.

I remember Larry O'Gorman sitting in the dressing-room, singing and humming away to himself. Every so often he would throw in a whistle. He was singing that bloody awful Eurovision entry *Why Me?* by Linda Martin.

I started taking the piss out of him. Let's face it, the song isn't exactly a classic. But Larry's logic was simple: 'I'm marking Teddy McCarthy today. He's down in the Cork dressing-room dreading the prospect of marking Larry O and he is thinking to himself, "Why me?" '

What could you say to that?

After five minutes, Teddy had three points scored off him. Larry O was then moved to wing back and then up to centre forward out of the way.

'Why Larry?' we wondered. That was 'The Brother' for you. We called him that because he used it to salute everyone else. He was some hurler and a real character as well. His one-liners became legendary over the years, and the Wexford camp would have been a much quieter place without him.

While Larry struggled that day I could hardly have gone any better and though I started off marking Tomás Mulcahy in each game, I ended up on six or seven different lads before they eventually brought up Corcoran from corner back to say hello.

Brian was an absolute class act then, and we really did feel for poor old Eamon Scallan, who had to try and mark him at his peak. Though I'm surprised, by the way, that Brian came out of retirement for Cork in 2004 – he had a lot to lose in terms of reputation. The gamble, however, clearly paid off.

Anyway, John O'Connor was in the thick of it again for the replay when he mishit a late 70-metre free that would have given us the game and again we drew; we got 1-8 while Cork nabbed 0-11.
We scored a goal in each half of extra time, which should have been enough to see us through but Cathal Casey hit balls over from all angles and Jim Cashman got a dramatic equaliser before John O had that chance with the free.

John O didn't know it then but he would later more than make up for those two misses in a much more important game.

Once more, extra time failed to separate us and Jim Cashman pointed for them in the last seconds to leave us locked at 3-9 to 0-18. They were an arrogant old team, Cork, and you couldn't fault them for that – success breeds that sort of an attitude – but we were slowly getting some respect from them.

The League was a huge competition back then and not surprisingly, those games dominated the media, who lapped up the excitement of it all. Once more, good old Wexford were championed as the underdog and we had 90 percent of the country shouting for us. But Cork had the last laugh and we just didn't get a sniff on the third day.

I think we had nothing left in the tank, and they beat us by five points, 3-11 to 1-12. The Cork lads were so used to winning that they didn't even bother to stay out on the field while Brian Corcoran lifted the Cup. We would have partied for the year had we won it.

And yet, defeat didn't feel all that bad. We trooped off the field, out but not down. The crack had been unbelievable over those three weeks and we all enjoyed the buzz. To this day, I have some wonderful memories of those games, which were played in brilliant spring sunshine and with the whole country looking on.

After the saga eventually ended, the plan was to meet in Mary Willies pub, just outside Thurles, for a clear-the-air discussion. I was sure there would be plenty of strong words from the management; after all, we had thrown two good chances away and the fans were crushed. But instead what we got was a party. Like I say, no-one knew how to celebrate defeat like Wexford.

Don't get me wrong, we are a great sporting county and have had plenty of heroes. This past while alone, we have seen Gordon Darcy dazzle the world with the Irish rugby team, Matty Forde set the Gaelic football fields alight and Niall Griffin, Liam's son, make the Irish Olympic equestrian team. Before them, Nick Popplewell from Gorey was the main inspiration. I loved rugby union ever since Nick put Wexford on the map and took great pride in seeing a Wexford man on the world stage. Billy Walsh competed in the 1988 Seoul Olympics and another countyman, Jim O'Sullivan, won the Irish senior boxing title 10 times.

I just wished the county hurling team could start to make a bit of headway but that was unlikely while we hailed moral victories.

Mary Willies was waiting for me as I arrived, one of the last to make it in, still wondering what might have been. The first thing I noticed was a huge commotion inside, and as I opened the door, I was greeted by a sea of purple and gold, the fans congregated around Christy Keogh.

Now I expected Christy to be in a foul mood, pissed off that we failed him yet again, and I half-anticipated we might get a bollocking. But as the great man stood up and sang *The Hucklebuck*, it seemed unlikely we would.

There would hardly have been more excitement if we'd won the final, and I knew in my heart that even though they had the League trophy, the Cork camp weren't having half as much craic.

And that was the crux of our problem. We wouldn't know what to do with a trophy.

I hadn't heard Christy performing this song before, but by God, he was now the centre of attention and knew every line of it; it was great stuff. The crowd loved it too and cheered like hell as he showed off shakes and moves that Elvis would have been proud of. In fairness, despite the disappointment of losing, it was one of the most memorable moments of my time with Wexford.

Christy gave his heart and soul to Wexford hurling and even though he had fallen short after coming so close to guiding the county to a major title, he was still able to look on the bright side.

He had been in charge in 1981, 1984 and 1988 and each time ensured the set-up was much more professional. He brought Jimmy Furlong and Jimmy Prendergast in as selectors, which proved to be a success as we reached the final. And so it hurt that we couldn't do the job for him.

Dave Bernie had really developed the Supporters' Club and Jim Bolger, the racehorse trainer, was delighted to be involved. I remember coming out of training a few times and Jim would call you over for a chat, which usually ended up with Jim digging deep into the boot of his car and putting a few pairs of Puma King football boots into your gear bag. He enjoyed the League saga immensely and looked after the players out of his own pocket. Lads were always delighted to get the nod from Jim – they knew it usually meant coming away with a bit of gear.

The players also knew it was time to repay the faith so many had invested in us, and in the lead-up to the 1993 Championship we put in an enormous effort. It was mostly hurling with Cyril Farrell, but there was a huge emphasis on running this time, and Christy, who ran with us, put his own plan of action on the table.

Training may not have been as intense as it is now but we put in savage preparation, doing bleep tests in the Showgrounds in Enniscorthy, where the county senior footballers also trained, and undertaking those long stamina runs.

I always thought the Wexford footballers must have felt aggrieved because they trained a lot harder than us but missed out on all the glory. They had one star player, John O'Gorman, who would have made any team in the land, but the hurlers had the much bigger profile so the fans went for us. This has changed a bit in recent years; at least in 2004 they made something of a breakthrough.

It seems crazy to say but after the buzz and high jinks of the League, we went back to the 'humdrum' of the Championship and yet another meeting with Dublin – we beat them 1-14 to 0-10 – and Laois, who by now must have been sick to the back teeth of us.

There was a bit of expectation there this time and the media had really warmed to us so it was no surprise that a massive Wexford crowd drove to Nowlan Park to see the Laois game.

Adrian Fenlon, who had played no part in our League saga,

waltzed straight into the team as a fresh-faced 20-year-old. And I was delighted that Tomás retained his place on the team at wing back.

We hurled well enough on the day and were never going to lose if our heads were right.

Kilkenny were waiting for us in the Leinster final and I reckoned we'd win. Christy had done a marvellous job preparing us and we were primed and ready for action against our biggest rivals.

We gave it everything and had them on the rack for the entire first half. John O'Connor skinned Eamon Morrissey and Tomás skinned DJ Carey, but in a different sort of way. DJ seemed to spend a lot of time on the ground that day. Tomás claimed he had no part in that at all, but in fairness, he gave DJ a few leathers (something the Kilkenny superstar has had to get used to) just to unsettle him. But there were battles like that right the way up the field and we dominated most sectors against a damn good team.

Close to half time, we led by seven points and it looked like a breakthrough finally beckoned until Eamon Morrissey pinched a goal back just before the interval. That score changed the game as we only led by three at the break after hurling them off the pitch.

I think we were a lot like the current Limerick footballers, who came so close lately to slicing the old firm of Cork and Kerry apart but ultimately failed.

We stayed in touch in the second half and, with the game drawing to a close, DJ fell to the ground one more time and I looked across to see Tomás standing over him. My marker, John Power, went ape shit but I hit him with the end of the hurley under the ribs and told him to stay where he was.

He drew a box at me and hit me straight in the jaw.

I wasn't expecting the left hook and he drove me back nearly to the previous week. It was the last time I hit Power with the tip of the hurley – I decided to get on with the game after that.

John and I waged some real heavy battles and some of the spiciest encounters were under the dropping ball. I often cut the hand off him but when the next ball came down, he would pull twice as hard. Sometimes a lad would learn not to put his hand up against me more than once but not John Power.

With a few minutes left I went over to take a free we had done well to win and pumped my fist at the Wexford crowd. I was high on adrenalin and the crowd absolutely erupted onto their feet; they were now with us all the way and I sensed we could finally do the job.

But although I drove the free down the field it came back twice as quick and Kilkenny engineered one of the best points you will ever see to draw level. I was in a circle chasing after them as Liam Simpson, Adrian Ronan and Eamon Morrissey all combined. Morrissey finished off the move to make it Wexford 1-17, Kilkenny 2-14.

That was it: another chance blown. We headed back to Gorey that night and the kick had gone out of us. Totally depressed, Tomás and I hit the town and rumour spread the next day that we were seen punching each other's lights out in the early hours of the morning. If the truth be known, we were holding each other up. We knew our chance was gone.

Deep down Christy knew it too, and we got skinned the next day, 2-12 to 0-8. John Power destroyed me; I had done okay on him in the drawn game but he was a proud man and this was his answer.

The one Wexfordman I felt never got the recognition he deserved over those two games was Tomás, who had held DJ scoreless in the drawn game and limited him to just a goal in the replay.

It was the end of a busy year for the county. We had come so close but in the end we blew it. Kilkenny had ambushed us in the provincial final. To add to our misery in Oulart, the club was knocked out of the Wexford Championship by Buffers Alley.

I was only 25 but I still felt the years were slipping by and while other counties were busy writing romantic and elegant pieces of history, Wexford's contribution to hurling seemed to be one depressing chapter after another.

The 1994 Championship pitted us in another potential bloodbath against Dublin. It was always going to be stormy following the wars of 1990 and 1991, and again controversy was the order of the day. A good few lads were booked early in the game but it got worse. We went on to have George O'Connor and Tom Dempsey sent off while they lost Shay Boland and Tommy McKeown. The game ended in a draw: Wexford 3-13, Dublin 2-16.

Those Dubs were dirty bastards but they showed they could play a bit of hurling – two goals and 16 points is a nice haul. But they were out to get Tom Dempsey, no doubt about it, and I don't think they cared how badly they hurt him as long as he was out of the game. I suppose the fact Tom was sent off was mission accomplished for them. And it upset us because Georgie also lost his temper and walked.

Christy Keogh had given up being upset by their tackles; he was genuinely afraid one of our lads would lose an eye or get the fingers smashed, and when he saw Georgie getting a red card he sat down in the dugout and buried his head between his arms. The subs thought he was going to crack up.

'Poor Georgie, poor Georgie,' was all he muttered.

When he lifted his head, he found an even nicer surprise waiting: Tom Dempsey was there beside him.

'What the fuck are you doing here?' roared Christy.

'Never mind your poor Georgie – I got the line too,' snarled Dempsey.

If an intercounty Championship match hadn't been in the balance just then, it would have been hilarious but there was deadly serious business going ahead on the pitch.

We didn't want to be the team that lost to Dublin again but we were struggling, because even though they played nice hurling in patches, they also dragged us down to their level and we couldn't put them away.

Two days later, a number of players from both teams, including of course your truly, were summoned to a Leinster Council meeting and as we walked in the Dublin players came over to us. For 70 minutes the previous Sunday, they had tried their best to kill us, but we are all only human and we knew that each player who was in the dock wanted desperately to get off.

We reckoned we were lucky that we had Tom Dempsey on our side because he would sweet-talk a raging bull and we saw him as our trump card in the meeting.

But in the end, the Wexford lads didn't have to say much because Ciarán Barr, the former Antrim and then Dublin hurler, spoke for everyone and rambled on for half an hour.

When he finally stopped waffling, the bemused members of the Leinster Council went in to consider their verdicts. They handed Tommy McKeown a year's suspension and gave Georgie and Tom Dempsey a month each. The rest of us got off with severe warnings but the funniest part of the night came when they announced the county boards were fined £7,500 each.

With that news our county chairman, Paddy Wickham, nearly choked on the cigarette he had just lit. Spluttering with shock, he started ranting on about the cost to the county board. Wexford didn't have that sort of money and Paddy was doing his best just trying to keep the ship afloat so he wanted to know where in the name of God would he find the extra seven and a half grand?

But maybe the county board need not have worried. Some will argue that the money eventually went back to the two counties anyway. The Leinster Council slammed on the fines but once the fuss was over there was a fair chance that the money found its way back in the form of coaching grants to both county boards. The Council got their bans, the press got their headlines and the Wexford and Dublin committees probably got their money back in some shape or form.

You could never be up to the GAA!

These days the Council make sure a lot more goes in the direction of the players and I must say in passing that I got to know one of the current Leinster Council officials, Michael Delaney, very well over the past number of years, and he's a real players' man, which is nice to know.

But the bans Michael's predecessors handed out failed to do the job and things were no better in the replay, where Dublin had three men sent off.

This time we held our heads, came out of it with a bit of dignity and progressed easily by 3-22 to 1-11 to meet Laois in the next round. Again we demolished Laois, this time by 18 points, 4-24 to 4-6. I felt for Laois; it was an absolute disaster for them, one of their worst days ever.

In the Leinster final, though, we were on the receiving end. Offaly pulverised us by 1-18 to 0-14 and that match was the end of Christy Keogh's reign – he resigned after it.

Christy felt his time was up and so too did a few other guys who never played for Wexford again, including Garrett Kavanagh.

My heart went out to Christy and many others sympathised with him too. He had been so close at times to landing us either a League or Championship title. Over the years I had often wondered what he thought about when he went home after losing another final or big match by just a point or two.

I still feel he was the unluckiest manager in the game and while this was his third term, we were still being beaten by a point or two each time; there was no respite. Luck is a precious commodity – not everyone gets a taste of it. But he could eventually take heart from the fact he had built a team that would soon go forward and represent Wexford in style and some of the lads he had brought in would perform for the team for the next 10 or 12 years, something he can be justifiably proud of.

Christy was never far from my mind. At the end of the day, he was the one who gave me my first break. Incidentally, Christy had won county senior medals with both Shamrocks and Raparees and I often wondered what club he would support if push came to shove. Several times I asked him what medal would take pride of place on his mantelpiece and he always just smiled. Knowing him, I suspect they would have been side by side.

I also wondered if things would ever start to happen for me. By now, I had lost three Leinster finals, three League finals, two county finals and, damn it, I had even lost two Walsh Cups and two Oireachtas titles.

There was some respite from all the doom and gloom when Martin Storey, Tom Dempsey, Larry O'Gorman and I were picked for the Leinster Railway Cup team and we actually won a trophy. I'm not joking. We beat Connacht in the semi-final and then Ulster in the final. I was absolutely delighted because it was my first proper medal at adult level and the bonus arrived when, at the end of the year, I found myself in the running for an All Star again.

The hype had begun around the county but I ignored it because although everyone was telling me I was a certainty, I had heard the exact same in 1991 and had been devastated to lose out.

Anyway, the morning before the 1993 team was announced, Larry O rang my mother and told her I had made it. I refused to believe it and went to bed early but made sure to be up early to listen to the radio and actually hear my name being called out. In 1990, the hurling awards had been announced 'live' but it was the footballers' turn this year and so this time the hurlers knew their fate the day before.

Martin Storey made it on the team as well and up we went to the All Star function and had a great night.

Individually I suppose it had been a good year for the likes of Storey and me but what good is that? We needed success for Wexford. While I was delighted to win a Railway Cup, the second All Star meant more because I was still sore with Wexford for being dropped a few years earlier. As I said, winning personal awards just wasn't good enough anymore – I wanted to do it with the boys I grew up with.

There seemed to be little I could do about Wexford's slump but off the field, I decided to freshen things up a little by switching jobs. By now I had been 10 years with Andy Roche, who encouraged me to use my profile more.

The soft-drinks industry was an area that interested me; I had seen Billy Byrne working as a sales rep for one company and had been attracted by the company car and mobile phone that came with the job so I began to look into it.

Breda Flood had arranged a meeting for me with Liam Griffin, a Rosslare man who had a reputation as a big fish in the hotel business. I didn't ask any questions – people just said he was the man to talk to – and when we met, he told me I would have to bide my time because such jobs were hard to come by.

It was no surprise then, that I ended the 1994 intercounty season frustrated and wondering when our luck would change. At this stage all I had was a bit of respect, something I would lose a few years later.

I suppose when the county team gets knocked out, I did what every player does when reassurance and confidence is needed. I turned to my club.

What the Jaysus do you want going down to those louts for?
It's boxing gloves you'll need for them, not hurls.

Wexford follower to Tom Neville
when he agreed to manage Oulart-The-Ballagh

– CHAPTER NINE –
Oulart-The-Ballagh

It took over 100 years for Oulart-The-Ballagh to win a senior Championship but what chance of success had the club when we were cursed? Legend has it that an angry priest put the hex on our club in the 1930s when the boys on the team refused to go to a funeral Mass and went training instead. The story goes that the priest told them they would never win a senior Championship, though we were only a junior club at the time.

Now the 'curse' was a load of rubbish but some people began to believe it after we lost final after final and certainly the Buffers Alley men delighted in sewing it into us and laughing at this so-called enchantment.

I think a few of our players started to believe in it as well because before we reached the 1994 decider, we had already lost five county finals and, believe me, that puts a few doubts in your mind.

Oulart could always produce plenty of intercounty players. Tom Byrne captained the Wexford minor team to an All-Ireland title in 1968 and Martin Storey led the seniors to the promised land 28 years later. In between, we had countless other great players but other clubs used to laugh at us because we never pulled together at club level. They saw Oulart players travelling to county training individually and laughed at the sight.

How could you win anything when lads you were playing

alongside wouldn't even talk to you sometimes? That's the way it was with us; you were never guaranteed to have everyone pulling in the one direction.

Still, the advert on the telly reminds us it's 'One life, one club' and that's the way I have always felt about Oulart-The-Ballagh. It's my home. I grew up here playing with my brothers and best friends and while there was a certain amount of bravado in our battles over the years, this is where it all started. And this is where it will all end in 2006 when I plan on completely retiring from the game.

We were never short of heroes growing up. Mick Jacob was the main man, but as I said, even he couldn't lead us to the breakthrough. We were starved of success, regularly losing county finals down the years. I was there to experience the feeling when we lost 3-16 to 2-13 in 1989 and again in 1992, when Buffers Alley beat us 1-11 to 1-5. And so when 1994 came around a few of us felt it was time to get rid of the old wives' tale for once and for all.

In fact we were desperate to win a county title. We felt like second-class citizens of Wexford, especially when we would meet teams like Buffers Alley, who were well used to winning. Maybe it was that desire that prompted us in the end to go ahead and bring in an outsider, something many would consider treason, a slur on those loyal club stalwarts who had spent years trying to get things off the ground.

Back then especially, the idea of going for an outside coach was treated with disdain. It was a case of is there no-one good enough in the club and if there's not, well we still won't appoint an outsider.

But that's not always the best view to take and in 1994 we needed a blow-in to lead us to our Holy Grail. Like it or not, we would not have won our first county title without Tom Neville.

In 1993 Brendan O'Connor, a guy who was heavily involved with the club and would have given his lung for the cause, called to the house and explained to me that he had a plan in mind for the Oulart-The-Ballagh senior team. But he didn't provide a huge amount of detail, and so when in January of 1994 Martin Storey and I travelled to Carlow with Brendan, on the basis that he had a pleasant surprise in store, we were not sure what to expect.

As we arrived closer to the town, Brendan told us we were meeting Tom Neville, who had won All-Ireland medals with Wexford and had trained them in 1976 and 1977.

Brendan had a fairly detailed brief on what was needed to manage our team and it was just as well because Tom bled him dry for information on the set-up. It was clear straightaway that if he was coming down, it wouldn't be for the fun of it.

It took a few meetings to persuade him that we had something worthwhile to offer but eventually Brendan broke through and was able to make the proposal at board level.

Inevitably, there were a few dissenters in Oulart, including Mick and Robbie Jacob and Pat Dempsey – guys who, in fairness, would have had the club's best interests at heart. But Tom's name somehow got through and we had a new manager.

From day one, Tom took no shit. On his first meeting with us, he revealed that people around the county thought he was mad coming to train us.

One wag had said to him: 'What the Jaysus do you want going down to those louts for? It's boxing gloves you'll need for them, not hurls.'

That was the perception people had of us. The Dunnes may have been no angels but the rest of the lads on the team were well able to look after themselves too. We had a name for being well up for a boxing match. Sadly, when it came to hurling, we didn't always end up winners.

Tom decided he had to change that mentality. He demanded a lot from Martin Storey and me, the two resident county players, and gave us no special treatment just because we were wearing the purple and gold. We had to go training with the club like the rest, and even when we were with the county two weeks before the 1994 Leinster final Tom expected us to train with the club – there was no layoff.

That hadn't happened before, Martin and I being on a par with the rest. But it was Tom's way or the highway and he got the respect he deserved.

The man just wanted to win every match he played and he changed how we trained to help achieve that ambition. If he wasn't running the shit out of us, we were doing ball work for a couple of hours at a time, and while it was heavy going, the results were clear for all to see.

Tom's training methods were unusual but effective. The first thing he did was penalise indiscipline; a guy could lose his place for persistent fouling and he would certainly have to do extra training if Tom wasn't happy with him. The result was we went the whole year without getting a man sent off.

He also hated the idea of five or six players looking for a pass from a team-mate at the one time so he introduced the idea of 'silent training', which meant you couldn't call a lad when he was about to offload. It was frustrating; lads who broke the silence had to hit the ground and give 20 press-ups and the boys on the team didn't like that. It led to fits of coughing being introduced into the Oulart-The-Ballagh training sessions. You would cough if you wanted a pass and cough even harder again if you wanted it more desperately than someone else.

Passers-by thought a flu epidemic had broken out in the village; here were the 30 fittest men in the parish coughing and wheezing at each other. It's a wonder someone didn't put Wexford hospital on alert. But how could you question Tom's methods when we came through the early stages of the Championship unbeaten and ended up in a county semi-final against Crossabeg-Ballymurn.

With a little bit of arrogance in us now, we cruised past them by 3-12 to 2-9 and qualified to meet St Martin's, backboned by the Wexford legends George and John O'Connor, in the final.

In previous years the village went ape-shit whenever we reached a county final but this time the build up was much different. Tom insisted on keeping it low-key, and you would have thought the club had been knocked out months earlier. There were no new togs or gearbags for the game. We didn't even get a pair of socks. Tom wanted no fuss, and he got his wish.

Off the field we were tighter than we'd ever been. There was always a good social element to the club but Tom had put a special bond between the lads.

We knew there were fellas who had lost finals going back 20 years and still didn't talk to each other, and we didn't like the notion of that.

As I write this in late 2004, we have one of the best club teams in Wexford, but we still have the odd guy who won't row in or pass the ball and that attitude won't win a county title for you.

You see, while the club is the be-all and end-all for many people, it's also the easiest place to fall out with your neighbours, family or friends. The amount of politics that goes on in clubs all over the country is crazy.

Tom and his selectors, Willie Sutherland, Jimmy Prendergast and Mick Jacob changed all that. They recognised the pitfalls right away and saw to it that we all sang from the one hymn sheet.

I enjoyed 1994. Tomás was captain and corner back and my other brother Seán was corner forward. In between them, I was centre back, and my old friend Martin Storey was wing forward.

As the days led up to the decider, I couldn't help comparing it to the 92 decider, when there were about 500 red and black Oulart flags hung on telegraph poles the whole way into Wexford town. This time, there was just one flag up; people wanted so badly for us to win that they were afraid to put anything up in case it would increase the pressure.

When the final came around, we were well drilled for the Martins, but the game itself was touch and go the whole way, a battle between two teams that had forgotten how to win and wanted it desperately – St Martin's had been out in the cold for almost as long as us.

I marked James Quirke, a good hurler who scored 10 points from frees and one from play. Then Rory McCarthy came in on me and he was another tough test. We were going down to the wire.

But Martin Redmond, Martin Dempsey, John Stamp and John Cleary were flying for us and we went into the half-time break a point up. With time almost up, and Oulart a point down, I was about to take a free from 80 yards out. Just as I made to lift the sliotar, Tomás came racing up like a lunatic looking for a short pass: 'Play the quick one! The quick one!'

I looked at him as if he had two heads, wondering where the silent hurling had gone, and replied: 'Will you ever fuck off – haven't I enough to be worrying about.'

Fortunately, the free was on target, though the sliotar barely cleared the keeper's hands and laboured over the bar. We were level again. Storey then shot a great point to put one between the teams. But the referee, Brian White, gave St Martin's two close-in frees, no more than 45 and 50 yards, the type of handy frees that can rip the guts out of you, but thank God they missed both. Fuming, I went over and told White what I thought of him and shortly after that he blew for time.

All mayhem broke out. We had won our first county title, by 1-14 to 0-16. I can honestly say it was the best feeling of my sporting life and when I rewind the memories, it still is. It's a moment I'll never forget, to see the looks of joy on the faces of friends and neighbours – it meant so much to them. Tomás got the man-of-the-match award and, as captain, lifted the cup too; it couldn't get much better for him.

I went over to George O'Connor and embraced him. I put my head on his chest and I don't mind saying a few tears fell out of my eyes. George had never won a county title either and his emotion was obvious.

Lifting my head up, he said: 'It had to be one of us, Liam. It had to be one of us.'

Four years later St Martin's went on to win the title but George wasn't playing, though I was delighted that John still was.

Meanwhile, we hit the town that night and partied for a year after. Even some guys who had carried grudges from previous losing teams put aside the bitterness and joined in the celebrations.

At one stage I looked around and I saw family, friends and neighbours; we got back to Oulart and thought that the village had never looked so well. There was a cup home now to make everything seem complete.

While we partied hard, Tom had a tough job reminding us that there was a Leinster title to be played for. In fairness, we put the pint glasses down for a few days and managed to beat Castletown in the semi-final, which meant we would meet Birr in the final.

As luck would have it, Birr were on the cusp of becoming one of the greatest club teams in history, with Brian Whelahan, the Pilkingtons and Joe Errity on board. It was no shame on us that they needed a replay to win.

Needless to say, Tom was by now the main man around the village. He had made it possible for us to at least look a Buffers Alley man in the face and say: 'Hey, we have a county title too.' That feeling was priceless. The curse was lifted. We knew it was a load of crap but the Alley lads had milked it all along. For good measure we shut them up again in the county League final later that year to put another trophy beside the Bob Bowe Cup, which now looked to be almost half the size it was when we first got our hands on it.

I went through so many emotions that year after playing with lads so long and then actually winning something together.

Winning that cup prolonged some lives in the parish by three or four years such happiness did the locals get out of it. A few of them went to their reward in the past year or two but I'm convinced they would have gone much earlier if not for that win.

I'm talking about lads like Lar 'The Boiler' Dempsey, a man who passed away recently but saw it all with the club over the years. Lar was club president for a long time and had watched us go from the junior ranks to senior county champions. After so many bad years, he finally got a taste of the big time.

We went on to retain our title in 95 when we beat Glynn-Barntown, who were playing their first county final, 2-15 to 2-9. We beat them again two years later to win our third title.

They were magic times. I was delighted that the club finally came good. For years, there were five major families in the village: the Cooneys, Clearys, Roches, Penders and Dunnes. And people like Brendan and Butch O'Connor, PJ Harris, Tom Byrne, The Boiler Dempsey, Paddy Keogh and the Jacob brothers all helped steer the ship in the right direction. But it took an outsider to get us to the top.

Tom Neville will always have the freedom of the village and maybe in a way he helped us adapt to outsiders coming into our parish. That's the way it's gone now. A generation ago everyone knew each other, but so many people have moved in lately it's no longer so.

The great thing is that 95 percent of them are lovely and have got fully involved in the community. My hope is that many of them will contribute to the club for the next generation.

Just lately we played a match and Tomás brought my young lad, Billy, into the dressing-room afterwards. It hit me then that, when I retire in a year or two, for the first time in over 30 years there will be no member of the Dunne family playing for Oulart, and I suppose that's the way it is. Playing for the village was always something special to me; for a long time it was much better than turning out for my county.

And then in late 94 we heard that Liam Griffin, a guy who had been involved in the underage set-up was taking over the Wexford team. Jesus, he was a committed man at underage level and had played for Clare, but what would he know about managing a Wexford senior hurling team?

Stick to frying rashers you long nosed hoor.
Disgruntled Wexford fan after the county's
loss to Meath in the 1995 League

– CHAPTER TEN –
A prophet in his own land

I spent the first meeting Liam Griffin had with the Wexford hurling team staring at the size of his nose – I was fascinated by it. He was a skinny bloke but, by Jesus, was he well equipped in the nasal department. And did he love to talk, a chattering cyclone. As he stood there in front of us, it was clear as day to any outsider that he was the only winner in the room. Although we could all spot his big hooter, we took in little or nothing of what he said. We were losers, you see. We had thrown away every final we had reached and didn't really want to listen. We were just too used to losing.

Griffin was born in Rosslare in 1946 and is one of a family of 10. His father, Mick, came from Clare and Liam went there to study at the Shannon College of Hotel Management and joined a nearby club, Newmarket-on-Fergus. He had played all grades of hurling and football for Wexford apart from senior but soon found himself on the Clare senior hurling team that reached the National League semi-final of the 1967/1968 season.

He made his Championship debut that same season and scored 1-2 against Waterford but his career at the top ended when he had to travel to Switzerland to continue his hotel training.

His hurling ambition had, therefore, never been fully realised but we were hardly going to help him either. This Wexford team had lost every final it had reached and maybe we didn't even want to listen. But not least because he had helped me in the past, I felt I owed him something. Thank God I opened an ear and kept it opened through the bad times because we went on to share a piece of history together.

He didn't know me when he helped secure my first job; he didn't really know much more when he made me captain of Wexford, but it's fair to say he had learned a little when he quickly took it back again. It was never going to be a straight road.

I didn't know Liam from Adam when I first met him in his family hotel at Rosslare in the summer of 1989 and even now it's hard to think that one person could have such an effect on the rest of your life. Around the county, Griffin was seen as the man in the know, the guy to talk to if you wanted something, and if he trusted you or thought you were worth the effort, then you were on the way.

I badly wanted a job as a soft-drinks rep, mainly because Billy Byrne had a similar position and I liked the look of the lifestyle. Breda Flood arranged the meeting with the blessing of my employer at the time, Andy Roche, who encouraged me to move on in life and use my profile. I had decided the joinery business was not for me and had no intention of setting up a business on my own so it looked like I hadn't too many choices. I was only a kid, nervous as hell, but out Griffin came from the hotel offices to talk to me and I almost wet myself thinking how much he looked like Pinocchio. But I managed with a mighty effort to look him in the eye as we made a bit of small chat, and then it was straight down to business.

'What age are you, Liam?' he asked.

'I'm 20.'

'Well, it could take you five years to get this job, you know,' he continued, before scribbling down my details.

He didn't have to help. Liam Griffin owed Liam Dunne nothing. But that day he treated me like one of his own family. And a short while later he wrote off to Cantrell & Cochrane, Letts, Coca-Cola and all the big drinks companies on my behalf.

Of course I recognised that as a successful businessman he had enough to do without writing letters on my behalf, and I resolved that if

I ever got the job I would pay him back by working hard.

Little did I realise that five years later, when I eventually got the job and we got to know each other better, Griffin would maintain his incredible habit of making dreams come true on and off the field.

I suppose my first impression of him was that he was an ordinary Joe, apart from the nose, but he took a great interest in my career. Through the years, we'd meet every so often and he would stay in touch just to let me know he had not forgotten.

The news I'd been waiting for finally came in February 1994, when a position came up with G.H. Lett Ltd, the only independent drinks wholesaler in Ireland.

I hadn't a clue what the job entailed because I had given up all hope of getting it but they still gave me the nod. That was down to Griffin. Dougie Lett brought me around with him on a run for the day and as I had to fill in the order sheets I couldn't keep track of where we were going or what direction certain pubs were in, so when he left me on my own for the first time, I didn't finish the run until 9 pm. It was pitch dark but I felt like I was someone at last.

That was down to Griffin too. By that time, he had served as manager of the Wexford football team and had long been involved in the underage set-up and with his own club. He was known as a passionate GAA man but didn't have any real reputation as a miracle worker, so when word filtered through that he was the new county senior hurling manager, the team was surprised and didn't really know what to expect.

Word reached us that Griffin had absolutely bamboozled the county board, scarcely allowing them a word in edgeways to ask him any questions. After talking up a storm about tactics, players, discipline and training techniques, he himself ended the interview by saying: 'If I were in your shoes, I wouldn't appoint me. I'm a loose cannon. But I will help you find somebody else.'

It was too late – he had the job.

We had known Christy Keogh so well but here we had someone different and it must be said that not all the lads danced with joy at his appointment. He could well have been a great player but for injury and his studies but the lads wanted a bigger name as boss. I wanted to give him a chance but part of that goodwill disappeared three weeks into October of 1994 when he rang to tell me that I wouldn't be centre-back for Wexford in the following year's Championship.

'You're a better wing back than you are a centre back,' he insisted.

It was a strange enough phone call to get before the season even started. He softened the blow by telling me I was his captain but reiterated I would not be played in the heart of the defence. And then he hung up.

I felt both decisions were wrong. Centre back was my best position and Tomás should have been made captain instead of me. I didn't really want it and felt most of those in the club wanted Tomás for the job anyway, but from day one Liam thought he wouldn't get the necessary commitment from Tomás and that was the end of it; my brother was not in his plans.

Liam sent me a letter confirming I was captain and what was expected of me. He pointed out what a great honour it was for me and my family and added that he expected full consultation between both of us for the year ahead. I felt no added joy or elation at getting the job; we had to start winning things – that was more important.

Convincing the public we could be winners was going to be the hard part. Many in the county felt Griffin should have been let nowhere near the job; he had a lot of critics and still has, but then again, if you voice your opinion often enough people get envious or resentful and that's what happened with him as the years went on.

Liam does things right 99 percent of the time but we Wexford people have an awful habit of shooting ourselves in the foot and it seemed we resented anyone who would get off the fence and stand his ground for the county. We didn't know Liam had been offered the job previously and had turned it down, although he will tell you now that he regrets spurning the chance of taking us over a few years earlier.

He devised an individual training programme for each of us. There was no collective preparation until after Christmas. Griffin simply trusted us to work away on our own before regrouping after the holidays. I don't believe for a minute that anyone did the programme, and when we came back after the break it was clear we had taken a step back in terms of physical conditioning.

My brother Seán, Martin Storey and I did the training every so often but we would wash it down with a great haul of pints in one of the local pubs just as soon as it was over. To say the preparation was poor in 1995 is like saying modern Ireland is a rip-off, an understatement.

Liam also tried to take a psychological approach with us but it went in one ear and quickly flowed out the other. We were a macho lot at the time and had no business listening to this philosophy crap and reading the handouts he gave us. Most of the lads thought Griffin was a lunatic and it would take a full year for them to cop on there was method in his madness. He brought in Rory Kinsella and Séamus Barron as selectors. Those two were well respected but after beating Cork in the 1994 Oireachtas final by 2-7 to 1-8 and losing to Dublin 2-6 to 0-11 in the Walsh Cup final, we went through the whole 1995 season playing like children.

The week before our League clash with Meath at Belfield our club went away for a weekend in Killarney as a prize for winning our first county title. To get the ball rolling, Tomás and I started the session in the Danny Mann pub on Thursday at 1 pm and we went at it all day Friday and Saturday before eventually calling it a day in the early hours of Sunday morning.

Just a few hours later I lined out for Wexford against Meath. Seán and my friend Bartle Sinnott lay unconscious in the car as I drove to the match and they never had as much craic at a game in all their lives as they watched us go down by three points, 1-16 to 0-16.

As captain, I led the side out and went up for the toss, but that was the closest I got to leadership or action in that game. I don't remember hitting a sliotar in the first half, although my marker had scored a goal and a point. You'd think I would have grabbed a point or two because I had the choice of three balls – at least that's how many I was seeing most of the time.

Once, trying to run out for a ball, I tripped and fell, only to hear an old man in the crowd tell his pal: 'Dunne had never been the same since he broke his ankle.' If he knew how much Dunne had drunk in the previous 72 hours, he might have had more respect, or not.

The Meath lads were overjoyed at the result and as he walked off the field, Griffin was spat upon by a Wexford supporter. That was how bad things were; it was clear we had done nothing before Christmas and it was twice as obvious we were still only pissing around.

But we still didn't hurt enough. A few of us even chuckled at the result. It would have hurt more if we had cared enough, but then we would have had to do something about it.

As the Championship loomed we hoped for a change but failed to look within, where change was most needed. Griffin continued preaching but we would not be converted. While he wanted us reading articles on sports science and sports psychology, most of the lads wouldn't even bother reading a menu. We wanted to hurl alright, but weren't prepared to put the work in before games.

Griffin would give us handouts on diet and nutrition, but most lads threw them out the windows of their cars on the way home, though Storey and the two O'Connors used to take note of them. We were the fools though. Our new manager was trying to make changes but we had been around for a few years and thought we knew it all. We were set in our ways but they were not winning ways.

Surprisingly, Griffin never lost the rag with us and so we edgily progressed to the 1995 Championship. My debut as captain went well and we walloped Westmeath 6-23 to 1-7 to qualify for the Leinster semi-final with Offaly. That game proved to be more controversial in its build-up than anything else.

Oulart-The-Ballagh had a League game with Crossabeg-Ballymurn fixed for the Tuesday night before the Offaly match and, as we were under pressure to play from the club, I told the Wexford secretary, Mick Kinsella, that if the game was on we would play. He disagreed and told us to concentrate on the Leinster Championship as county board regulations suggested. I dug my heels in and made the point it had been seven weeks since the Oulart club had played a competitive game and our club officers wanted the complete panel together to get ready for the Championship match with St Martin's. I told him I felt the board could have put our Championship game back by two weeks like they had done for two clubs the year before. But this was Oulart, we were unfashionable and the board refused to switch.

But the club didn't budge either; we wanted to defend our League title so we took a stand. Tomás, Paul Finn and I all played against Crossabeg-Ballymurn – Martin Storey was injured and didn't play – and we won by 20 points.

But the sewage really hit the fan in county training the following night. It was clear when Griffin arrived that World War Three was about to break out.

Looking desperately hurt and deadly angry at the same time, he came up and really tore into me.

'I haven't slept a wink all night over this,' he said through gritted teeth. 'Playing a League game days before a Leinster semi-final. What in the name of Jesus are you at? I have to do something to you but I don't know what. I have to take some action.'

I had to say something but what could I say?

'Liam, whatever you decide to do, I'll back you 100 percent,' was all I could think of.

He walked away but some 45 minutes later, still with a face like thunder, he came over to me.

'I have to make a stand,' he sighed. 'I'm taking the captaincy off you.'

In fact he took the captaincy off the club completely and Martin

Storey was very angry with that because he hadn't played in the League game with Oulart. But Georgie O'Connor became the new leader of Wexford.

What followed was not pretty and there were meetings about meetings for days afterwards. I pointed out that we had a game ahead and we should try to focus on that but it split a lot of people in the camp. The club was very bitter and there was fury all around the village. It had been Oulart's first time winning the county title and our first shot at having a county captain and many of our members and supporters were disgusted at Griffin for taking it away from us. In fact many would still hold it against him. They would have settled for any of us, Tomás, Martin Storey or myself, leading the team out.

South East Radio read a statement from our club on the matter but the county board and the management team were furious they didn't get a chance to respond and the matter flared up all over again.

I didn't mind losing it, I really didn't, but I felt Liam made an awful blunder giving the captaincy to Georgie because he was too close to both him and John O – they were cousins and good friends as well.

I also felt he had put Georgie in an awkward position. And even though I didn't particularly want the captaincy, I was a bit annoyed. I remembered Griffin's phone call the previous October, when he told me I would not be centre back for the season ahead and began to put two and two together and get seven. Now I was getting paranoid.

I saw Georgie at centre back and captain of the side and knew it should have been one of our club members. Worse still, others on the team clearly felt the same and were grumbling behind Griffin's back. Most of the lads agreed the manager had to do something about the controversy but not all believed Georgie should have been captain. There were huge differences of opinion.

And so it was in that alarming frame of mind that we approached the Offaly match. We didn't have a chance. I knew it and Griffin knew it.

'Dunne sacked as captain' was the headline in the *Irish Independent* in the lead-up to the Croke Park clash. I was hounded by journalists looking for stories but I remembered all the effort Griffin had put in getting me a job and so I kept my mouth shut.

John Conran rang me and said it would be better to turn my phone off and go to Morriscastle beach for a walk. He was right; the fact I kept my views to myself would later stand in my favour. But one thing was for sure: as match preparation went, you could not find any worse. It was typical Wexford.

There was enough bitching between the players and the county board as it was without this. They would hardly even let us swap jerseys with opponents back then and there was a bad vibe towards the fixtures committee, who had refused to switch that club game.

When Sunday's televised game with Offaly arrived, the Wexford team was a total shambles. The game began but we might as well have been still in the dressing-room, and by the time we got back there at half-time, we were a beaten team.

Georgie tried to rally us by going around and roaring encouragement but I went into the toilets and didn't even listen. I was wrong but Seánie Flood and a few more of the lads followed me; it illustrated the split in the camp.

Despite everything, and even though I had been in the public eye all week, I had remained pretty focused and was actually happy with my game. And yet it wasn't worth a tinker's curse that I picked up a man-of-the-match award because they beat us again, 2-14 to 1-10.

Controversy would dog me for the rest of my career but this was my first experience of it. I was a key player in the further decline of Wexford hurling. We had become a pathetic, sad bunch, incapable of taking our chances.

In the early 90s, we had come so close to getting somewhere but here we were on our arses, having lost three Leinster finals in 1992, 93 and 94, and now this latest slump.

The 1995 season could have been the start of a new era for

Wexford hurling, what with live TV coverage and all that, but it had caved in on us and we could not get out of that dressing-room quickly enough – I doubt some lads even waited to have a shower.

As for the row surrounding the club, I felt I had let Liam Griffin down, but at least he had been given a two-year term and I hoped there would be a chance to repay him the next season.

I had been adamant I would stand by my club, even though I mightn't always have received their full backing when I was a minor. To this day I maintain it would have caused little bother for the Wexford fixtures committee to make a switch but they didn't bother their arses and we all were in the doldrums again. Good old Wexford – open a window and we'll jump out.

All sorts of jokes at our expense flew around the place but it wasn't funny at the time. By now the fans had had enough and wanted Griffin out. Oddly enough, the players had seen him take a stand on the Oulart incident and respected him for it, and they knew there were more to blame than just Griffin.

But the public failed to see it like that and on Monday September 4 about 20 members of the Wexford Supporters Club convened at Murphy Floods hotel to voice concern at the way the team was being handled.

Sensing a good story at a dead time of the year, the *Wexford People* newspaper rubbed their hands in anticipation and sent a reporter along.

'Griffin must go' was their headline the following week over a report on the supporters' meeting, where it was claimed, among other 'heated' exchanges, that Wexford would be a third-world county if things didn't change.

But the county board ignored the rebellion and Griffin, Rory Kinsella and Séamus Barron were ratified the following week for a second year in charge.

A proposal to get rid of the three was rejected when board chairman Paddy Wickham asked they be given a year's grace and there were only four dissenting voices.

Once he was safe in the knowledge he had a job for another year, Griffin travelled west to attend the 1995 All-Ireland final Clare homecoming. He had played for them for over two years – his father hailed from there – and understandably felt some affinity. It was a different Liam Griffin that came back from Clare the following day.

Meanwhile, the club-versus-county controversy had ensured that once again Oulart-The-Ballagh were Public Enemy Number One and we were under pressure to retain our title and shut our critics up. But after such a terrible year with the county, Tomás, Martin and myself were only too glad to get back to grassroots.

Tom Neville was waiting to get his hands on us again, of course. He insisted we had to compensate for the disasters on the intercounty front and off we went with another match against St Martin's, beating them by two points in the first round of the Wexford Championship. I got a lovely piece of crystal from South East Radio for winning man of the match and it was good to get back to playing decent hurling again.

Storey was captain this time and did a super job for the entire season. Although reigning champions are there to be shot down, it was no shock to me that we were in the county semi-final again just a year after winning the title for the first time. We were a damn good team. Our old friends Buffers Alley waited for us there and while they badly wanted our blood, there was no way we were going to bow to them, and so for the second year in a row we took them. Earlier that year, we had also beaten them in the League final but this Championship win was like all our Christmases and birthdays coming together.

The Alley had 12 county Championships but they would have given them all back just to deprive us of one – that was the extent of the mutual hatred at the time. It's not as bad these days because all the young lads play soccer together but back then it was fairly saucy to say the least. We beat them by seven points and didn't hold back in celebrating as they trudged off the field. In your face!

There was no talk of a curse now as we faced into our second county final in a row against Glynn-Barntown, a new team who had just reached their first ever decider at this level. They were peppered with good players, including Shane Carley, Eugene Furlong and Gary Laffan, but the occasion got to them and you could see it clearly even during the parade, as they waved and smiled into the crowd like pure novices. I knew there and then Oulart were more focused and we beat them 2-15 – 2-9. For the second year in a row, the Bob Bowe Cup came to the village and Martin Storey lifted it with a huge smile on his face.

This time, I wasn't completely satisfied just to win a club title. I still felt we were throwing everything away with the county, shooting ourselves in the foot.

Anyway, like Liam Griffin, I watched half in delight and half in envy as Clare went on to win the All-Ireland and change the face of hurling forever. Storey and I were so intrigued by their achievement that we agreed to go down and play them in the annual GOAL charity match on the Wednesday after their win over Offaly in the All-Ireland final. Oulart had a challenge game pencilled in for the Thursday, so the two of us had every intention of getting back for it, but we didn't factor in the danger of getting wrapped up in the celebrations in Ennis.

Over 16,000 turned up to watch the game, and Liam Doyle, who by now could hardly move, came over to mark me and chatted away, whenever the sliotar was down the far end of the field, about the countless early-morning training sessions they had put in. By the end of the match, I was under no illusions about Ger Loughnane's success – their All-Ireland was far from a fluke.

Daithí Regan and Kevin Kinahan were two of the few Offaly players to turn up and they deserved great credit for that and I remember thinking how down they must have felt but the Clare boys went out of their way to thank them and the rest of us for making it down. They were heroes for life but could still spare time for the ordinary Joes like ourselves.

I met Ger Loughnane and he asked me about Wexford, and seemed genuinely stunned when I told him my club team was better-prepared and fitter than the county squad.

It had done the Wexford team good to see Clare burying the so-called curse of Biddy Early and enjoying all the fruits of their success because it renewed our own hunger and showed us what winning an All-Ireland could do for you. At the same time, we weren't fully convinced we could get to that level because, quite simply, we were way off the pace. So our admiration of Clare was heavily mixed up with a fair bit of the green-eyed monster.

Griffin, however, thought the exact opposite. He began to draw up a plan and called an emergency meeting of the Wexford panel just a couple of weeks after the Clare win.

A few days before that gathering, I bumped into my sister-in-law Paula Sinnott, who worked for Liam at the Ferrycarrig Hotel, and spoke to her about the great year it had been for the club. I also remarked what a shambles of a season it had been for the county. Paula's response was immediate, emphatic and totally unexpected.

'I guarantee you,' she smiled, 'Liam Griffin will not leave this job until he achieves what he wants to do with that team. He will leave no stone unturned.'

To be honest, I seriously doubted he could achieve the miracle. Of course I didn't know then he had already plotted much of the way to the summit. It was an odyssey only Griffin could foresee, the road to emulating the Clare team of 1995 and laying hands on the MacCarthy Cup.

So come on ye full-time, small-town heroes, cast away your inbred fears/
Of standing out from all the rest, the cynics and the pessimists/
The self-indulgent, almost rich, the blatant hurlers on the ditch/
Time is passing so come on, face the ball, the game is on/
To win just once, oh to win just once, that would be enough.
The Saw Doctors, To Win Just Once

– CHAPTER ELEVEN –
The final countdown

The first sign that things were about to change in Wexford hurling came the Tuesday after the 1995 All-Ireland final when every squad member got a short phone call from the management.

There were no little chats or small talk; instead they issued us with a blunt message: Training resumes next week in the gym. This was new. Never had we gone back so early. But we all agreed something different was needed to dig Wexford out of the hole, and though we usually approached training with all the eagerness of someone going to a dentist to get a tooth yanked, this time there was a sense of willingness. In a sense it was imposed; you got the impression that now they weren't asking you to come in but were demanding it.

The Oulart lads were left alone, however, until our involvement in the Leinster club campaign ended. Our season finally ended after we were knocked out of the club Championship by Glenmore and beat Rathnure in the county League, and so just before Christmas Griffin asked us to the final two training sessions with the Wexford team.

The lads had been going strong for weeks, pumping iron in Dominic Kiernan's gym in Wexford town, but we had notions about ourselves – sure hadn't Oulart men long been the fittest in the county? We decided there wasn't much point to it and gave it a miss.

It was a big mistake because when we eventually did go back to

Dominic's we got the fright of our life. The lads had muscles on their muscles and were working like machines. There was no messing or joking as they threw themselves into their circuits and pumped iron to dance music. Seán Collier, a former international boxer and Ireland team trainer, was timing them at each station before moving them onto the next machine.

I looked at John O'Connor, who was paired with Damien Fitzhenry, and was astonished. John O had always been fit but he was absolutely flying now and Fitzy was all guns blazing too.

The pairs had been decided at the first training session and there was no slotting in with a lad just because you arrived together, no way. There was no-one getting between Fitzy and John O, or Tommy Kehoe and Adrian Fenlon, who was fast becoming the star performer in the gym by a country mile.

Storey and I went in together but we found working out to the music strange and didn't know the routine anyway, so like bold children, we did only half the repetitions and wouldn't be anywhere near finished when the boys were already on their next drill.

It was as clear as day Griffin had raised the bar and the Oulart contingent had failed to hurdle it. We were left embarrassed because it would take two days to get the soreness out of our shoulders and the back of our arms, but by then we were back in the gym again.

Weights are a part of life for the modern-day GAA player but for most of the Wexford panel this was their first hardcore experience of the gym. As it turned out they loved it. They seemed to rise to the bait Griffin, Collier and Kinsella had laid down, responding to the urgency of the drills, where everything was done at high speed.

Each player was asked to fill out a sheet on what he thought of Wexford hurling. In return, we were drowned with more handouts – sports literature, diet sheets and so on. Each player was told to drink four pints of water each day and stay away from alcohol.

Griffin told us that while other teams were running up hills we would be running down them as well to enhance our speed, but he said the gym work would continue for months until he was happy with our upper-body strength.

Wexford Wanderers gave us the use of tackle bags and suddenly I was going home with data on each muscle in my body tucked into my kit-bag. It was the first time I even knew I had muscles, to be honest.

There was no guesswork with the training; everything was done scientifically – well more or less everything. I remember Dave Guiney really getting into it in a bid to nail down his place on the team. He asked George O'Connor how much training he should be doing on his own and was duly told he should be doing at least 1,000 press-ups per day. It was a wind-up, of course, but a few days later Georgie got a phone call from Dave.

'Do your arms not get sore after a few days, George?'

The rest of us might have fallen around laughing but it just showed that Dave was ready to do what it took to make the team.

The issue of the captaincy arose around then. I ruled myself out because it didn't particularly interest me after what had happened the year before. Storey had replaced Tomás as club captain and had succeeded in getting everyone to row in behind him. He had to be the man to lead Wexford and I said as much to Griffin, reminding him of the great job Martin was doing with Oulart.

The announcement was made that Martin was the man, and though he and Liam may not have been bosom buddies, that had little or nothing to do with hurling and so they simply got on with it.

Early in 1996, when we played Offaly in the Walsh Cup, you could see everyone was starting to pull together. And of course the reason was that it was either Griffin's way or the highway.

It had all started with the pre-Christmas sessions in the gym, but the new attitude wasn't confined just to the gym. Just after the holidays, for example, he brought us up to the old golf links in Bunclody for a run. The course was unkind; it was hilly and bumpy and there was lots of it, the kind of place you'd bring an Army Ranger, or someone you didn't like, for training.

The Friday night before one of our first sessions there, Oulart had its club dinner dance, where we got our medals. Many large bottles of Bulmers were consumed as we gloated on the great year we'd had but the only drink we were involved with the following day was what came up through our throats and out our mouths.

As we arrived at Bunclody, we estimated it would take us 15 minutes to go around the course and we were not far wrong, but we didn't bank on having to run around it four times at nearly full stride.

It was a deadly course; there were little banks hidden everywhere and as I staggered onto my second lap I could see lads were well into their third. I swore then that never again would I drink before a session and do this to myself.

Yeah, it was a nice little learning curve, and as Tommy Kehoe, Larry O'Gorman and Adrian Fenlon were stuck at the front, the aim for me was to get up there within a few weeks. I was helped when I saw Ger Cushe, not normally known for his stamina, also improving with every outing.

You find out lots about your team-mates in these situations and it was clearer now who would make the cut and who was interested in going to a higher level. Cushe was not the fastest but he was pushing the boat out and staying at the front for as long as he could before drifting back a bit; the winner in him was coming out.

Under this regime, the games were a welcome respite from the training, even at this early stage of the season. We wanted to win every game we played and were thrilled to win the Walsh Cup against Offaly. It may not have seemed any big deal to outsiders at the time but for us it was massive. For good measure, we hammered them again in the League quarter-final, by 16 points, unheard of for a Wexford team.

People wondered what had changed and of course it was the players' attitudes. In a League game against Meath, Larry O'Gorman was whipped off the field in the first half because he didn't conform to

Griffin's game plan, and to ram the point home, he was dropped for the next game as well. He had been handed a specific job to do at half back but had tried to run the field and play his own game, and the manager was having none of it.

Griffin tried Ger Cushe at centre back and gave Damien Fitzhenry a run out the field, leaving Séamus Kavanagh in goal. He made sure all his theories and formations were tried out early in the year and assured us that by the time the Championship arrived everything would slot into place.

After games he would chat to us, rattling us with statistics compiled by John O'Leary, who'd been brought into the back-room team. The stats don't lie. I remember coming off the field many times chuffed with myself only to be told I'd been doing my own thing and not conforming to the team plan, which demanded more hooking and blocking and clearing the lines and less of the fouling and flaking.

Once we had absorbed the lessons, it was back to the heavy training during the week: two or three sessions in the gym and plenty of stamina running.

It had taken me six weeks to get the hang of the weights but then I became addicted to them and loved the buzz. For the first four or five weeks, I had found it hard to get out of bed with the pain and could hardly turn sideways, but I soon noticed my body changing, and my days of playing catch-up in the sweaty studio were over when I joined the lads who were doing the most reps on the bars.

Seán Collier used to bring us into the ring at Dominic's and invite us to spar with him and while a few chanced their arm, the rest of the lads were at the weights and machines. With Griffin and Rory Kinsella treating the exercises like hurling drills, it was move, move, move. The backroom took a huge part in the sessions and gave us a one-minute breather between every set but they took no shit whatsoever.

One night, Tom Dempsey was doing his usual job of entertaining the troops while we suffered in training. As one of the funniest men I ever knew, Tom was invaluable to us on and off the field, but this particular night Griffin felt he was too much of a distraction and gave the signal to Collier, who beckoned poor old Tom into the ring for a bit of sparring.

We were all pumping away when Griffin ushered us ringside to admire Tom doing his best Sly Stallone impression. Suddenly, Collier let fly with a left hook and drove him into next week with a box. Tom hit the floor, blood dribbling down his mouth. It wasn't a bit funny – he had taken a fair old smack – but he didn't say a word to anyone.

In fairness to Tom, I don't think anyone else on the panel would have taken a box like that and stayed involved in the set-up. Eventually, everyone saw the funny side but the only thing Tom was raging about was that when he hit the floor, the first thing he could see was my red and black jersey of Oulart-The-Ballagh. Buffers Alley men always hated to see that shirt looking down on top of them.

From there, no-one was under any more illusions about what the management would and would not take and so we moved forward together, keeping the little transformation in the team quiet and well away from the Wexford people, who were expecting another disaster that summer.

Early in February, we travelled to Limerick for the League and they beat us 1-13 to 0-8 in the rain. The shocking thing was that they not only beat us on the scoreboard but also absolutely devoured us physically. Tommy Kehoe, a classy forward, was beat around the place that day.

I rarely saw Griffin angrier after a game, and he promised the team would never again be intimidated.

Despite the defeat, the Wexford fans must have had their hopes up once more.

We had gone through the early stages of the League in impressive fashion and, as I said, walloped Offaly before falling to Galway in the League semi-final.

We were not too downhearted about losing that game because we knew progress had been made; the team was still evolving and the dynamics of it were changing from week to week.

But the night I realised we really meant business was an evening late in April when we beat Cork 2-17 to 0-10 in a tournament game in Waterford.

There, the skeletons of the team of old were swept away into the night and replacing them was a psychological backbone that would carry us on for the remainder of the year.

Damien Fitzhenry was back in goal after his spell outfield, lighter and with an enhanced touch thanks to his stint there. Ger Cushe was on the edge of the square again but this time with the knowledge that he had played most of the year at centre back and had done fine there. If he survived that far outfield, he'd have little bother so close to goal.

I was at centre back, a position I loved because I felt I could have a big impact on games from there, and beside me was Larry O, who had played in so many positions by now that no-one could actually read the game better than him.

At midfield, the experience, skill and determination of Georgie was merged with the energy and ground hurling of Adrian Fenlon. Up front, Martin Storey and Tom Dempsey were fitter and stronger than ever and it was no coincidence that we absolutely blew Cork off the field that night. You could tell they had no idea what had happened to them but we knew and we wanted more.

For the first time in my era, the Wexford hurlers were pulling together. At least, most of us were. The Guiney brothers, Rod and Dave, hung together and there was always a little gap between them and us, but once we went on the field, I would give 100 percent for both of them and vice-versa.

Drink really did go out the door this time. For a few years, we had introduced phoney alcohol bans but this time, you carried the guilt of a serial killer on your shoulders if you guzzled even one pint.

Smoking, although it didn't affect me, went on the back burner as well, which meant purgatory for Seánie Flood and Martin Storey. Seánie used to love cans of coke as well and he could drink five or six of them every day in his tractor, but they went out the tractor door, replaced by water.

Our diet was completely changed at this stage. No more butter, no bread or anything sweeter. I lived on chicken, fruit, pasta, water and spinach after training; I ate so much of the bloody stuff it was little wonder I started to feel like Popeye.

Once training was over, we would head to the Talbot Hotel in Wexford town, where Griffin would usually have a five-minute meeting that lasted about two hours. While we waited, he would go into the chef and instruct him to take all fattening oils or creams off the menu. But being from Wexford, we couldn't do everything right and despite the fact that there was a huge BSE scare in the country back then, we shovelled juicy steaks into our mouths after each training session, just in case we wouldn't get infected.

The steaks were sponsored, would you believe, so to support the local farmers Larry O and Georgie were asked to pose for a picture and reassure the nation that beef was your only man. All around the county, you could see huge posters of the two boys loading steak into their big gobs. Priceless.

It wasn't just diet and physical preparation that we needed, though. Perhaps Liam Griffin's cleverest stroke was the introduction of a sports psychologist, Niamh Fitzpatrick, into the camp. Around six weeks before our Championship started, against Kilkenny, Niamh was presented to us in the Ferrycarrig Hotel and proceeded to tell us what Griffin had told us exactly a year earlier – only this time we were taking it in.

She went through every detail of our lives and each player was allotted a 20-minute slot to discuss things with her; you got half an hour if your head really was in bits. Once more, a circuit-like approach was adopted at those meetings; you had to be on time and ready to go in and talk to Niamh when your team-mate came out.

Niamh started to become more than just a sports psychologist for me. Gradually she got my life story. I wouldn't talk much about my father to anyone, about why he left home and so on, but she got it all and a lot more.

I spoke of bad things like the pressures of work and good things such as my upcoming wedding with Eithne. I told her stuff I wouldn't have told my mother but each time I felt a weight being lifted off my chest.

As well as the chats serving as great preparation for games, Niamh gave me real peace of mind as well and I found myself still chatting away when the time would arrive for the next player to come in. She would press pause and simply carry on the next time as though the conversation had never been interrupted in the first place.

We were given tapes, to be listened to especially before games, for mental preparation and relaxation. We would listen to them going to and from Croke Park as the year unfolded.

On top of that Liam Griffin gave us tapes of positive or motivational songs like *Search for a Hero* from M People, *We are the Champions* by Queen and two popular Wexford tunes, our 1996 anthem, *Dancing at the Crossroads*, and the ballad *Boolavogue*.

We had been way too manly to ever consider such airy-fairy methods before 96, but now I would close my eyes before training or a game and relax for five or 10 minutes at home, but at the same time suspecting that if my brothers or sisters could see me they would commit me to the men in the white coats.

One day I put the motivational tape on in the car for my brother Seán, and he was fairly wound up himself by the end of the journey.

So, as we headed into the Championship, there wasn't a stone left unturned and though a few months earlier we had believed Griffin to be insane, we could now see it all coming right in front of us.

Seeing these hard men going in front of a woman they hardly knew and blurting out their life stories to her, well, it just showed the change of attitude in the squad.

On the field our selectors, Rory Kinsella and Séamus Barron, who both knew everything there was to know about the game of hurling, hounded us in training, and our challenge games were reaching a ferocious tempo. After each match, with the help of John O'Leary, they pinned the stats up on the back of the door – just how many frees we won and conceded, how many line balls we got, scores, blocks and so on. There was just nowhere to hide.

With the Kilkenny game looming and Croke Park recently rebuilt and radically transformed, Niamh decided we should send a delegation to the stadium to report back on the alterations so we wouldn't be distracted by them on match day. Unfamiliarity, she said, can be seriously unsettling.

After her visit there with our PRO, Pat Murphy, she provided us with a comprehensive virtual tour of the place, describing the big yellow doors into the dressing-rooms, the inside of those changing rooms and the feel of the pitch.

Pat would lay out the jerseys from one to 15 in our virtual dressing-rooms so each of us knew where he would sit. Already it felt like we knew the stadium, though we had never seen it since the redesign. That was the sort of preparation we needed for Kilkenny because I and many of the lads had never beaten them in the Championship.

If we were doing our bit, Griffin was almost going overboard. That man was up some nights until 5 am dissecting videos, and though we would have played Kilkenny several times, he always had a new angle on them after watching those tapes.

We knew also that there were a few internal issues with their team, so when the game finally arrived, it really was shit or get off the pot, because we had never been so well prepared.

That game was in the melting pot for so long. We went five points up but back they came to within a point and we had to bring Billy Byrne on to rescue us with a goal – it wouldn't be his last time saving us that year.

When Billy came on, our game tactics went from: 'Get the ball in to the forwards quick and low' to 'Get the ball in any old way to Billy', because the man just seemed to gobble up any sort of supply that came his way and we were glad to see the Kilkenny net rattle soon after his arrival.

Griffin had told him to win the first ball and stop Pat O'Neill from lording it. When Billy got the sliotar, he was to jink one way and shoot the other.

He followed the orders to a T.

His goal came from a quick Adrian Fenlon pass and changed the game. A minute later, Feno took a quick line ball to Larry O which resulted in a point, and we hung on to win 1-14 to 0-14, a sensational result.

Only afterwards did it occur to me that we had never once even contemplated defeat. There was just no fear of losing; it was something that was never spoken about and that was incredible because we had discussed just about everything else.

But Griffin reminded us that the win was one step on the ladder and despite the fact county board officials had shed tears of joy in the dressing-room, we soon returned to normality on the following Wednesday night.

As with every game, we would sit down and pinpoint where we went wrong and then in training afterwards try to rectify the errors. There was always a huge emphasis on tactics in those sessions; Griffin insisted on six defenders marking eight forwards, which meant one defender would have to leave his man and someone else would have to look after his patch. It ensured cover play was always a strong part of our defence. Damien Fitzhenry's puck-outs were also analysed, and whichever way he stepped, every guy out the field knew where the ball was landing.

Niamh brought us back in to work on our minds so we were well prepared when we met Dublin and, after a desperate second half, just held on long enough to beat them 2-12 to 1-9, a poor winning margin considering we had played them off the field in the first half.

Just before the break, they got a penalty. Eamon Morrissey mishit the sliotar, but it somehow managed to get past Ger Cushe. After a few kind words were said to Ger, we went into the dressing-room and stayed there for the restart, because Dublin destroyed us in the first 15 minutes of the second half before we made a few changes, regained our shape and got through.

Our collapse in the second half was a sharp lesson because we had endured a scare. But rather than panic like we would have done in the past, we reacted well, made a few changes and played a get-out-of-jail card to ensure we would meet Offaly in the Leinster final.

I had watched Offaly destroy Laois in the other semi-final at Croke Park and when John Troy scored his second goal, I and Bartle Sinnott got up to leave – I had seen enough. The former Offaly hurler Pádraig Horan saw me leave and, pointing to Troy, heckled: 'That's your man, Liam.'

I kept my mouth shut but Bartle heard me mutter: 'He'll be my man alright.'

Troy scored 3-5 against Laois but with every score he and Offaly got, I wished them another one, which may be cruel on Laois but I wanted to build up the men in green, white and gold to the last and let them think they were invincible for the six weeks that remained to our big game.

We needed them to feel infallible because we had our own problems to iron out. It was clear as the spring water we were slugging by the gallon that our display against Dublin would not cut the mustard.

Sensing this, Griffin brought Niamh in to meet us shortly before the game. She asked us all to write down the reasons we felt Wexford were going to win the Leinster final. I had been talking to her a few days previously about the same subject, and when she didn't hear me speak up at the meeting she asked me why.

At this stage, we had heard the views of the whole squad: we're fitter; we're better prepared; our team is stronger. They were the theories but Niamh still wasn't satisfied.

'Liam,' she said, 'will you tell the lads the story you told me last week?'

I went red but proceeded to recall that a few days previously when I went home for dinner after one of our best ever training sessions, Mam asked: 'How did ye get on?' and my reply was: 'Mam, today we decided we're going to beat Offaly.'

As soon as I uttered those words, Niamh scribbled them on the board; it was the mantra she was looking for. It might sound cocky now, but I knew there was no way we could be beaten – we were just too well prepared.

With that, we were sent onto the training pitch in Wexford Park and as soon as we had done our warm-up drills, Griffin came up to me, caught me by the neck and growled: 'You don't forget what happened to you two years ago when the first ball came down between you and John Troy.'

I was taken aback. He had never spoken to me like that before. But he didn't have to remind me; my memory is long and I hadn't forgotten that Troy 'did' me with the first pull of the ball – he pulled early and caught my hand – when they hammered us in 94.

A while after the reminder about Troy, Griffin came back to me again, this time less pumped up.

'What do you think about Tom Dempsey?' he enquired.

Tom's brother-in-law had died just before the Offaly game, and Tom felt he wouldn't make the team and was anxious all week beforehand, so I felt maybe he might not be mentally right.

'I wouldn't play him,' I said. 'He's not right.'

Of course, Dempsey went on to have the game of his life and scored 1-5. It was his perfect game but the same applies to the rest of us as well. The memories and stories of that day will never be forgotten.

Going up to Croke Park on match day, Griffin stopped the bus on the Wexford-Wicklow border just past Inch and before the Arklow by-pass and asked us all to get off and move over to the ditch, where cows were mooing and passing cars were beeping their horns.

I'm sure the hundreds of Wexford supporters who passed us that day must have thought we were gone in the head but none of them dared stop to ask what the hell we were doing.

Griffin stood almost in the ditch and gave a speech – Christ, it still sends shivers down my spine! He gave a rendition of who we were and where we came from. He brought us back down the centuries to Vinegar Hill. The passionate way he spoke about Wexford brought tears to our eyes. It got worse when he spoke about our families and neighbours and ancestors and all the battles they'd had to fight over the years. And the fact they had risen, almost alone, in 1798 to give their blood in the cause of freedom.

By now there wasn't a dry eye on the ditch and to tell you the truth, the speech was so inspirational even the cows came over to have a look and listen. He asked for a complete focus and eventually, standing by the bus, brought his oration to an end.

'Lads,' he roared, 'we are walking out of our own county today but we are coming back as Leinster champions this evening! And we are walking out!' he reiterated, slapping the side of the bus and instructing the driver to move up the road and over the border.

Seánie Flood strolled alongside me and the two of us were in such shock at Griffin's speech that we scarcely heard the cars blowing their horns. When eventually we reached the bus and hopped on, there was complete silence – the lads were still trying to take in what had happened.

Larry Murphy looked over at me and while neither of us breathed a word, we were both thinking the same thing: Griffin was awesome. And so off we drove, heading to the Stillorgan Park Hotel, our pre-match base, to go through the usual ritual: pasta, Niamh Fitzpatrick, potatoes, Rory Kinsella, chicken and beans, Liam Griffin. You could eat what you wanted and speak to who you chose. In former times, we had been eating Mars bars on match days but now it was all hot food, full of energy.

On the way to Croke Park on the bus, Griffin showed us a video of his old favourite blockbuster *Braveheart*, which we watched every time without fail on the way to a big match. I was so entertained when I first saw the film before the League quarter-final against Galway that I didn't want to get off the bus.

The tape was switched on when the whole team was on board, but again, he never let us watch the end of it – just as the film entered its final stages, we had to hop off, tog out and warm up.

The lads used to love seeing bodies fly through the air, but Griffin was clever enough not to let us see the finale because the hero, William Wallace, dies in the end and we were so wrapped up in the film, it could have affected our minds. Seriously, that was the way we were thinking.

Of course *Braveheart* was a classic and all that, but by the time I got it for a Christmas present I was fairly sick of it.

Another part of the pre-match ritual was reading the newspapers. Nowadays, managers are paranoid about their players speaking to the press and if a team loses, the papers get the blame, while winning teams get accused of losing the run of themselves while talking to the press.

We didn't give a tráithnín what was said about us and would talk away to any journalist. Griffin knew the media had a big role to play and he knew how to handle the reporters, so he instructed everyone to talk away, and even before matches he would bring us back to newspapers by showing us the difference between photos of winning and losing players.

Adrian Fenlon was really the only guy who didn't like chatting to the press and, while I understand that, I can't fathom this bullshit of managers appointing two players to talk to the press before every game. It's manufactured and it's only putting more pressure on those lads who are chosen.

I read all the papers before the Offaly match and the pundits were split on the outcome but we were confident. Griffin called us into a huddle and did his usual prophecy act by predicting we would score a goal but within two minutes they would get one back. He warned us not to panic when that happened.

It had been 19 years since we won a provincial title so panicking should have been about the first port of call if we fell behind in a game.

Amazingly, though, Griffin's prediction came to pass. Early in the game, Gary Laffan, our big full-forward, flicked a lovely ball over to Tom Dempsey, who rifled a sweet goal, but almost straightaway, Michael Duignan cancelled it out by hitting one for Offaly. How could you panic when your manager had predicted exactly what would happen? Was it any wonder we had such faith in the man?

Soon after the goal, the first ball that landed between John Troy and I broke harmlessly between us but I pulled hard on the second ball alright and caught him in the mouth with the end of my hurl. It looked legitimate to the referee but I knew I had got him.

Blood spurted out of his mouth, but remembering what he had done to me two years before that, I didn't feel one bit of guilt. He was good at pulling off the ball himself; he had it down to a fine art.

Anyway, he was soon moved off me and into full-forward, where the big, welcoming arms of Ger Cushe opened for him.

'What happened you, John?' Cushe enquired politely.

'You know damn fucking well what happened,' Troy snarled.

Ger used to joke that lads would come in to mark him after a spell on me with bits of hurls stuck in them but this time we had a game to win and, with my revenge exacted, it was back to focusing on the ball.

Hassle! Next ball! Those were the key words in 96. They were drilled into us.

We started to pull away in the second half thanks to some heroic defending and even though Billy Dooley got a second goal for them, John O'Connor leapt around the full-back and half-back lines like a leopard, clearing ball after ball.

With time running out and Wexford leading by four points, Troy, who was back out marking me, decided to test me and leaning over, said: 'Congratulations! You deserve it.'

I didn't answer straightaway, aware he was probably playing mind games, but then we went six points up and I replied: 'Thanks, John.'

Just at the end, Brian Whelahan came out with the ball trying to make a huge clearance as he so often did to inspire his team, but for the umpteenth time that day Larry Murphy appeared out of nowhere and drove him back, as we had been instructed to do by Griffin before the game.

If we could plough their best player back and stop him from clearing ball, it would dishearten them, and seeing Brian being hounded, with time just up, drove our lads on to the final whistle.

For the first time in my career, I got a real sense of satisfaction as the seconds ticked away, a feeling of accomplishment. When the whistle blew, I just sprinted straight to the stand. I had been waiting so long for this moment and I just wanted to look on at the mayhem back on the field.

Storey was the first player I met and we wrapped our arms around each other. He walked up the steps to lift the Bob O'Keeffe Cup and Seánie Flood and I quickly followed him.

Maybe we got a little carried away. The two of us started swinging out of the little podium up there, and a steward told me to sit down.

'I will in my fuck,' I replied. 'I'm waiting 19 years to get up here.'

Looking back at the video of those celebrations in 96, well, it often raised the hairs on the back of my neck. Jim Berry, a Wexford man, was chairman of the Leinster Council at the time and he started us off talking about the 19-year gap and telling the nation we had done the county proud.

Below us, the crowd went nuts, and it took me ages to get back down to pitch level. I stood talking to reporters and when I did make it to the dressing-room, the mayhem had died down. But it was great to see the Bob O'Keeffe Cup inside.

The only thing that dampened the thrill that day was that I soon got one of my blinding headaches. In the 90s I suffered badly from post-match migraines and used to have to sit in the dressing-room and take painkillers after games. I would often feel sick with the pain and because of that I would avoid travelling back on the team bus. I just wanted peace and quiet so I used to go back to the car, which would be parked in Clonliffe College, munch on a few sandwiches, drink a pint of milk and slip home quietly on the back roads.

Those blazing headaches were deadly. Seánie Flood suffered from them as well and the two of us used to sit with our heads down after games. People must have wondered why we sometimes looked so upset after winning matches, but there was a reason.

It's a good thing there were no drug tests back then because I had so many painkillers inside me, I would surely have been done. But there was so much nervous energy entailed in playing in Croke Park that I used to get overwhelmed with pain once the final whistle blew.

And so while the rest of the team went mad in Wexford town the night of the Offaly game, I did my own thing. I was at home in bed early that night and didn't meet up with them until the night after, when we gathered for a reception in the town again.

We were back training on Wednesday and went for a run at Curracloe. It was great to see everyone on a high, and for good measure, Liam told us if we wanted a few pints that night there would be no problem, though in the same breath he warned us that training would resume in earnest the following night.

Of course, we needed no second invitation and retired to Hanrahan's of Curracloe, where the video of the game was still being replayed. Free pints were handed over the bar and we didn't hold back, but we suffered for our indulgence the next day.

Griffin ran the shite out of us, nearly killed us with those deadly 200-metre and 400-metre efforts. Ned Buggy was there watching and said he felt green at the gills just looking at us. We were back to reality, as if nothing had been won. Griffin told us to hit the showers and said he would be in with us in a few minutes to ask the squad one simple question.

With steam rising everywhere in the changing-room, he was hard to see but his voice was unmistakable.

'How many All-Ireland semi-finals are you guaranteed to play for the rest of your lives?' he asked.

No answer.

'The answer,' he replied, 'is this – you might never play in another one'.

Silence again. Just the sound of water splashing and guys trying to come to terms with what he had just said. And with that, we began to look forward to Galway, next up in four weeks' time with a confident manager, Mattie Murphy, who was talking up his men as the best in the business.

In the interim, the county really started to get behind us and at an A-versus-B training match, we spent hours just signing autographs for kids. It gave the lads a feeling of what life could be like for them, which was important as well. Banners and flags united the county and club rivalries went out the window. Our players were recognised everywhere they went. Of course my job entailed meeting publicans and shopkeepers, who were only too glad to collar me for a chat and go through the Leinster final blow by blow all over again.

Mam was sick in the run-up to the semi-final against Galway and I hadn't been in to see her. Maybe I was putting off going to the hospital – it's a trip I dislike at the best of times.

Anyway, I eventually got in to see her. None of the brothers or sisters had arrived, so though it soon came time to go training, I didn't want to leave her on her own and hung back. When the family eventually poured in I left and headed for training, arriving late. Griffin told me to do a few laps and then ate the face off me. I told him Mam was sick but he wasn't taking excuses and told me the next time I was to leave earlier. It was his way now.

The morning of the Galway match, Mam was still in hospital and Martin Storey and I went to see her.

'Martin,' she said. 'I won't make this game but make sure and give me a chance to see the final.'

Martin told her he'd do his best and we set off to Croke Park.

The game was only minutes old when John O'Connor was knocked unconscious after a tackle with Joe Rabbitte. The referee awarded a throw-in and Joe made the serious mistake of going in beside Georgie for it – he ended up with a broken bone in his ankle.

Another thing I recall about that game was the trouble I had with Cathal Moore. He scored 1-3 off me, and though there was nothing I could do for the goal, he really caught me for the points.

They were awarded a penalty in the second half and you can imagine my shock when I saw Ger Cushe alongside Damien Fitzhenry and Larry O'Gorman for the penalty. Cushe's record for saving penalties was not the best, and when I told him to get out of there he seemed fairly happy to do so.

I turned to the boys: 'Lads, if we stop this, we're in an All-Ireland final.'

Joe Cooney took the penalty and Fitzy dived, but I stopped it with my hurl and cleared it down the field.

For the rest of the game, we looked the better team and Tom Dempsey, Rory McCarthy, who got a brilliant goal, and Martin Storey gave us a bit of a cushion as the final minutes ticked away.

Galway looked rattled and drove loads of wides and while I still feel they wouldn't have beaten us, they did spurn a huge number of chances. But we got there.

Back home, everything went crazy and that night Bartle Sinnott and I came out of Phil Redmond's pub. I pointed across the road to a group singing and dancing at the crossroads, just like the song suggested.

'We might never see it again,' I said to Bartle.

Within three months, we had become the heroes of the county. We had a back-up team to look after our every need and ensure no-one was taking advantage of us. Not that it was likely to happen. Any step we took, there was someone waiting for us to put a blanket on the ground before us. It was incredible. You would get a punnet of strawberries sent over to you after training; people were coming over to us in restaurants and asking what way we wanted our steaks cooked; there were free boots for everyone. It was unreal and I had never seen anything like it. We even got free suits and shoes – some of the lads are still wearing them.

The management stopped us from taking the Bob O'Keeffe Cup around the county, however, and Griffin made sure we knew the journey wasn't over yet. He called us back into training after the Galway game, brought us into the room and told us we didn't have to train if we didn't want to. Most of us gave it a skip and tried on our new boots but that was the last night the showbiz stuff was allowed into the camp.

There and then, he spoke to us about every aspect of All-Ireland final day. I still reckon this was the night everything fell into place. He went as far as explaining how to greet President Mary Robinson before the game, instructing us to stand with our hands behind our backs and look straight at her. After that, we were to focus on the Liam MacCarthy Cup above on the podium, and that was to be our point of visual contact until we were called to walk behind the band with our socks up and look into the crowd to remember who we were and why we were there.

That night, there and then, two and a half weeks before the game against Limerick, the All-Ireland final was won. He had a list longer than Santa Claus himself, the most comprehensive guide to playing in a big match you will ever see. We knew our every movement from the talk that night to the moment the ball was thrown in against Limerick.

In the lead-up to the big match, I was best man at the wedding of my cousin Robert Dunne, and as old habits die hard, I got home from the Tuscar House hotel at a quarter to five the next morning.

It was a great wedding. Robert and I were close; he had lost his Dad, my godfather, in a car accident in 1972 and we had played a lot of hurling together. I found the occasion a great release from hurling, Griffin had relented and given me a dispensation from training, but I still felt all eyes were on me in the residents' bar to see if I was having a drink.

I took a few Budweisers and thought I had behaved fairly well, but Griffin didn't appreciate my honesty one little bit when I told him about it and I got another earful.

And so the training went ahead for the biggest game of our lives. We just worked hard and listened. Griffin reminded us how Tommy Kehoe had been pulverised by Limerick's Seán O'Neill in a League match earlier that year and how the home crowd in Kilmallock jeered Tommy.

Rows broke out everywhere that day but we didn't come out on top in too many and when Griffin brought us back into Dominic's Gym the day after that game, he demanded it would never happen again.

'No intimidation!' he roared.

'As long as I live, what happened you in Kilmallock will never happen one of my players again,' he screamed at Tommy Kehoe.

'What's the word, lads?' he shouted.

'No intimidation!' we roared back, and with the music pumping in the background we must have looked the unlikeliest bunch of thugs. From then on, if Griffin ever felt training was slipping, he would haul us into a big circle and get us to roar that mantra at the top of our voices.

But we were disciplined and maybe the idea of bringing us to an Army tent at Ballytrent beach had the desired effect. We had been there earlier in the year but a couple of weeks before the final we were back, sleeping in a huge tent erected by the backroom team.

It was straight out of boot camp with little camper beds just six inches off the ground. We slept there on Friday nights, travelled to Rosslare to train the next day and played a match between ourselves. Afterwards, we would go for a walk together and then it was back to camp, where one of the manager's friends, Tony Kehoe, was cooking a big barbecue with lashings of sponsored food. Martin Storey and John O'Connor were his commis chefs and helped him prepare the mountain of steaks. Some more of the lads set a big bonfire, and while we waited for the main course, we drank Ballygowan water, tea and orange juice by the litre or dug into large baskets of fruit. It was the best of grub and the best of times.

At night we would huddle up around the bonfire and Tom Dempsey would lead the way in a singsong. Of course Larry O was the headline act, belting out the numbers, aided and abetted by Seánie Flood on guitar. It was a great bonding, serious stuff.

Blankets were thrown on the bed and the lights went out. Then the real fun started. Boots and other heavy objects flew through the darkness and there were desperate roars and gasps as men were suffocated by pillows. What do you expect from 30 redblooded chaps deprived of a social life for so long?

At 5.15 the wake-up call for Sunday sounded. Griffin said he was calling a team meeting to discuss the Limerick players, but first we had to train. We went for a run, and then started pulling hurleys on rows of old tyres to develop our weak sides.

When he was called in to give us a hand, Griffin actually brought us back there again in 2001, the week before the All-Ireland semi-final with Tipperary. It was the same set-up only this time we didn't stay overnight.

Billy Byrne, the two O'Connors, Tom Dempsey and Martin Storey, who had retired by then but was drafted back into the squad, all came and we tore into the mountain of steaks and sandwiches.

Griffin got up at one stage and arrived back with crates of Budweiser and Heineken.

'Have a drink, lads,' he said. 'Next weekend, we will beat Tipperary and reach the All-Ireland final.'

He would be proved wrong of course, but it was close – the man is never far off the mark.

But the two camps we went on in 96 were the brainwave of a genius. You could see everyone growing closer together. The chats, the sing-songs, the grub, the fun – I will never forget it.

But when we got the wake-up call at 5.15 am before the final with Limerick, I wasn't too delighted with the whole thing.

'For Christ's sake, could he not have called us at half nine or something?' I moaned. No, he wanted to do it then.

We dragged ourselves out, battled our way through the training and settled down for the theory bit. Griffin proceeded to go through the Limerick team, dissecting them one by one.

'Joe Quaid, a great shot-stopper so try and place your shots but his puck-outs are predictable and won't go too far away from Gary Kirby. Ciarán Carey, will run all day but try to drag him out of position and he won't like it.'

Martin Storey was to play his usual game and we were to be confident that would work. He came to Gary Kirby but didn't get a chance to voice his opinion on him because George O'Connor interrupted: 'Liam will take care of Gary Kirby – we don't have to worry about him.'

Griffin looked up and moved on. I was a bit taken aback at the faith George and the boys had invested in me. But there was no fuss and the rest of the Limerick team quickly got the once over before the manager switched on a video.

He showed more highlights of the Clare team coming home after winning the 95 All-Ireland final. We could see the crowd going nuts and the joy that greeted them, but again, just as we got carried away with the footage, he turned it off and told us it was ours if we wanted it badly enough.

We did, of course, so there was no better time to spring a weights session on us while the squad was still starry-eyed from the Clare footage. Seán Collier had a mini-gym built around the tent and we used boots, tyres and sandbags to reinforce our muscles.

As we beavered away at all hours in the morning, Griffin and the selectors went around to each one of us individually.

'While we are down here getting ready for Limerick, they are asleep in Dublin. They are up there in a cosy hotel trying to get used to the pre-match routine but look at us and what we are doing. We are ready for them.'

And he was right. We were fine-tuned now. We went back to bed for a while and then turned up for breakfast before being 'released' back to our families. Amazingly, no stories or tales of our camp were leaked to the press; it showed the loyalty that existed in the set-up. By now lads totally believed in Griffin; they would have done ballet dancing for him, Rory, Séamus, Seán and Niamh. It was a time of confidence and belief.

But we still had to win the All-Ireland final and it wasn't all claps on the back; there were a few disappointments on the road to the big day. Our build-up had been marred by an injury to Seánie Flood, who had to retire injured against Galway. Seánie was one of the team's best and most tigerish players and we needed him as much as he desperately wanted to play himself. With a fortnight to go, he tried to give himself every chance by running but he wasn't able to and it was heartbreaking to see. His biggest problem was trying to find out what the injury was. A number of specialists offered opinions, but by the time he realised he had a hairline fracture it was too late – Seánie was going to miss the biggest day in the county's history.

Another upset for me was the fact that Tomás was not on the squad. I felt he should have been because there were others there not half as good as him. Of course he was no saint. I don't know if he would have stuck to the same torrid training regime as the rest of us, but Liam Griffin certainly cannot have been sure he wouldn't knuckle down. I had asked the manager about Tomás early in the season; he didn't get back to me, and Tomás's hopes of making the cut just seemed to fizzle out.

I didn't allow it to affect me and didn't sulk but I was disappointed he wasn't there. We had grown a lot closer travelling to matches in and around 93 and 94 and it would have been great to go in and out of training with him. But I got on with it and Griffin never raised the matter again.

So that was it, the All-Ireland final checklist was drawn up. Liam even had a local artist draw cartoons of us beating Limerick. But he had the serious stuff sorted out as well, and that included the scenario where one of our men, or one of theirs, was sent off.

Anytime we sat down to eat, Griffin had a man come over and take the butter off the table. Instead of apple tart and cream, we got spinach. We had lovely new shoes and suits – some of the lads even looked respectable. I had enough boots, togs and socks to kit out a whole team. I knew the personal statistics of every man on the team and would spend training matches trying to clear more and more balls so I would have a higher average than anyone else.

We all knew the Limerick team inside out. Gary Kirby was my man. The in-form forward in the country, he had scored 1-33 on the way to the final.

But when I woke up on September 1, the morning of the 1996 All-Ireland final, I was ready for him. I switched off the alarm and the first thought that came to me was the film *Braveheart*. I wondered if we would finally get to see the end of it, and if it would after all have an heroic ending.

I suspected it would.

MAKING HAY AT HOME IN OULART: Kieran, Tomás, Seán and I in the back garden in 1972

THE FIRST OF MANY: I won my first ever hurling medal in the Nicky Rackard League

THE RED AND BLACK OF OULART-THE BALLAGH: I am pictured here playing against St. Martins in the county final. The club means everything to me.

GRIN AND BEAR IT: Myself and Seánie Flood at the 1996 All-Ireland Final banquet. Seán was so unlucky to miss the final through injury but was an exceptional hurler.

FROM WEXFORD PARK TO ST PETER'S SQUARE: Six Kilkenny men surround me at the Vatican. John Hoyne, James McGarry, Derek Lyng, me, Michael Kavanagh, Noel Hickey and Henry Shefflin during our Railway Cup trip in 2003.

HENRY THE GREAT: I am pictured here at the 2003 All Stars with my friend Henry Shefflin, one of the game's greatest hurlers In the foreground is the late Cormac McAnallen whom I had the pleasure of sitting beside that night.

HOME IS WHERE THE HEART IS: With Mam and Dad after winning my first All Star award in 1990

WOULD YOU BUY A USED CAR FROM THESE MEN?: Martin Storey, Larry O'Gorman and I at the 1993 GAA All Stars

WORLD AT OUR FEET: I'm pictured here with clubmate Martin Storey and Dublin football legend Charlie Redmond picking up my second All Star award in 1993.

MINE'S A PINT!: Tipperary legend John Leahy and I have the craic at the 1990 GAA All Stars banquet. I found him to be great company.

ACROSS THE BORDER: Wexford men at the 2004 Wexford/Carlow dinner dance
Back row: Mick Doyle, Darragh Ryan, Tom O'Keeffe, Liam Dunne, Jim English
Front: Jim Doyle, Ned Wheeler, Tom Neville

REACH FOR THE STARS: Life really changed for me after I won my first All Star award. Two years previously I wasn't even good enough for the Wexford team.

Rise and follow Charlie! Here I am receiving my first All Star from GAA President John Dowling, Frank O'Rourke from Bank of Ireland and Taoiseach Charlie Haughey

Two tribes come together: A Buffers Alley man in Oulart. Only Tom Dempsey would get away with it!

THE WEXFORD WAGON: This car followed us everywhere in 1996. How, I don't know!

THE START OF THE CONTROVERSY: Gary Kirby and I get ready to pull on the first ball that came our way in the 1996 All-Ireland final. We all know what happened next!

WHAT MORE COULD YOU ASK FOR: A glowing bride, Eithne, and the Liam McCarthy Cup. It doesn't get better than this.

SAFE HANDS: Damien Fitzhenry with Billy

WELL ARMED: With my Man-of-the-Match trophy and the Liam McCarthy
Cup and below with my brother Kieran

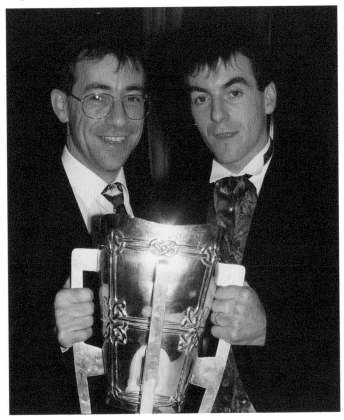

CRAMPER VAN!: David Beckham may have a Mercedes but in 1996 all Martin Storey and I had to bring the cup around the county was Paul Finn's Renault 5 van!

HATS OFF TO THE BROTHERS!: Seán and Tomás play the whistle at one of the homecoming celebrations in Oulart in 1996

Eye on the ball: Making my international debut for Ireland in the 1988 U-21 Shinty Championship against Scotland

On the run: Dashing out of defence against Offaly in the 1991 League Final. Michael Duignan and Daithí Regan are behind me while George O'Connor waits in support.

CHASING DJ: This was not the first or last time I was left trailing in DJ's wake – one of the best hurlers of all time

CHASING MICKEY: Rory McCarthy and I in pursuit of Cork midfielder Mickey O'Connell in the 2003 All-Ireland semi-final

FAME AT LAST!: Signing autographs for fans in the run up to the 1996 All-Ireland

BEYOND THE TUNNEL: I run out into a sea of purple and gold at Croke Park for the 1996 All-Ireland semi-final with Galway.

THE END OF AN ERA: Shaking hands with Cork's Joe Deane after they had defeated us in the 2003 All-Ireland semi-final replay. My last game for Wexford.

SEEING RED AGAIN: Picking up my second red card from Pat Horan after a clash with Tipperary's Brian O'Meara in the 2001 All-Ireland semi-final replay. Brian missed out on a final appearance after this dismissal.

FROM RED TO TOE: Ger Harrington issues me with my third consecutive red card in the 2002 Leinster hurling final against Kilkenny. This signalled the start of my decline.

DOGS OF WAR!: Kilkenny's John Power and I had many saucy battles over the years. I came out on top on this occasion in the 1997 Leinster Hurling Final.

LOOKING AFTER MY OWN PATCH: While my teammates follow the ball, Tipperary's Liam Cahill and I get to know each other during the 2001 Championship.

BROTHERS IN ARMS: Celebrating qualifying for the 1996 All-Ireland final after a thrilling win over Galway.

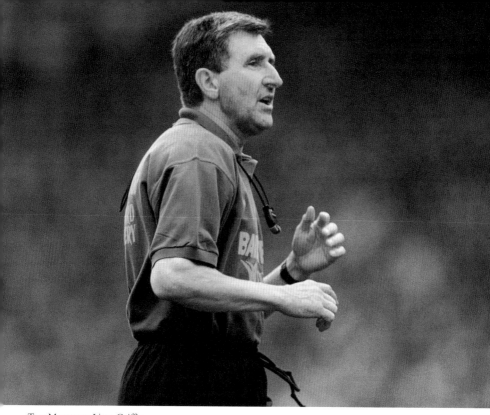

THE MAESTRO: Liam Griffin

IT'S MY FIELD BULL!: L–R: Bartle 'Jacks' Redmond, Bartle 'Foxten' Sinnott, Martin 'Sport' Dempsey, Ned Evans, Tom Sinnott, Pat 'The Boiler' Dempsey, Liam Dunne and Johnny Hayden at the new Oulart-The-Ballagh GAA pitch

OULART'S GREATEST SUPPORTER: Stephen Hayden is surrounded by a likely lot! Seán Dunne, Liam Dunne, Tom Byrne, Jimmy Prendergast, Martin Storey, Paul Fnn, Mick Jacob and Tomás Dunne.

IF YOU WANT IT, PHIL HAS IT!: Phil Redmond and I at his pub and shop in Raheen Duff. He sells everything from pig meal to curry powder.

HISTORY ON THE DOUBLE: The Oulart men who won All–Ireland titles for Wexford in front of the 1798 Rebellion monument. Front row L-R: Darren Stamp, Liam Dunne, Christy Jacob, Seán Dunne, Jimmy Prendergast; Back row L-R: Rory Jacob, Paul Finn, Keith Rossiter, Martin Storey, Mick Jacob, Tom Byrne, Tomás Dunne, Michael Jacob

FAMILY TIES: Eithne, Aoife and Billy

TIME OUT: Taking a stroll on Morriscastle beach

In every bar down on the Main Street, they were hanging from the rafters,
And they sang the Boys of Wexford, like it was going out of style,
All the bingo halls were empty and the Masses finished early,
Sure no-one ever saw the like of it since the time of JFK.
The Wild Swans, Dancing at the Crossroads

– CHAPTER TWELVE –
Heaven can wait

After thinking of Gary Kirby and *Braveheart*, my next memory of All-Ireland final day was being called to the telephone to speak to Christy Jacob, who had won an All-Ireland medal with Wexford in 1968, the last time we had won the Liam MacCarthy Cup.

It was strange for me to get a call from Christy because we hadn't always seen eye to eye but it was a nice touch and it sort of put me in good humour for the day.

When I looked out the window after that conversation, the day got even better and I couldn't help laughing. At the start of the season, around 20 people from the village would gather in the middle of Oulart to see us off to Croke Park, but this time there were close to 200, all of them looking for autographs.

It wasn't hard to enjoy their enthusiasm; again it left me feeling positive and bright. I smiled as I looked at the tractors that had been painted purple and gold, the beloved Wexford colours in all their glory. These were your neighbours, the people you grew up with, the ones that were looking out for you, and if they didn't inspire you nothing would.

I joined up with Storey and we hopped on the team bus. Once we were all present and correct, Griffin slapped on our favourite flick for what felt like the 100th time, and yet the lads were still glued to it. We didn't need to look at William Wallace to have legs flying around the

163

place; we had John O'Connor, who did the job just fine on his own.

The lads were tense and as we pulled into the Stillorgan Park Hotel in Dublin, the amount of support for us was frightening. Each of us individually attended to his various little rituals before we came together for one last team meeting.

And strangely, Griffin took no part in it. After steering us through the year and showing leadership Martin Luther King would be proud of, he left us to our own devices. He just said the work had been done and it was now up to us, quickly went through the game plan and was gone. Jesus, we'd have to do it on our own after all!

Niamh Fitzpatrick said her few words, and it was over to us. The meeting had a nervous edge to it, but soon players chipped in with their tuppenceworth. Then Seánie Flood stood up.

We had seen Seánie break down in Wexford Park as he tried to push himself into All-Ireland final contention and we broke down with him; it hurt us as much as it hurt him. Each time he had tried to string two runs together, he had just made the problem worse. He knew himself he had no chance but would find out exactly how serious the injury was only after the All-Ireland final.

As he stood up, the room went totally silent. What followed was something I will never forget. For years after, people would talk about the rousing and passionate speech Seánie Flood had made and how he'd inspired us to victory, but if the truth be told, he said hardly anything at all because he soon broke down, and I'm not ashamed to say I quietly let the tears well and almost broke down with him.

'Lads,' he whispered. 'You will never realise what you have until it's taken away from you.'

And with that, he wept. I put my head down so no-one could see me at it, but there were plenty others in the same boat.

Seánie couldn't continue; amid total silence he went over to the window and gazed out at the legions of Wexford fans on their way to Croke Park.

After what seemed like an eternity, that eerie stillness, more at place in a library than a team meeting, was finally broken by a loud thump on the table. It was Georgie O'Connor, of course.

'Come on to fuck, lads! We're going to win this! We have to!'

He stood up, and with that the mood in the room changed completely.

Defiance.

Lads went over to Seánie to console him. It was tough, but the tears were not finished yet. Before we took off from the hotel, Griffin held us in the team bus and read out a telegram he had received. He read the whole thing from start to finish: about what the team had done for the county and people of Wexford, about the pride and delight we had inspired. And he finished with a few words that basically wished us every blessing in the world for the big match.

'And that telegram,' Griffin concluded, as he placed his hand on my shoulder, 'is from Eileen Dunne, Liam's mother.'

Bang! My mother. Jesus, if he was looking for a weak spot, he had found it. She was the one person who always had full faith in me. There all the time, when my father had left, she was the one who picked up the pieces. Each time I got into trouble, my mother stood up for me – it was someone else's fault, you see.

A strong woman, she had guided eight of us through life with the help of little but a wooden spoon or poker, both of which she used to good effect. She and my aunt Ann used to travel to games; they were enthralled by the whole Wexford thing. They would gather on the Friday before the game, my aunt Ann having travelled from Cork, and I would spend Saturday trying to avoid them because all they wanted to talk about was the match and that was the last thing I wanted to chat about. Each morning of a game, I would pop up to see them but the first thing they would ask for was inside gossip and the latest match tactics.

Now Griffin had caught me again, just hours before the match. I thought back to how Mam had been sick for the semi-final; it was heart-wrenching stuff. I half expected Griffin to put on *Sleepless in Seattle* instead of *Braveheart*. But what more motivation could you ask for? Somehow, I stayed focused. This was the chance of a lifetime. None of us had ever reached an All-Ireland final before and there was no guarantee we would get back. As it happens, I never did play in another one after that.

The bus started and with the rev of an engine began the final part of our odyssey. I looked out the window and took it all in. Larry O and the rest of the lads were also taking everything in. Every good-looking woman that passed was subjected to an admiring whistle from him, with support from the rest of the crew. In fairness to Larry O, he could spot a well-formed woman a mile away, and on big match days the scenery always seemed to be exceptional. Nerves always play a part but the Wexford players were too busy spotting talent to suffer unbearable tension.

As we drew nearer the stadium, I tried to memorise everything I saw. Sometimes, when I close my eyes at night, the thoughts are still there, only a dream away. Thousands of fans waving at you with their eyes wide open and full of hope, the colour of it all, the mix of purple and gold and green and white jerseys, as they made their way to the ground.

The start of the minor match; we hankered for it to end but had to let on to have some sort of an interest in it just to keep our minds off the big game for a while longer.

It seemed like an eternity to throw-in. The wait was a lengthy definition of what my life was all about up to that point. Over the years, I had asked many questions of myself and now it was time for answers.

In the dressing-room, it was as tense as I had ever seen it. I made 10 visits to the toilet and kept meeting the same lads the whole time, Seánie Flood, Ger Cushe, Larry O.

'Jaysus,' I thought to myself, 'are they still pissing?' But I could have sourced a river myself that day.

Our PRO, Pat Murphy, handed the jerseys out, and I went into the jacks again, found a cubicle, sat down on the seat and pulled on the jersey. Before all big games, I used to lock myself in the toilet cubicle. The rest of the lads probably thought I had the scutters, but I would just sit down, pull the Wexford shirt down on me and spend a few moments thinking about my Dad. For some reason, it always helped me do the job on the field.

It goes without saying that I thought of my mother but I also thought of my father, whom I hadn't seen for so long. Why hadn't he called? Jesus, he started me off hurling. It would have killed him to miss a game like this. I couldn't understand why he didn't get in touch. But of course Dad had a different life now; working in St Helena, off the coast of South Africa, he didn't want to come home. And although we found it hard to take, we had to move on.

Dad had missed everything but we had missed him too. The gap between us grew wider each year from 1992 onwards as we began to see less and less of him. At first, it was a six-week gap but that soon became three or four months and then we were lucky to have him home once a year. When he started to skip Christmas time, we knew it was all over and just rallied around Mam.

It seemed to be a blow each time Dad missed a big game, like when we won the club's first ever county final in 1994, when Tomás led the team home. Tomás and I used to travel to training together and spoke about Dad a fair bit, but what could you say really? Here he was, missing us reaping the harvest after he had helped to sow the seeds.

I had my own thoughts on the whole situation but it must have been hard for the old man as well. When he would make the rare journey home, people in the parish were blowing him up, telling him what a great tan he had and saying that he looked twice as fit and healthy as his sons. But that soon changed too, and when he came back the year after we won the 94 county final, the locals reminded him of what he had missed. The fact he was now missing the All-Ireland final, well it hurt a little bit.

There were no letters or cards, and yet we just carried on. And

while I would spend time thinking about him before matches, my
mother was the last person I would think of before going out of the
dressing-room. The cubicle is a quiet place. It's small and may not smell
the best but you can lock yourself away before you go out and place
yourself in front of the whole country. I did a lot of thinking there
before games, personal thoughts. The team stuff was confined to the
dressing-room. People never came looking for me – maybe they knew I
had my own routine to act out.

The Wexford jersey always lifted me; it was an honour to put it
on and when I locked that door, it was all about the county, my family
and myself. Let's just say I wasn't short of motivational tools when I
went out to hurl.

Snapping out of the zone, I left my hiding place and stepped back into
the dressing-room, where the atmosphere was even more tingling than it
had been in that little cubicle.

'Jesus, Brother,' Griffin was telling Larry O'Gorman, 'get us
going! Come on, Brother!'

Then Larry brought us into the warm-up room and started to
inject a bit of humour into proceedings. We huddled together fiercely,
like best friends out to say their goodbyes for the last time. While the
Limerick team were jostling lads out of the way going into their
dressing-room and beating their hurls like lunatics inside, we were
saying prayers. They were way too hyped up; we were controlled. The
look in our eyes said it all: it was shit or bust, and after offering up a
prayer, we nearly took the hinges off the doors when the call from the
stewards came to vacate the room.

The run out onto the field will stay with me for life. While I was
hyped, I couldn't but sneak a little smile into the TV cameras that
greeted us at the entrance to the tunnel.

Boom! Jesus, the roar was deafening. I'd never heard anything like
it. I gave one big sprint out of the tunnel. My helmet barely stayed on. I
ran nowhere and ran everywhere at the same time, tried to get water in

and then remembered I couldn't go to the toilet anymore so I stopped. I was in the middle of the pitch. My legs were strong. That was good. Yet I wanted to hide and there was no hiding place. I was never as dumbstruck in all my life. The fright I got when I ran out onto the field that day will live forever with me.

The noise, the people, lack of space, it shocked me and I turned around and saw Seánie Flood, which didn't help me much either. Seánie went to walk to the bench but I dragged him back, like he had defiantly pulled us out of the fire all year.

'No way, Seánie!' I told him. 'You're in this with us.'

He was a real character, a witty, funny lad who made his money as a self-employed contractor and tried to make it to Slane in his spare time with his rock band Running on Empty. They were no Beatles, but all the same they were a fairly lively bunch and would go on to get a fair few gigs after this match.

Seánie had been unflappable in defence for so long and there was no chance we were letting him go now. So I caught him by the neck, marched him over for the team photograph and threw him in the middle of the bench. But of course, Larry O had decided to go missing, and to this day people still think it was a Griffin ploy to leave out a team member from the photo just to confuse the opposition.

That theory is crap, because Larry O was off somewhere getting his own few photos taken, I think. Anyway, it was important to have Seánie in the picture; he was a big part of our camp and had quietened Johnny Dooley and Kevin Broderick in previous games to help us get this far.

Would you believe that the nerves then started to disappear a little, and as I warmed up, I thought what an awesome feeling this was to be here pucking around just before an All-Ireland final. I envied the Kilkenny lads who got to sample this occasion most of the time.

This may seem a trivial matter, but when the call then came to stand for President Robinson we felt we were seasoned professionals at this lark. After all, Griffin had coached us for this moment a fortnight earlier. As per orders, I stood with my hands behind my back and looked for the Liam MacCarthy Cup, but it was not on the podium.

'Never mind,' I thought. 'I'll see it soon enough.'

It's only a little thing but it matters on All-Ireland final day, and if you contrasted the Wexford and Limerick teams on their presentation to the President, you may have picked the winners out before the ball was even thrown in. We stood in a straight line, chests forward, backs straight, and even paid her compliments.

Amid all the tension, it was one of the funniest moments of my career when Larry O even praised Mary Robinson on her choice of dress, while nearby the Limerick lads hopped nervously in and out of line, bending and stretching and looking seriously on edge.

I looked up and down the line at our lads and my heart just thumped; I marvelled at the way they appeared so calm and focused. How great it had been to travel the road alongside these lads over the past year! Fitzy, then only 22, was beside me. From day one, we knew he was possibly the best goalkeeper in Ireland. What I didn't know while standing there meeting the President was that later in the day he would create one of the defining moments by laying his body on the line and stopping a certain goal.

Then there was Cushe, sound and solid, a lionheart. He could not have been blamed if he'd thrown his hat at it when Griffin dropped him in 95 for John O'Connor. We had to win for the likes of him, who had always watched out for others.

After Larry O had finished giving the President fashion tips, I sneaked a look down his direction. Free entertainment, they were the words that popped into my head when I saw his big grin. But the hoor was also the best hurler I ever played alongside.

John O'Connor was in contrast to Larry O because he was a serious fellow and didn't take any messing. Like Georgie, he was superfit. Looking along the line at the two of them, I was glad they were on my side.

Adrian Fenlon, another iron man, was also a key reason why we had to win this match. He hadn't even been on the team for the League but here he was, vital to the cause, inspiring other youngsters for the future. He would lead us from centrefield. I was sure of that.

Colm Kehoe was cut from the same mould. He was someone I didn't really know until 96. Now, when I looked over at him, he was quiet as usual but you could see the desire.

And then I looked over at Rod and Dave Guiney, or the Gooneys, as I used to call them. They didn't mix that much with us, but Griffin had a great hold on them, and just as with the rest of the team, I was willing to burst a gut for either brother.

Just because you don't always get on with someone doesn't mean you can't hurl with him. At this stage, I was trained to keep away from them in the warm-ups before matches. They were like rocket-launchers, firing the ball from one to the other, trying to kill each other; I almost laughed aloud as I remembered the constant competition between them.

Dave didn't start that day, and alongside him on the bench was Billy Byrne. Jesus, if you couldn't try to win for that man, you had no hope. Here he was, 36 years old, eight years older than me, but he had done all the training with no bother and there was no complaining out of him. Win, lose or draw, he had left his mark on the Championship.

We got the call to fall in behind the Artane Boys Band, a part of the proceedings we had rehearsed from way back. As we marched, I spotted some local photographers by the Canal End and gave them a nod – they'd been with us all year as well and it meant as much to them as it did to the rest of the county.

The big TV screen glared down ominously at us like Big Brother. Niamh warned it would be a daunting experience but had prepared us well, and so we were calm and assured marching around the field, which is more than can be said for Limerick, who had broken away and run into their field positions before we were even halfway down the Cusack Stand side.

We didn't bat an eyelid. Wexford were staying behind the band all the way around and that was it. Around by Hill 16 we rallied on our own, right over to where the Wexford fans dominated the terrace. You can imagine the lift we got passing in front of them on our own. At the same time, Limerick must have felt like spare pricks at a wedding, because I looked down and saw Mike Nash, Declan Nash and Stephen MacDonagh jogging on the spot, running over and back to each other. They didn't even do a half lap of the field. Too impatient.

One thing we neglected to do was to listen to Martin Storey's final few words after we broke. Martin called us back but Fitzy was off like a rocket and down to his goal. Four of us stayed back, but then we said to hell with it, the time for talking was done.

I ran to my position and shook hands with Gary Kirby. I had my homework done on him. I had studied videos of Joe Quaid's puck-outs, so each time he went to deliver a ball on the left, I knew it was coming my way. Two weeks before the final, I had phoned Griffin to ask him how I should deal with Kirby and he warned me that discipline was the key. He rammed home the fact that from frees Kirby had scored almost everything he'd hit so far that season. By the end of the conversation, I was in no doubt that this guy could well beat us on his own.

'If we keep Kirby to four points from frees, we'll win the game,' Griffin said and added that he had every confidence in me. Before he hung up, he finished: 'Liamy, the great Liamy Dunne, you will be man of the match on All-Ireland final day.'

I wasn't exactly sure about that but now there was no time to think. Seconds after the ball was thrown in, Seán O'Neill, who had flattened Tommy Kehoe in the League earlier that year, hit Georgie a right shot. The referee, Pat Horan, awarded a throw-in between the two and Seán ended up on the ground and I don't think he hit a ball after that or since; he had met someone who was mentally and physically strong and Georgie absolutely flaked him.

Soon, the second puck-out of the day landed between Gary Kirby and I. We both pulled on it at the same time, and as I pulled he came in sideways with that unusual style of his. We made contact and the ball broke to Martin Storey, who gave a 70-metre free away.

I didn't feel there was anything out of the ordinary during our exchange; Gary didn't go down and there wasn't even a break or stoppage in the play. He went over to the Cusack Stand side instead and pointed the free.

A few minutes later, Rod Guiney gave a free away and he stuck that over as well. Later, a young lad came in with a towel to wipe blood from his finger, but Gary was fine and played on. He had two points from frees by the break.

But a lot more dangerous at the time was Ciarán Carey, who really seemed to be getting into his game. Joe Quaid started off brilliantly but his tactics didn't work for him. Joe started hitting the ball as far as he could, raining puck-outs down on top of Georgie and I, who just retreated as far back as we had to and mopped up.

I didn't hit the ball five times during the second half but I didn't have to; in my opinion, my opponent's body language suggested that he was going to do no damage. And yet, they left him centre-forward for the entire game.

But still, the picture wasn't much rosier for us and we trailed by four points, 0-5 to 0-1, early in the game. Mike Houlihan broke his hurley across Larry O'Gorman, John O'Connor was having trouble with Owen O'Neill and Ger Cushe gave Damien Quigley a slap to test his reaction.

It was a stormy opening and, not surprisingly, both John O and Owen were soon booked. As Horan wrote their names in, I drew his attention to Houlihan's tackle on Larry O and, in fairness, he booked the second Limerickman as well.

At the other end of the pitch, Joe Quaid made a great save from Gary Laffan. I thought it was going to be one of those days but then a row started involving 15 lads. We were supposed to be minding our discipline but here we were again, fighting all over the place.

This time, Adrian Fenlon, Martin Storey and Ciarán Carey were booked. Then, after a throw-in, our corner-forward Eamon Scallan followed them into Horan's notepad.

Play continued and Scallan and Stephen MacDonagh pulled across each other but Scallan pulled again and, after 23 minutes of the first half, the referee decided this was going no further. He called our man aside and flashed a red card.

Now, three weeks before, we had spoken of this possibility, but you could have got some odds on Eamon getting the line. We were good friends over the years. He was very witty and good company, but he was far from being the giddiest guy on the team and was the last fellow I would have expected to walk the line.

We needed something to save our All-Ireland and we needed it quickly. Griffin calmly created a two-man full-forward line and instructed them to keep switching onto Limerick defenders so they couldn't settle. He kept the rest of the team intact.

Limerick decided Davy Clarke was their loose man but we threw one of the lads over on him and they seemed to play him all wrong, leaving him in defence, instead of switching Ciarán Carey into that role and moving him up the field, where he could have drawn one of the defenders out and created space for someone else. They left Clarke where he was and allowed Joe Quaid to boom huge puck-outs down on top of our defence. We lapped it up.

And the Man Above, this time, gave us a sign that it could yet be our day when he helped John O'Connor float a 91-yard free over the bar soon after Eamon was sent off. It gave us an awful lift. John O had missed a similar score that would have won the 93 League final, but here he was, doing it when it counted most.

Like a rolling stone, the momentum continued to gather. Almost immediately Tom Dempsey got a goal that was like an organ transplant for the team because it handed us back our belief. Larry O added another quick point. We were thriving in the face of adversity and went to the dressing-rooms a point to the good.

The halfway house was calm and controlled, but it was hard to keep cool because we were like bulls, raging and frantic to get back into the ring. The one thing that kept things in perspective was the sight of Eamon Scallan, and we took turns to offer words of comfort to him. The buzz word was discipline for the second half. Kirby was still capable of winning the game from frees, but not if we didn't concede any. And with the game half over, we could concede two more frees and still meet the challenge Griffin had set us. Up stepped the manager.

'You have put your lives on the line for this!' he roared. 'This is it. I believe you are 35 minutes away from destiny. We have that feeling lads – it's been building up all year and you know it. Believe in one another. We had guys up at five in the morning training with us and they didn't even get a jersey today but look at them, part of us.'

He referred to guys like Thomas Codd, MJ Reck and Joe Kearns, who had trained their arses off all year and didn't even have a jersey on match day.

Griffin was right, we owed it to them as much as each other.

'You've put in 187 sessions from day one to today, the All-Ireland final,' he reminded us. 'That's a lot of time. But today is payback for your families.'

And out we went, the light blinding us as we ran head first into destiny, not knowing how we were going to get there but determined and confident we would arrive.

Gary Laffan ran the show in the opening minutes, hitting two bad wides but eventually nailing a point that settled us. Quaid made another great save from him, though, and all over the field, Limerickmen were clashing swords with us. Rory MacCarthy was struggling with Mark Foley but working his ass off. Barry Foley, who had scored a point off Larry O, was called ashore and we breathed a sigh of relief that Limerick had no Mike Galligan to bring on.

As the game became more frantic, our full-back Ger Cushe went down injured. There was nothing wrong with him but from his vantage point he could see we needed a breather. As Cushe hit the ground, John O went over to Hill 16 and got the massive Wexford crowd going, and we breathed in what little inspiration our lungs would allow us to.

Playing with 14 men was starting to take its toll. Yet we didn't give away one free in defence for the 35 minutes of the second half. I always maintain that if we had fouled, Kirby would have pointed six or seven frees, but we showed some bottle to rein in our violent urges and cut out that aspect of the game, which I'm sure contributed to Gary having a stinker of a final.

Going into this game, I had developed a reputation for not being a tight marker but that game I shed the label, and a few yards behind, Ger Cushe, who was said to be too big and too slow for the top level, was having a stormer. There was no better day to shut people up.

As the game entered the magic moments where life will change either way, we clung onto a two-point lead, more precious to us than any gem or jewel in the world. With time almost up, I got the ball, soloed out of defence and waited for a Limerickman to come and clatter me. It was the only time in my career where I wanted to be upended, and I kept hobbling away, waiting for the free to come.

But no-one fouled, and suddenly Seán O'Neill arrived and whipped the ball away as I lost control and slipped. Trying to catch him, I found my legs would not move – they had gone to jelly – and I just sighed in colossal relief as Storey came to my rescue and won the ball back.

'The hill-running in Bunclody stood to him anyway,' I thought, before realising I was on the ground, dreaming, in an All-Ireland final.

I prayed to God and shouted at Pat Horan in the one gasp: 'Jesus, Pat, time must be up.'

I think he heard me because though they won a free, he blew the next whistle. Unsure that we had really won the game, I looked up at the scoreboard to double-check. WEXFORD 1-13 - LIMERICK 0-

14. Yep! The first thing I did was shake hands with Gary. I genuinely felt sorry for him. It was their second time losing a final in three years. What a pill to swallow!

Still, we had waited 28 years ourselves and that was no picnic either. In a daze, I walked to the stand, all the strength sapped out of me. I met Bartle Redmond on the field, my old pal, put my hand on his shoulder and started crying.

We walked side by side over to the Hogan Stand, until fans got me and threw me on their shoulders. I got down again and kept walking. It was strange: supporters were running past me, ignoring me, and in the end I had to turn around to a few of them to try and get in with the rest of the team.

'Jaysus, I'm after hurling here. Will some of ye try and throw me in,' I begged.

Eventually, I reached the inner circle and saw Storey lift the Liam MacCarthy Cup. What a funny feeling to see your own clubman lift the cup! I tried to take it all in but I could barely see Martin, there were so many ribbons on the piece of silver.

For a moment, the team went back under the Hogan Stand because the gardaí wanted the crowd to break up, and in those few moments we bonded with each other – the pictures in Monday's papers would show Oulart and Buffers Alley men crying in each other's arms – and the team just reflected quietly on what we had achieved before going back out onto the field.

Thousands were milling around out there, but in the middle of the purple and gold blur, among the legions of whooping and back-slapping supporters, I saw my mother, crying with delight. I looked her in the face and saw pride. I felt the very same. Hugging her, I bowed my head. 'Mam,' I said, 'I have no more tears left for you.'

I was told before the game that they were going to do me.

**Gary Kirby of Limerick on the 1996 final,
which left him with broken fingers**

– CHAPTER THIRTEEN –
Victory and Kirby

Life just changed. The win was for ourselves and for the supporters, who just put us up on a pedestal. From then on, nothing was the same. Wexford: 1996 All-Ireland champions. The win was made all the sweeter by the fact that I was named RTÉ Man of the Match. I don't know how because I cleared only four or five balls all during the game. The TV cameras hovered ominously around me all night so I realised Jim Bolger must have known something in advance when he told me I was getting the nod.

Commentator Ger Canning called my name and everyone stood up and clapped as I received my award, crystal worth £750, so they told me, but I still couldn't figure out why I had got it. Sure I had stopped Gary Kirby but I hadn't hit five balls all day and felt my hurling had been sacrificed for the purpose of that specific job. Even going in to that winners' banquet in Malahide, the extent of what we had done didn't sink in, but as we met great hurlers from a past era and saw their eyes twinkle with delight, we knew we had achieved something rare and wonderful.

The Wexford fans had taken so much hurt over the years, and it was great to be able to sit back and watch them enjoy this with us. I thought in particular of our number one fan, Marcella Meehan from Charleton Hill, who was in the audience wearing her beloved Wexford geansaí.

I had met Marcella for the first time when I was presenting medals to the winners of a pool tournament in New Ross. She was confined to a wheelchair, but we got to know her well because she would never miss a game. Her bedroom was a shrine to Wexford hurling and she would send birthday cards to all the lads – how she used to get the dates I don't know.

She got on particularly well with Damien Fitzhenry, who always reckoned he could hear her behind his goal, no matter where we were playing. He gave her his jersey, Ger Cushe presented her with his hurley, Rod Guiney gave her a purple tiger teddy and George O'Connor was only too happy to make a presentation of a bronze statue of a hurling boot. Tom Dempsey and she shared tears of joy after the All-Ireland final win and the Wexford Supporters Club named her their official Number One Fan. From time to time, she would ring Eithne and chat away and even though she went through several operations for her illness she wouldn't miss a game.

Larry Murphy wrote her a lovely note once saying: 'We will keep your courage in our hearts forever.' And he was right.

Her wish was that, when she died, the Wexford team of 96 would carry her coffin. Sadly, that moment would come to pass in January 2003, when Marcella passed away.

The funeral was terribly sad. In fairness to Rod Guiney, he did a marvellous job and went up to the altar to speak on behalf of the players. His words were poignant and real. The team took turns to carry the coffin, and walking down to the graveyard I was beside Rory McCarthy and in front of me were George and John O'Connor, Billy Byrne, Martin Storey, Tom Dempsey, Seán Flood and Larry O'Gorman. They were all devastated. If I ever needed a reminder that we had all shared in something special, this was it.

'I can't understand why we didn't win more, Rory,' I said. 'Just look at those lads around you.'

Marcella would have approved. She was buried in New Ross and as we left the church, the strains of *The Purple and Gold*, her favourite song, carried across the churchyard. It was one of the saddest experiences of my life.

Thank God she saw the good times! The night of the 96 final would have been the happiest of her life. The team got a glow when we saw people like Marcella beaming from ear to ear.

The rest of that night was a blur to me. I do remember, however, the Wild Swans getting up on stage to sing *Dancing at the Crossroads* and we enjoyed the formalities and informalities of it all. The years 93 to 95 had been rollercoasters but to win an All-Ireland after 28 years was incredible, especially when you considered how many Leinster titles we had lost along the way.

The fun stopped momentarily when we were informed there would be a team meeting, at 11 am the next day in the hotel, and true to form, no-one was late. With the breakfast eaten and the papers read, we gathered in a room to listen to Griffin one more time. By this stage, if he'd told us we should become transvestites, we would have gone shopping for bras and nylons, so the whole squad attended, all eyes and ears, to hear his thoughts on what had just happened. Not for the first time, his words were loaded with meaning.

'This,' he whispered, 'is probably the last time we will ever be together as a group.'

Again, he had caught our attention, and again he would turn out to be right. At least one guy didn't even make it to the official medal presentation later that year, and one or two didn't make it on the team holiday the next year either. I can understand holidays, but missing the medal presentation was a crime. One of our subs, Liam Turley, a Galway native, was the man who missed out.

Liam was a nice lad and a decent hurler who had transferred to St Martin's and had managed to attract the selectors' attention, and to his credit, he trained and hurled away with us all year. But I felt his absence showed just what that All-Ireland meant to him. It seemed a little bit of a snub when he didn't turn up to the medal ceremony.

But Griffin had predicted someone would miss out and there we were, startled to hear such a stark prediction hours after we had won an All-Ireland, the fruits of slaving together for nine months on the trot. And he wasn't finished there. He went on to warn us of the dangers of booze. He hadn't been wrong once all year so we listened intently as he advised us not to go near the winners' podiums all over the county if we had drink taken.

'You are All-Ireland champions now. Conduct yourselves like All-Ireland champions,' he concluded.

After that, we had to go to the Burlington Hotel for the traditional post-All-Ireland banquet for both teams, which I always felt was terribly unfair on the losers. I shook hands with Mike Nash from Limerick and Davy Clarke but we didn't speak much.

Then Gary Kirby came into view and just as I was about to go over, because obviously he was disappointed, I saw he had a big bandage on his finger and his arm was in a sling. That just turned me off, and I didn't bother approaching him.

Of course, that's when all the innuendo started: the rumours that we had agreed in training that I would break his hand so he wouldn't be able to take frees, the theory that I had deliberately pulled on his fingers as the second ball came our way. And that's all I've heard ever since.

'Ah yeah, you're the man who broke Kirby's fingers in the 96 final. Stopped him from hitting frees.'

Word got back to me that Gary had been telling people he knew it was going to happen, but as far as I'm concerned, Limerick beat themselves that day. I haven't a clue if he broke his fingers or not. If he did, I certainly didn't set out to break them. The two of us pulled on the ball at the same time and, as far as I'm concerned, if he had struck correctly he would have got no contact from me. There was nothing said about the 70-metre free he pointed from under the Cusack Stand a moment or two after we had pulled. And there was even less said about the fact that the Wexford backs gave away no free in the second half of the final, which I reckon is a record.

Nothing was premeditated. No Wexford player went out to take any Limerickman out of it. The whole incident was blown out of proportion. To anyone who still doubts me, I would say take the video out, slow it down when it comes to that notorious exchange between us and you will see there was no malice on my part.

A few years later, I was in the Anner Hotel in Thurles when Philip Ryan, a C&C sales rep, said there was an old friend of mine nearby that I had to meet. He ushered me into a room and left me there with none other than G Kirby. We spoke for about 10 minutes, chatted about hurling in general and shook hands before leaving. There was no awkwardness.

But then, in 2003, I was told of an episode of the TV series *Laochra Gael*, where he had plenty to say about me and the incident. It was in that broadcast he told the world Wexford had a pre-match plan to go out and do him.

He said: 'As I pulled, my hand met a hurl and broke a bone in my finger. If I was pulling on the ball, it meant that the ball was a hurley length from my hand. So whoever hit me was pulling low below the ball.

'You lose games, but we all have to go to work the following morning and you don't do things like that.'

It's clear he was very sore over what happened; I can't do much about that. What annoyed me more was the insistence by the Limerick players that they had thrown the 1996 final away. Thrown it away? Who were they trying to cod?

We were on the wrong end of an 0-5 to 0-1 scoreline and reduced to 14 men for about 35 minutes of the game, yet we cut the free count down to almost zero and they say they threw it away. What about the 1994 final when they had it in the bag but let Offaly take it from them? Maybe Limerick threw that one away – they certainly didn't in 1996.

I have to say the whole affair didn't occupy much space on my mind at the time but I was damned angry when it all flared up again from 2000 onward when I got my first red card. That's when it really got to me.

I hope this finally sets the record straight. I didn't go out to 'do' Gary Kirby. There was no preconceived plan to take him out. In case you think I protest too much, maybe consider Liam Griffin's purist philosophy when it comes to hurling. He would rather you miss a point from 70 metres than cheat by moving it forward five metres and score. To suggest he would encourage me to do something that went so strongly against his principles is defying all logic.

Another defender would never have heard of the incident again but my reputation landed me with this. That's my take on the affair. It also seems to me that whenever you win something, there will always be people who want to take from it.

It was no wonder that we enjoyed the homecoming so much. On our way to Gorey, Billy Byrne told me he had often imagined coming home as a winner and wondering if the streets would be packed. He didn't have long to wait for his answer because from there to Enniscorthy and on to Wexford town, the county was thronged.

Heading into Enniscorthy, we negotiated the corner around Cinema Lane and there I saw the Kilkenny hurling legend Christy Heffernan, clapping and cheering the team bus on. To see a Kilkenny man obviously delighted for us was something to behold; he was really enjoying the craic.

The entire panel went up on to a platform and were introduced one by one to the crowd. By this stage, we were almost fed up of the ritual, which had to be performed in every town the team bus stopped in, and so it was a relief when we reached the Ferrycarrig Hotel, where the team stayed and enjoyed a buffet dinner.

I don't know what got into me but the next morning I woke up and drove into Wexford town in search of a flower shop. The woman who worked there hadn't a clue I had played in the final but she must have thought I was soft in the head when I asked her to create a bouquet of purple and gold flowers and requested they be sent to Liam Griffin and his wife, Mary, at the hotel.

The GOAL match was the next item on the agenda, and of course a drinking session broke out in the Talbot Hotel before we even got to play the Rest of Ireland outfit. About 12,000 turned up and, to their credit, a lot of the Limerick guys showed their faces as well, although I only managed a half hour against them because I was green to the gills from drink. But it didn't stop me from heading back to the Talbot after, where we rocked the night away until about 5 am.

Sometime during the celebrations I had to nip out to find a hole in the wall and extract a few quid, and passing the County Hotel, I was invited in by the manager. The place was jointed and before I knew it I was hoisted shoulder high and planted on stage by a crowd of cheering supporters, who demanded I sing a song with Joe Monaghan's band.

Joe started singing some tune – I still don't know what it was – but all of a sudden I was centre stage with a microphone, not knowing the words and looking like a right clown. I had to do something.

'Up Wexford!' I roared, and the place went bananas.

I said I'd push it a bit more.

'Yyuuupp Wexfooorrrd!' I shouted even louder, shaking my fist in the air. It wasn't the most original stage performance of all time, but the crowd nearly went through the roof before shouldering me off the stage in triumphal procession.

Eventually, I managed to sneak away and rejoin the lads. It would be like that for the rest of the year.

Going back to your roots is always special, and so I wanted to be clear in the head when Martin Storey, Paul Finn and I visited the schools in Oulart, starting with Church of Ireland, Kilnamanagh, and then set off to meet the villagers.

Now style was not a big thing with any of the three of us and while the likes of Manchester United are used to limos and Mercs, we piled into the back of Paul Finn's old van with the Liam MacCarthy Cup to meet the club chairman, Fintan Cooney, and all the various families and aunts and uncles.

Joe Quaid was gracious enough to come down to us that night and stayed over with Tom Dempsey. The TV cameras were also around and no-one ever saw a livelier buzz around the place. That evening, we went over to Storey's end of the village, the Ballagh, and it was the same all over again.

For six solid months after we won the Cup, the celebrations continued and only then did I get a chance to bring Liam MacCarthy back to Raheen Duff, where he was warmly received.

For any lad who likes the taste of a few pints it was a dangerous time, though. I was working with GH Lett Soft Drinks of Enniscorthy before moving to C&C, and with both jobs I was expected to be at certain pubs at night if the Cup was also there.

I never disliked the taste of drink anyway but this didn't help and I was too conscientious to refuse anyone an appearance. I feared word would go around that I was too big for my boots.

But the reality was that I was being asked out to pubs every night. I should have drawn a line but publicans I dealt with in the line of business took it as a personal slight if I was not there to bring the MacCarthy Cup to them.

And so I had more 5 am sessions than an Olympic athlete and although I had never been looked after better in my life, not having to pay for drink or food, I was falling into a trap, an easy one to slip into. Still, it was better that we had a piece of silverware than to be stuck in the doldrums, I thought, and I got on with it.

There were one or two tricky and uncomfortable moments, including a day when I visited a pub in Ferns, and asked the owner to open an account with my new employers, C&C. He refused, saying I had given him a kick in the teeth by not making it to his pub the night the Cup arrived and now it was his turn to give me a kick back. What could I do except apologise?

But that was an isolated incident and generally we were worshipped and treated like heroes, and we made no bones about using our new-found status to boost the Wexford hurlers' holiday fund.

The squad raised so much money for that American holiday in January 1997 that the married guys received £2,500 spending money each, the single players with a girlfriend got £2,000 and the totally single chaps received a nice £1,500 in their back pockets.

Of the 13 of the side nominated for an All Star award, seven of us got the nod, though Ger Cushe should have been the eighth – I remember Brian Lohan saying he had taken Cushe's All Star.

But it didn't stop there. Martin Storey got the Players' Player of the Year award; Larry O'Gorman got the Sports Writers' Hurler of the Year; and I got the *Star* newspaper/Waterford Crystal equivalent. And just about every Wexford hurler got some recognition for his efforts.

We were gods and the freebies just kept on flowing in. The night before the 96 senior football All-Ireland final between Meath and Mayo, Martin Storey and I were invited by Guinness up to their corporate box to watch the game. We were put up and handed £100 spending money and watched the two teams box the shit out of each other and play a little bit of football as well.

There was also a three-week holiday to the US coming up and the trip with the All Stars after that. Suddenly, everything had clicked into place and although I was still a little upset not to have heard anything from my Dad, who hadn't contacted me after the final, I was getting married in a few weeks' time to Eithne and hoped he would make it.

Suddenly there seemed to be no need to worry anymore. The vouchers, holidays, gifts and stuff were only small tokens but life could not get much better. We were All-Ireland champions for the first time since 1968. These were the days that every player dreamt about. Only now, there was no need to dream.

A real friend is one who walks in when the rest of the world walks out.
Friendship is one mind in two bodies.
Mencius, Confucian philosopher

– CHAPTER FOURTEEN –
From feast to famine

On October 18 1996 my mother finally had a challenger for the role of leading lady in my life.

I first met Eithne Sinnott in the Hydro nightclub in Wexford in 1989 although I had known her brother, Eamon, who hurled for Wexford, a long time before. Eamon was a fine bloke but the Sinnotts came from Buffers Alley territory so there was no way I could have been seen around any of them. Nevertheless, I found Eithne, who worked at the time as a hairdresser in Kilmuckridge, to be easy on the eye and wonderfully easygoing and so it took off from there.

There's probably never a convenient time to be introduced to your future in-laws, and so my initial visit to the Sinnott household was clouded in fear and discomfort. After a few pints to pluck up the courage, I eventually made my way in and Eithne's Mam and Dad, May and Paddy, were having tea.

Paddy was in dire form because Eamon had shipped a right smack in a county training match in which I was involved with the other team. Paddy was big into hurling and not too happy about it.

'Get me out of here quick,' I thought.

The Sinnotts loved their hurling. Stellah, Eithne's sister, had played in an All-Ireland final with my sister Siobhán, so that was a link straightaway. Eithne herself had played a bit and represented Wexford at under-14. Her sisters Paula and Kate also played and Eamon was a class act; he captained Wexford at one stage and did really well on minor and under-21 teams before then. But though the family were hurling-mad and naturally friendly, they probably would have preferred anyone but an Oulart man to be arriving in courting the lovely Eithne.

Of course love conquers all, or so they say, and gradually I got totally comfortable with the Sinnott family and always got a warm welcome anytime I called.

I proposed to Eithne at the end of 1995. It was a real romantic moment as I popped the question in my car. Eithne was surprised; she hadn't seen it coming at all, but to my colossal relief she said yes.

We bought the ring in Waterford, arrived back at her house and said nothing. Her Mam got a right shock when she saw the gleam on her finger.

The wedding was fixed for October 18 1996 at the Ferrycarrig Hotel and to be fair to my fiancée, she excelled herself with the preparations and did most of the work. I was a disaster, totally consumed by hurling. All I really contributed to the effort was to ring Liam Griffin and book the hotel.

Liam was great to us. For good measure, Paula Sinnott worked in the Ferrycarrig, so from my point of view it was ideal – it was only a matter of me turning up with the ring on the day.

But as I say, I'm a laid-back person and not much fazes me, not even the fact we had nowhere to live three weeks before we got married. I found it amusing but few others did. All I could do was tell them not to panic, and add that it was actually too late for that anyway.

Eventually, I asked a friend, Kevin Cooney, about the living quarters over Phil Redmond's pub in Raheen Duff and he said there was no problem; we could stay there till we got sorted out. Little did I expect we would spend three years there, boosting Phil's bank account by a huge amount along the way.

Our wedding was like a hurling match; there were 10 of the 1996 All-Ireland team invited and many of my Oulart team-mates were there as well, as were the cousins and the usual circle of friends. My brother Seán was best man. Carol, another of Eithne's sisters, was bridesmaid.

We had sent the invitation to my father, unsure if he would travel. But even though he was working in St Helena he made the long journey home. He had been home around the time of the 1996 Wexford-Galway All-Ireland semi-final but we had lost touch completely apart from that. It was great to have him there for the big day. Mam had been sick around then so it was nice to have her up and well and enjoying the wedding also.

I really enjoyed the ceremony and it flew by, to be honest, although the day after was just as pleasing, when most of the party headed into the Centenary Stores, a popular hostelry in Wexford town.

Mind you, Eithne was seriously displeased to see me disappear into a corner of the Stores for several hours for an interview with Tom Williams, a local writer who was compiling a book, *With Hand on Heart*, the inside story of our All-Ireland win, at the time.

But the woman was a saint and still is. I have to confess she has put up with a lot from me over the years. I overstepped the mark several times, but she has never given up on me.

Before I went to chat to Tom, Dad phoned me from Dublin Airport to tell me he was on his away again and we chatted for a few minutes. I didn't realise it would be five years before we would speak again.

Dad wished me luck and went off to his other life but there was no time to get down about it. I went ahead to do the interview and join in the sing-song that was after breaking out.

We had a great day and as the Wexford team and their partners would soon be heading to the US for three weeks, there was no point in honeymooning straightaway, so instead we retreated to the West of Ireland and visited Galway and Ennis with our friends Bartle and Josie Sinnott.

We enjoyed that little trip. It was the start of our new life together and when we came back to our new home over Phil Redmond's pub, we tried to make it homely and lived in. Well Eithne did. My main contribution to homemaking was to set about 200 traps around the place to keep the mice at bay.

There was some craic in that house when we first moved in. We loved it there, though my frequent trips downstairs to the pub nearly killed me and my bank balance. It was way too handy.

It was also too accessible for the thieves who broke in and robbed us blind while Eithne and I were asleep some time in March 97. I had a number of work-related cheques in the house but they were traceable and of no use, so the burglars just lined them up on the sink and left them there. But they took just about everything else.

When I came downstairs the following morning and saw we had been fleeced, my first thought was of my All-Ireland medal. I dashed to the press and went searching for it but dropped my head in despair when I saw it had been removed.

Shocked, I turned to sit down, and was astonished to see an array of medals lined up along the edge of the table with my All-Ireland medal taking pride of place in the middle.

The thieves had opened the box so that the medal sat gleaming out at me. They had more or less put it on show. I was just relieved they hadn't swiped it.

They got away with cash, other belongings and a lovely Wexford tracksuit I had just received from the county board. I reported it to the Gardai but the culprits were never found.

Amid the fuss over the All-Ireland final triumph, which still hadn't died down, the wedding and the hullabaloo over the robbery, it was obvious something had to give, and this time Oulart-The-Ballagh suffered. We could all see what was happening; there was still too much rejoicing about the place. Tom Neville tried to get it going again for the 97 club championship but what could he do?

We ploughed away and got to the quarter-final against Glynn-

Barntown, whom we'd beaten in the final just a year before. It was a miserable evening, I remember, but we managed to get past them before losing to Rathnure in the semi-final.

The team had suffered because of the All-Ireland win. Paul Finn and I were dragged all over the place with the Liam MacCarthy Cup, but I really felt sorry for Storey, who was asked to go everywhere and even had to take a few weeks off work to cope.

From here, things started to get worse for me and Wexford. In January of 97, the team went on holidays to the US. Near the end of the stay, Griffin called us together for a meal and meeting, to which wives and partners were also invited.

He made a one-hour speech but it was not as morale-boosting as the rest of the talks he had given us over the past year, for the simple reason he told us he was leaving. He went through all of 95 and 96, analysing the ups and downs, the highs and lows. And at the end of it all, he said he was stepping down.

Disappointment seeped through all of us, but strangely, we kind of knew that this was coming because Mary had been sick. So we accepted his decision.

What could we do? He had made his move.

Straight away, I wound my mind back to a chat I had with my sister-in-law Paula Sinnott and remembered how at the end of 95 she had told me Liam wouldn't walk away until he felt the job had been done. Well, here we were now, undoubtedly with the job done, and although Martin Storey stood up and made a passionate plea for him to stay on, it was never going to happen.

Liam had to devote everything to Mary, who had given him so much encouragement when he took the job, and his decision was quite understandable after all the time he had given to us the year before. We knew there and then things would never be the same again. Fair enough, the set-up was good and there was a decent base there for us to build on, but there would never be another Liam Griffin.

Plenty of counties would, though, have killed to have a man of the calibre of Rory Kinsella as their manager, and we were damn lucky to have him. Rory had been there as a selector with Séamus Barron, who also stepped down, and was widely respected as a real hurling coach among all of us. He introduced Eddie McDonald and Paudge Courtney to the set-up.

It was a comical sight to see us going back to the grindstone a few weeks after the holiday and it was no wonder we had a terrible League. I felt sorry for Rory because the expectation levels were huge and yet we were absolutely way out of shape when we returned.

We played our first League match against Galway and what a shock the crowd must have got. The last time many of them had seen us togged out, we were like whippets: lean muscular machines who had reached the top of the summit. We stood out and so did the muscles and veins in our necks and calves. You could tell at a glance we were fit and bursting to go.

Well, when we trotted out onto Wexford Park for that first League game, you could almost hear the disbelief that greeted us, because most of the team were like Oompa Loompas.

Ger Cushe had gone absolutely huge after a winter of enjoying life as an All-Ireland champion. But he wasn't the only one doing impressions of Mr Blobby. Gary Laffan and Tom Dempsey certainly bore no resemblance to Kate Moss and I was a good stone overweight myself.

I looked around the dressing-room that day and could see Griffin's words in the Burlington Hotel had already rung true. We, the men that won the All-Ireland final for the county, would never be in the same group or room ever again and it was a numbing old thought.

There was no Georgie O'Connor. It was strange not to have him beside me in a dressing-room before a game, staring at some point on the wall and inspiring us just by being there in all his bloody-minded glory.

John O was not in the best of form either and had been demoted to the bench.

And we had a few new faces in the set-up. Guys like Eugene Furlong came in and went straight onto the team, which was a sign to all of us that no place was safe.

I immediately liked Eugene. He had initially arrived on the scene a few years previously but hadn't reappeared since. I asked what brought him back and could only laugh at his blunt reply.

'I'm hurling the shite out of Gary Laffan every night at club training and there he is with an All-Ireland medal so I thought I'd be well able for it.'

Anyway, by the end of the League, a blind man could see that Rory Kinsella had been a brave guy to have taken this job on. We were in bits and certainly not helping Rory fill the shoes of Griffin, which seemed to be getting bigger all the time. We needed to snap out of it if we were to get anywhere that year.

But you don't become a bad team overnight and I remember doing an interview with the journalist Martin Breheny just before the start of the Championship and telling him that at last the corner had been turned and this team meant business again.

First up were Offaly and though Griffin was gone, at least some of his structures had stayed in place. Niamh Fitzpatrick was still involved, and for the three weeks leading up to our first Championship game of the season we trained like demons.

The 96 party was still going on around us, would you believe, but for once we avoided the celebrations and knuckled down to support Rory for once and for all.

I suffered a bit of a blow on the eve of the match when Fintan Cooney, the man who had been so good to my family when I was a child, got a heart attack in Oulart and passed away. The funeral was arranged for the Sunday evening, a few hours after the Leinster semi-final, and it was hard enough to focus on hurling.

Surprisingly, we went 10 points up against Offaly, but they came right back at us and it took a flukey goal from me, which went in off the stick of their goalkeeper, David Hughes, and a Damien Fitzhenry save to get us through in the end by three points, 3-12 to 2-12.

Before we knew it, we were in a big build-up to the Leinster final, and if we thought the hype was big in 96, it seemed to be much more widespread this time around. Everywhere I went with work, it was hurling, and when you are trying to drum up new business accounts, you can't exactly be rude by trying to ignore it all and stay away from it.

But I have to say that I was a little bit drained from talking hurling at this stage and was shocked that I couldn't even get away from it at the funeral, where the club members formed a guard of honour in Fintan's memory.

People kept coming over to me, shaking hands and talking about the Offaly match. It just showed how deeply they felt for Wexford hurling but at the same time I thought it was a bit much.

I spoke to Fintan's wife, also my godmother, Clare. She said she just knew I got my goal earlier that afternoon for Fintan. When she mentioned the goal, I just remembered what a loss her husband was, not just to us but to the whole community. I was a bit upset and let the funeral go to the graveyard, a place I would not often frequent – that's just my way.

You never really get over losing someone close but time passes and lets you deal with it. So winning the Leinster final in Fintan's memory was the next priority and when we learned we would be up against Kilkenny, well, it made the challenge all the more spicy because our current crop of players had never beaten them in a provincial final.

Preparation had been going well; I think Rory had us fine-tuned.

And one week ahead of the game, an old friend came to visit us and have a chat.

Into a team meeting at Murphy Floods Hotel arrived Griffin with a big huge box. It was great to see him again and we wondered what he had in store for us this time. Maybe some new gear?

While we were wondering, out he stepped again, only to come back in with another big box. We thought we were in for a right haul here.

We listened to Liam as he spoke about defending our titles. Delving into one box, he lifted out the Bob O'Keeffe Cup and told us we had a choice – we could either hold onto it or give it back to Kilkenny. Then he lifted out the Liam MacCarthy Cup.

'You gave up your lives to win this,' he said. 'Are you going to let it slip away just like that, without a fight? The choice is yours.'

And looking around the room, I could sense we didn't want to give either of those cups back just yet.

The Kilkenny game was never going to be pretty and with Aodhán MacSuibhne refereeing, it was going to take a strong display from him to keep us apart. I say that because within a few minutes of the start, Andy Comerford took a go at Tom Dempsey and hit him a right belt. Not being shy on the field, I bided my time and drew a dart at him as he returned from a big solo up the field.

As Andy went down, my old friend John Power came over and sent me flying. I got up and had my name taken.

'You little bastard!' Comerford roared at me, with his two hands where you don't want to get hit.

'Andy,' I replied. 'If you want to act the bollox, you'll get plenty of it back.'

Anyway, the laugh seemed to be on the other side of my face when Kilkenny went into the break five points up thanks mostly to a PJ Delaney goal. Ger Cushe had been taken off with an eye injury and our backs were totally against the wall. Things looked bleaker than a

December Sunday in Tramore.

Rory sent on Dave Guiney. Jesus, I now had a Guiney brother on either side of me. I couldn't believe it. But they did well in what was a strange finale to the game.

Kilkenny didn't hold their places at all and we just decided to follow our men, meaning I actually ended up at full back for the last few minutes. It was strange to see Seánie Flood, who had recovered from injury, out at centre back. But that's the way we played them and it worked, because we hauled the lead back and won by six points: 2-14 to 1-11.

It was Billy Byrne's day. All throughout 96, he had come on as a substitute and done the business, but this really took the biscuit because he almost single-handedly won the match for us by scoring 1-2 in the space of a few minutes. Thank God he didn't retire!

Early in the second half, I was fouled and stood over the ball to take the free but Billy was coming on and told me not to take it until he got into position at the other end of the field.

'Wait till I get to the square!' he shouted, giving our game plan away in literally two seconds. Not that it was a surprise or anything. I lobbed it in to him and bang!, he rattled the net. Then we started to target him like Newcastle with Alan Shearer, and he scored another two points, which just gave us a massive lift.

We hung on to win and it was as good a feeling as I have enjoyed after a game. I went running off the pitch with my hands in the air. My brother Seán and a friend, Pat Dempsey, came toward me but I just smiled and sped past them like a hare on amphetamines. I wanted to get to the platform; there was a cup there waiting to be brought home again.

As I got up towards the stand, I stuck a Wexford flag in one of the flower pots and waited for Rod Guiney, our new captain, to lift the cup again. I just thought of what we had done: beaten Offaly in the semi-final and Kilkenny in the final. We deserved this and no-one could argue with that.

Tom Dempsey and Seánie Flood sang *The Purple and Gold* from the steps of the Hogan Stand, which didn't go down too well with some of the Kilkenny lads, but they are used to winning every year; this was still fairly new to us.

Something else that didn't go down too well was Rod forgetting to offer three cheers for Kilkenny, but I grabbed the mike and did the honours.

And still, I wanted a bit more. There was no point in getting too carried away. We were flying it and there was more to be won. I had a taste for it now and knew the team might never see days like these again.

After that game, people were queueing up to come over and hug me, shake my hand and chat about the final. But I took it all with a pinch of salt. I knew supporters were fickle and reminded them there would be plenty of days when they wouldn't want to hug me.

As I made my way back to the car in Clonliffe College for a quiet mug of tea and a sandwich, little did I realise how soon I would be proven right.

Although thousands turned up in Gorey to greet the team, the boys were by now seriously hankering after another crack at the All-Ireland and were determined to treat the drink with caution. So while they enjoyed the fun that night, the session didn't really linger.

It was back to training, and with the new back-door format now in operation, we had to wait a while before learning Tipperary were next up. They had lost to Clare in the Munster final and then beaten Down to get through to the All-Ireland semi-final.

And then something seemed to change. In the run-up to meeting Len Gaynor's team, you could sense things were slipping in our camp. The final proof was that while both Rod Guiney and Gary Laffan had injuries, they still ended up starting that game, which I saw as a big mistake on their part.

I admired Rod for wanting to play for his county but he was captain and should have stepped down. He had a fitness test on what turned out to be a cruciate-ligament injury. The test only involved running in a straight line and so of course he was going to be fine. One twist or turn on that area of the knee and you would have known it was all over, so from that point of view the fitness test was a waste of time.

And just to ram the point home, not long into the game the two boys were taken off injured, and that had a fierce unsettling effect on us. I'm not saying that we would otherwise have beaten Tipp, but we were wrong, everyone was wrong, the lads shouldn't have played and they shouldn't have been let play. The management and the medical team slipped up badly.

As if that wasn't bad enough, we had to endure losing Rory McCarthy at midfield, who was a great player for us. He got turned over in the air by Conor Gleeson. In my view it was an accident and Gleeson never went to do him, though an awful lot was made of it afterwards. At the same time, I felt Conal Bonnar should not have got away with kicking Rory over the sideline after the initial incident, and I know if I had drawn a kick like that, not only would I be barred from the game, I would probably be still hiding in my house as well.

Anyway, Tipp beat us, knocked us off our perch and qualified for the All-Ireland final. They beat us by seven points, 2-16 to 0-15, but it should have been more. I was marking Declan Ryan and needed all my concentration to keep tabs on him, but what really killed us off was when Brian O'Meara got a goal in the second half.

One thing that hadn't helped us was the pre-match build-up. The *Examiner* printed an interview with Ger Loughnane, who slated us for using 'roughhouse' tactics. Those comments went down like a lead balloon in Wexford. Even now there are people who will tell you he was way out of line. I'm sure Ger thought Clare could end up meeting us in the final, but it just wasn't the sort of psychological ploy Liam Griffin would have used.

Anyway, Tipp drew strength from those comments and on the day they physically blew us away, and the back-to-back dream was over.

The Loughnane thing was a huge controversy at the time and

while he claimed he was misinterpreted, we would have loved to ram those words back down Clare throats in the final.

That's one of the biggest regrets I have, that we didn't get to play them in the Championship after we learned so much from them and got inspiration from their breakthrough. The only time I had played against them was in GOAL matches. It would have been nice to meet in the thick of the Championship if only to see which really was the better team.

So here we were, out of the All-Ireland series, and yet I considered it to be a successful year though I don't for one second feel we got the recognition we deserved for retaining the Bob O'Keeffe Cup. That was evident in the All Star selection, where only one Wexfordman, Fitzy, got the nod and despite the fact we had come from six points down to beat them by six in the provincial final, Kilkenny got three awards.

I suppose we had another Leinster medal and that was the important thing, although I looked on, envious as hell, as Clare beat Tipp in the final a few weeks later.

Life had changed for me the year before, but it really went head over heels on August 23 1997. Little Billy Dunne arrived into the world and in the space of a few seconds changed the lives of Eithne and me forever.

We had been married just under a year and he came on the scene much sharper than we'd expected. I brought Eithne into the hospital on that Saturday morning at 4.30. Neither of us had much notion of what to do but we both knew the time had arrived.

I spent the day in the hospital until the hunger got the better of me and I headed for a Chinese takeaway in the Lotus House. In hindsight, I shouldn't have gone back to the ward so soon, because Eithne wasn't feeling well and the smell of me and my Chinese hardly helped her. But maybe it brought the birth forward a little. Either way, Billy was born at around 5.30 pm.

It's hard to know what to say when your first child comes into the world. I just kind of looked on, dumb-struck. I rang the two grannies, Mam and Eithne's mother, May, and told them their grandson had arrived.

Naturally enough, Martin Storey and the boys soon heard the news and the good wishes poured in, but I had to travel to Galway to play Sarsfields in a practice match the following day and for once my mind wasn't totally consumed with hurling, one of the few times I could ever say that.

Eithne and I hadn't discussed names, but the lads kept asking me what we were going to call the child, so just to give them an answer and keep them happy I replied: 'Billy.' And that became the standard response for those around the village wanting to know his name.

After I had missed most of the day because of the hurling match, Eithne's sister, Paula, was out for my blood so I hurried to the hospital to discuss names.

'We better call him Billy,' I told Eithne. 'The whole village thinks that's his name anyway.'

Of course, there was another reason. My uncle and godfather was killed in 1972 and I'd been thinking we hadn't seen a Billy Dunne in the parish for a long time. That all changed with the arrival of our son and, would you believe, a year or two later my cousin Robert had a baby boy and they called him Billy as well. Now there were two of them around the place. Uncle Billy would have loved that.

Buoyed by the arrival of the little lad, Eithne and I learned to adapt, but I must admit his mother learned a lot quicker than his father. I loved the idea of having him around and could not wait for him to see me hurling. That would take a few years, however, so as we got used to this third member of the Dunne family, and with Wexford out of the reckoning, it was back to the drawing board with Oulart for the rest of the year.

We drew Faythe Harriers in the semi-final and beat them in a replay to qualify to meet Glynn-Barntown in the final. They must have been sick of the sight of us. We beat them again, by three points, and I became the third Dunne brother to win a man-of-the-match award in a county final, following in the footsteps of Seán and Tomás, something else for Mam to boast about.

It was all still happening but things soon turned sour. There was plenty of hassle over having to play three Sundays in a row, but when we drew Castletown of Laois in the Leinster semi-final that scenario was on the cards. We played them at Rathdowney the same day the Wexford team were flying out on holidays to Spain. We sent our bags to Dublin Airport in the hope of meeting up after the game but – wouldn't you know it? – the game was a draw.

We wanted to go on holidays but Tom Neville and Mick Jacob didn't want that at all; they were afraid we'd go on the tear in Spain and not be right for the replay the following week. In fairness to Castletown, they agreed to put the match back for a fortnight but our own mentors would have none of it, and despite a spate of meetings, Storey and I were deprived of our holiday in the sun, a break we both badly needed.

We'd had too much hurling by now, and after 20 minutes of the replay, in Belfield, I went over on my leg and knew straightaway it was broken. The ball had cut loose; my clubmate Pearse Redmond went to pick it up and missed; he kicked it on and David Cuddy went in to get it; I shouldered David and as I jostled him my leg snapped and I went down in a heap.

I did not hear the snap but there was a shot of pain all the way down my leg and I suspected something was seriously wrong. That suspicion was confirmed a moment later when I looked down and saw a huge bend in the leg.

In agony, I put my hands under my calf and looked up at Brendan O'Connor and Martin Dempsey, who were roaring to the sideline for medical attention. It was a pain you wouldn't wish on your worst enemy. It was so bad I wanted to die.

My brother Seán came running to me. He knew it was serious because none of us ever stayed down unless we had to. Pat Delaney, the Castletown manager and former Offaly player, also came over but was less sympathetic.

'You fucking deserve that, Dunne. You fucking deserve that,' he sneered. It was raw and it was bitter. Pat obviously had issues with me. I wasn't able to answer but Seán was and told him where to go. I pleaded for a bit of silence; all I wanted was peace and quiet.

One of the women involved with the club, Mary Doyle, came running in with a tracksuit to cover me but the aroma of her perfume was too strong for me and I had to tell the poor woman to go away. I felt really sick and was in awful pain.

A few moments later, I was even less comfortable when they produced an advertising board and used it as a stretcher to bring me into the dressing-room.

'Jesus Christ,' I thought. 'Can it get any worse?' It could.

Dr Derek Forde came in and was about to give me a relieving injection. I almost grabbed the needle out of his hands so desperate was I to stick it into the leg myself but just as he was about to do so, he got another emergency call from the field, where the Castletown full forward had managed to get a bit of a hurley stuck in his jaw. Talk about a bloodbath.

'The boys are following the game plan to a T,' I smirked, half unconscious, half crying.

Anyway, Dr Forde sorted him out, came back and gave me an injection in the shoulder, which brought me more relief than I ever thought possible. It was blissful. The pain just went, and it demonstrated to me how important the presence of a doctor is at all GAA games. A stretcher wouldn't be a bad idea either; those advertising boards are not the best.

An ambulance brought me to Ardkeen Hospital, Waterford, where I was told I would need an operation the following morning. They put a cast on my leg but only for Derek Forde I probably would have been left waiting there and God knows what sort of an infection I would have got.

I looked at the date on the calendar, Saturday November 8, and decided I wouldn't forget it in a hurry. The pain had been extreme. But Pat Delaney's words, well, I would remember them too.

When my brother Kieran arrived at the hospital, I was still in my hurling gear and he was so concerned for my welfare that the first thing he asked for was my jersey. Brothers!

We started chatting and after a while I didn't feel too sorry for myself because I remembered the terrible story of a young guy from the village back home. It just came into my head.

In 1992, Stephen Hayden, a promising hurler, was rushing for training for the club under-21 team. I was a selector with the team and knew him well; Stephen was a lovely chap. As usual before training, he was finishing off his chores on the farm, inflating a tyre with one of those pressure machines when it suddenly blew up and hit him in the face. It was a freak accident and it drove him almost 25 feet in the air and left him with brain damage.

The accident had a terrible effect on the village. Stephen is such a top lad that we hated seeing something so terrible happening to him of all people. Stephen's Dad, Johnny, brings him to all the matches, and when we won our first county final two years later I gave my jersey to him, and Tomás dedicated the win to him. In fact, the entire team went up to Stephen afterwards. We knew that if things had turned out differently, he could have been there on the field with us as well.

And rightly so, thinking of Stephen stopped me from feeling sorry for myself. His bravery and his family's love for him should be an example for all of us because they look after him so well.

Me? Well, I got away lightly in comparison. The surgeon operated, put a plate and a few screws into my leg, and that was it. The whole of the village seemed to descend on Ardkeen and those wonderful women the nurses were driven mad because the phone rang so often.

I stayed there for a few weeks and all my old pals came down for a look, the lads from the county team, Griffin, Seánie Flood, Rory Kinsella, Paul Codd, John O, and it was great to see them. It relieved the boredom and took away the anxiety I felt over the injury and how it would affect my work.

Only four months previously, I had joined Cantrell & Cochrane, a job I had wanted for so long, and now here I was with a broken leg, not worth a shit to them. I had a new wife and little Billy, who was only three months at this stage.

With C&C, I had taken a cut in wages, but I had been pushing hard for the job as sales developer and knew it would take time. I was willing to bide my time there until my job prospects and wages improved.

Soon after breaking my leg, in an interview with Vincent Hogan, I articulated my feelings. I was 29, had no permanent job, had a four-month-old child and was newly married. The GAA insurance scheme was crap, absolute shite, and for the six months or so that I was out of work, I got £29.33 per week for all my efforts over the years. Cantrell & Cochrane were decent to me; they paid me a month's salary, which they didn't have to do. Furthermore, while I moaned about the GAA insurance scheme, I have to say that only for the people who make up the association at grassroots level, I don't know how I would have survived.

Pat Dempsey had been chairman of the Oulart club since Fintan's death and he organised a benefit night for me in Cooney's pub. I was humbled and grateful but embarrassed as well, so I kept well away from the bar the night of the fundraiser. And so you can imagine my shock a few days later when Pat arrived up to the house with a cheque for £4,500.

'Every penny of it is yours, Liam,' he said. I was stunned. But that wasn't the only kindness bestowed on me. One fellow I had never even met, Ned Kavanagh from Carlow, sent me £100 in the post. Pat 'Stack' Murphy, a businessman, sent me £350 in the post. Brendan O'Connor was also very good to me. None of these guys ever looked for thanks and I would have been too embarrassed to give it to them, but at the same time I never forgot.

The county board was excellent too and paid for my medical bills. So although it was a tough time, I was well looked after.

Once I left hospital I went back to our home over Phil Redmond's pub and, to be straight, I was a hard man to live with. There was the usual feeling sorry for myself; I just wanted to get out of the house and usually the first resort was the bar downstairs.

I probably didn't see what was happening at first but it didn't take long for the danger signs to start flashing. The winter nights are dark, weary and boring at the best of times, but when you can't walk it's even more depressing.

The first night I was home, Ger Cushe and his wife, Mag, came to see me and the two of us went into the bar downstairs. I wasn't in the form for drinking but ended up having a few anyway.

And that's the way it turned out for the next three months. Friends would call up to see how I was keeping and, inevitably, the bar was the first stop. It was just too handy for me: a 20-second trip to the stool.

All the boys visited, from Storey to Brendan O'Connor, and I started to get sucked into a rut. During the day, I was bored out of my wits and could do very little for Eithne and young Billy. I longed for the evening, the chance to chat to someone about hurling and have a few drinks.

Before long, Storey could see I was drinking too much and urged me to cut down because it would prevent my leg from healing properly. But of course I paid no notice; I was getting too fond of my evening sessions in Phil's bar.

Out of the £4,500 raised by the club, I would say Phil got a fair old chunk, which was fierce selfish of me, considering I was newly married and had a child only a few months old. But the same lads who were urging me to cut down were often there in the evenings helping me lower the hard stuff.

Phil's pub, there was something about it I just couldn't resist. For a stranger walking in off the street, there would be no great appeal to Phil's bar but stay there for a while and the man himself would have your family tree traced right back to its roots. You wouldn't be long feeling at home.

It's not much to look at: I suppose if push came to shove, 20 people might fit into it. But it has the spirit of a busy down-town New York bar. In such a place, not much bigger than a kitchen, you can be yourself, and it represents a part of Ireland that is untouched and honest to goodness. On the side of the bar is a little shop, where some lads prefer to sip their pint, and outside the actual counter is the fridge where the drink is stored. On the wall is a rings board, just in case you fancy a game, there were many nights when I was so drunk I didn't even connect with the board, but sure that was all part of the craic.

It just became too easy for me to drink the nights away there. Neighbours loved to gather there and the warm, cosy atmosphere made it a hard place to leave.

I was fast becoming 'the one' Griffin had warned us about. I slept during the day and wanted to get out of the house at night. It was mostly pints of beer and cider; at least I managed to keep away from shorts, but it didn't feel like that the following morning.

Other wives would have shown me the door or walked out but Eithne just kept the show on the road.

No wonder the injury took 16 months to heal properly and little wonder again that my hurling suffered for almost two years afterwards. I was digging a hole for myself and, as not a night went by without a visit downstairs, the hole would get deeper. Some lads would call over almost every evening. We would have a cup of tea, head downstairs for a few hours and then maybe come back up and watch a hurling video or something and eat the sandwiches Eithne had left out for us. Often, if the craic was good, we would even fill a box with a few takeaway bottles and bring them upstairs. It was the best fun I ever had while injured but for my life and career, it was a ridiculous scenario, and yet I could still persuade myself I hadn't gone too far,

Maybe that was the most worrying aspect. I was 29 and should have had more sense but I was in a ball of self-pity, and this was a way of dealing with the frustration: the night-time, the pints, the lads and a chance to get out of the house.

Amazingly, Eithne never said much to me; she had her hands full with little Billy. All I was concerned about was how tough it was to be out of hurling with a broken leg. Me, myself and I.

Worse again, the plaudits still kept flowing, though not for me, and awards like Wexford Sports Star of the Month and another All Star nomination reminded me what I was missing out on.

But I was to miss out on more than just awards. In fact the entire 1998 season went by without my involvement and that was down to inappropriate recovery methods; the leg was completely out of shape.

Eventually, I started to cop on and realised that unless I took care of myself the leg might never come right so I used the swimming pool at the Ferrycarrig Hotel. That in itself was a hassle. I couldn't drive so someone had to be at my beck and call to ferry me there, which I found hugely frustrating. Still, I stuck at it, and after 15 months I was at least able to walk properly again.

I had stayed on the crutches as long as possible to give myself some chance of playing hurling in 98 but, realistically, it was never going to happen. Because though I got the all-clear in August, I still couldn't even jog. that's what I got for skulling pints every night and feeling sorry for myself.

It was a conscious decision not to go to training in Wexford Park much that year. I kept my distance from the team during the week but still travelled with them to games, for my own sanity more than anything else. It didn't help my despair as I looked at them getting caught on the hop by Offaly.

Before the game, the team assembled for a photograph and left a gap of about two feet at the end of the bench. I used to sit there at that end, always had done for some reason. No-one ever sat there bar me, and Rory MacCarthy would have his space at the other end. Maybe it's just habit but when you're playing big games, it's nice to be able to look around and take it in.

This time, I waited for my spot to be filled but they left it vacant. My space was still there. If you look back at that team picture from 98, you will see what I'm talking about. Maybe the lads weren't aware they were doing it, and that little gap would have meant nothing to anyone else in the ground, but to me it came across as a great gesture,

Rod Guiney and Gary Laffan were also injured and yet I still felt we were good enough to keep the run going and pull off a win. I was almost right.

I talked to the lads before the game and recalled Pat Delaney's words of sympathy to me while I lay writhing in agony after breaking my leg. My intention was to strike a motivational chord with one or two of the team, and I could see Seánie Flood responding; he was just back from injury and knew the loneliness a player feels when his career is almost taken away from him. But it was all to no avail. Wexford had the game in their hands right until the final minutes but were caught by a Johnny Dooley sucker punch at the end of normal time and that was it, they were gone: 1-15 to 0-17.

Dooley's goal was brilliant but I felt Aodhán Mac Suibhne made some terrible decisions that day.

And so the season ended in disaster and I got little comfort even from Oulart-The-Ballagh, who were knocked out in the first round of the Wexford Championship. My sporting world had well and truly caved in, and I was learning all over again just how cruel and fickle sport could be.

Life is just one damned thing after another.
Elbert Hubbard, Author

– CHAPTER FIFTEEN –
Return to the fold

I got a chance to wipe the slate clean. Not everyone gets that opportunity. After a four-month slump of sleeping late, moping around the house and drinking even later, I managed to snap out of my self-pity and worked on my leg.

I gave it a right go to get fit again. I went swimming, used the gym, tried jogging in a straight line when I felt I could manage it and soon rejoined the Wexford squad.

When, in February 1999, I played my first game for Wexford since the injury, I decided, for the first time in my life, to put a shin guard on; I had already begun to worry about taking a belt on the site of the injury.

We played a game of Probables versus Possibles, but even though I had more experience than most of the new lads put together, I was way off the pace. I knew then it would be extremely hard to get back to the level of skill and fitness I had managed just a couple of years earlier.

I got through the League way below par but Rory Kinsella never criticised me, and I was in the half-back line when we played Dublin in Nowlan Park in the first round of the Championship.

Although we beat them by a point, 1-13 to 1-12, I was just awful. Their manager, Michael O'Grady, who had spent time with Wexford, was most gracious and said how delighted he was to see me back in the game. But Michael was too kind; the game had just passed me by completely. I was simply miles off the pace.

By the time our game with Offaly came around, I have to say the improvement had not been staggering. I was marking Michael Duignan, and in fairness to him, he came over to see how my leg was by letting a lovely pull of the hurl land just where I had broken it.

'I'd say it's fully healed, Mike,' I laughed.

I didn't mind taking a belt from Duignan because I respected him, and anyway there was no point in getting thick that day because they totally overpowered us and gave us a nice 3-17 to 0-15 beating.

It was clear as day that this team was starting to slip now and Rory was also coming to the end of his reign. The team was stale and, apart from Declan Ruth, no-one was coming through. Declan had broken onto the team in 1998 at wing back but was dropped in 99, so even he didn't look like setting the world alight back then, and the underage structures had produced no-one else.

In fairness, very few of the team had got completely carried away with the hysteria of 96 and 97 and I sensed most of the team still wanted more. Larry O would be the first to tell you he started to believe in the hype for a while and got a little excited by it all. But no man wanted more and he was as hungry as any of us. The trouble was that the team had learned to accept defeat all over again.

Everyone was working hard, so complacency could not be used as an excuse for defeat. Staleness could, however. Jesus, the truth is harsh, but the team just wasn't good enough anymore.

I started to look back and remind myself how lucky I had been, a bad move for any hurler. Apart from the trophies, I had the All Stars as well, which the likes of Ger Cushe somehow missed out on, so even though I felt the end was near, I had nothing to complain about.

Cushe should definitely have got an All Star in 96 or 97 or both but he was ignored. Griffin had called him into the bar of the Burlington the night of the 96 ceremony to warn him he hadn't made the shortlist. I remember praying that for once Griffin was wrong, but of course he wasn't. I never felt that Ger got the credit he deserved and here he was now, bowing out, and I felt that personally I was losing not just a great team-mate but also a loyal friend.

Rory Kinsella was another guy I felt for. He had shown huge trust in me while I was injured and even though I was struggling for form he kept me in the team and stuck by me. This was the end of him as Wexford manager and to me it felt like the end of an era. Once more, I remembered Griffin's prediction, the morning after our All-Ireland win, that we would never be together as a group again; it seemed unbelievable at the time but he was never more accurate.

It had gone from a famine to a feast back to a famine and, as I said, we held out no great hope of winning anything in 2000, when we heard Joachim Kelly was the new manager. He was a sound guy but he wasn't the man for us at all and it soon became apparent. It was a waste of a year and, as I look back now, I would give anything to have a season like that back, so you could try and make more use of it.

By the end of the year, we were lower even than we'd been in 95. Our League was terrible and the one Championship game we played was against Offaly, Joachim's own county, and they murdered us for the second year in a row, 3-15 to 1-8.

They had great motivation playing us because Joachim was our manager, but in truth, we could have had Seán Boylan, Brian Cody and Liam Griffin pulling the strings for us that day and Offaly would still have come out on top. We were the worst-prepared Wexford team ever. My mother would have breezed through some of the drills laid out for us in training.

It wasn't all Joachim's fault. My being sent off didn't help the team much either. So it's little wonder I have a sour taste in my mouth when I remember 2000. It was a long way from what we had achieved just a few years earlier. There was no queue of Wexford supporters lining up to shake my hand or hug me when I left Croke Park the evening of the Offaly game.

The following day Vincent Hogan wrote in the *Irish Independent* of my wild pull on John Troy, but to the grave I'll argue that I simply flicked the ball off him with one hand on the hurl. Then again, the way

Troy went down you would swear he had been shot.

I avoided Griffin for weeks afterwards for fear of the tongue-lashing I would get off him and sat back and waited to see who would leave the set-up.

There was a brief respite from all the gloom when Oulart won the 2000 League final against St Martin's but we had a lot of hassle in that camp as well by the time the Championship came around. Tony Cottrell from Kilkenny was our trainer and had raised plenty of hackles during the League final when he sneered at the fact that Anthony O'Leary and my brother Tomás were getting rubs from the physio at the interval.

'You wouldn't see that in Kilkenny,' Tony smiled.

Tomás must have been in serious pain because it would take a bullet in the back of his leg to see him wincing, and so Tony's remark pissed a lot of us off.

Nonetheless, we reached the Championship final, where we played Darragh Ryan's club, St Anne's, who had developed from the junior ranks since 96 and won the county senior football title earlier in 2000. We thought we were on the way after we'd gone six points up but they came back at us and brought it level. Again we went four points up and looked to have the game won, but they staged a late rally to win their first senior hurling title by two points.

They were a team of giants: most of them stood over six-foot-one, and the word went around that we had been horsed out of the title. People around the village couldn't accept that and we were slated, but I think Anne's brought more than just brute force to the game and deserved their win. Their club was on a roll from the football campaign and we were not good enough on the day to stop their momentum.

I believe 13 of them were on the football as well as the hurling team, and that's some achievement. But the people of Oulart felt we should have been able to push home our advantage on the scoreboard and so that season ended in a welter of disappointment as well.

The next time I saw the boys from St Anne's was when we were brought together for a Wexford hurlers' meeting with our new manager, Tony Dempsey. I found it strange to look at Tony and see Ger Cushe, now a selector, there beside him with the third member of the management, Davy Morris. I had battled for so long with Cushe and now here he was on the other side of the set-up. We had been great mates but Ger rightly kept his distance from me for a while.

It suddenly dawned on me that with Larry O, I was now the elder statesman on the team, and the point was made when Tony asked me to say a few words, something I would seldom have chosen to do in all my years with the squad. I was tentative enough at the start but I found what I wanted to say and it went something like this.

'We're fighting with the county board one minute and ourselves the next. We need enthusiasm for this now. The buzz has gone out of us and the set-up is stale, but it's down to us to get Wexford back on top.

'Tony will be a players' man. We will want for nothing and it's our responsibility from here onwards.'

I kept it short and sweet but Tony was a lot like Liam Griffin with words – you could stay listening to him all evening. He told us pride was the buzzword. He needed to bring pride back to Wexford and, true to his word, Dempsey would go a long way towards that end.

It was clear as day even then that Tony would wind up in Dáil Éireann because the man was always on the go. He was just starting his political career and it was amazing how he could combine both careers: sport and politics. But somehow he did. Probably the three mobile phones he was constantly talking into helped. One night, after training in Farmleigh, he was chatting with Adrian Fenlon and myself when he took out one of the phones; it had recorded 19 missed calls during the previous 90 minutes. Now that was pressure, and yet he never let the hurling suffer. At the time, Fenlon, Darragh Ryan, who had been the best player for St Anne's that season, and I were elected onto a players' committee, and because Damien Fitzhenry used to put so many great ideas from the floor, we decided to draft him in as well. The Three Musketeers found their d'Artagnan.

Fitzy became the head spokesman and anything we wanted we got. There was a county board chequebook there for us, and every so often he would produce a few gear-bags or other pieces of equipment to keep the camp happy. Some managers might have come back and said they couldn't do this or that but Tony would take out the chequebook and if a player was in trouble he would look after him. He was out for our best interests. For example, if a guy was having problems getting off work to make training, Tony would pay for a replacement at the workplace so the player could be freed up.

With such an approach, it's no surprise he was not only a successful businessman but also principal of Enniscorthy Vocational School. Anywhere he went, success followed. He had been chairman of the Wexford GAA board at 29, was on a number of high-powered committees in Croke Park and had also managed county under-21 teams, leading the 1979 team to a Leinster title.

It also encouraged us that we won the Walsh Cup within a few months of him taking over. It was my first time meeting Laois and marking David Cuddy since I broke my leg and we shook hands. I had never put an ounce of blame on him. But when the first ball arrived in, I drove it 10 yards out of his hand and when the second one came in, David was left shaking his paw again. Just to let all concerned know that my nerve hadn't gone.

With the game well won, I was taken off with five minutes to go and got a nice round of applause from the Wexford supporters, which was good to hear considering I had been jeered by the Offaly supporters the last time I had left a field early.

For us, it was just another Walsh Cup medal but you could see the disappointment on the Laois players' faces; the Cup would have meant the world to them.

We went into the League with a bit of confidence, and though we got nowhere we knew we would have the measure of Laois again in the Championship. And so it was no shock to anyone when we beat them by 17 points to 10. But it was all for nothing when Kilkenny destroyed us again in the Leinster final. They beat us by 2-19 to 0-12 this time; we seemed to be falling further and further behind them. Young Billy was baffled after the presentation and asked me why Denis Byrne from Kilkenny was lifting the cup when I had told him before the game that Wexford would be bringing it home.

I was almost afraid to explain; it looked like it would be a long time before the Bob O'Keeffe Cup would be home again. But Billy didn't need that harsh dose of reality at his age; I just told him Denis was borrowing the cup for a while.

With the back door looming, we tried to pick ourselves up the week after with a challenge match against Galway but might as well have sprayed graffiti all over the dressing-room because the writing was well and truly on the wall.

We went into that game aiming to restore confidence, and Galway beat us out the gate by 20 points. We were in big trouble and Tony Dempsey knew that the squad was more than a little short of the required standard. He decided it was time to bring Liam Griffin back on the scene. Boy, were we delighted when we saw the familiar skinny frame, preceded of course by that magnificent nose, walking back into Wexford Park! Griffin has some sort of an aura about him. There is no-one I know quite like the man. He is blessed with some sort of a reassuring presence that is enough for me any day of the week.

He returned to take a few sessions just before we were drawn to play Limerick in the All-Ireland quarter-final. Before he came in, we the players had a couple of heart-to-hearts, during which I pointed out to the rest of the boys that one man couldn't do it all for us. But of course he almost did. Before we knew it, after just a couple of coaching sessions, Griffin had us motoring well.

A few nights before we played Limerick, he brought us into a circle and started going through match tactics.

'Liam Dunne, where are you?' he roared.

'Oh, Jaysus,' I thought as I hesitantly stepped forward. 'What's going to happen here?'

Griffin grabbed me and put me in front of the squad.

'This is what's going to happen you on Sunday. A high ball will come down between you and the lad you are marking. You will pull on the ball and he will go to ground, holding his head. Their manager, Eamon Cregan, will run in from the line shouting "Dunne, you dirty bastard, you're at it again!"

'The referee will call you over and issue a yellow card. He might even give you a red card. But that is their game plan and no matter what happens, we will be ready for it. We are one step ahead.'

I stood there, not knowing whether to laugh or cry. This was Griffin's way of impressing on the lads that whatever the match threw up, Wexford would be ready for it.

That game turned out to be one of the most exciting and dramatic of my career, although the Wexford fans, suspecting we were in for a trouncing, stayed away. Without a shadow of a doubt, we were outnumbered five to one by the Limerick crowd, who were still hungry for glory.

The game started at 100 miles per hour and ended over an hour later at 120 mph. I never saw or played in such a sharp opening to a match. But Griffin had known this would happen and for weeks beforehand had us training on a tighter pitch and with two or three sliotars on the go at all times from the sideline or end-line.

After 10 minutes Ollie Moran, a sound guy, went to catch a ball and I pulled. I don't think I hit him, there wasn't much contact made anyway and the ball just broke in behind us. But as it did I saw Ollie was holding his left ear.

The referee, Michael Wadding, thought I hit him. His whistle blew and suddenly in came Cregan, roaring and shouting at me. Larry O made a run to stop him, and Declan Ruth lent a hand, while Wadding called me over.

'Michael,' I almost laughed, feeling like this was a snippet from *Back to the Future*, 'Liam Griffin told me last Wednesday night this would happen. Eamon Cregan is probably going nuts around here somewhere, but honest to God, I didn't hit the ball or the man.'

Wadding didn't listen. Out came the yellow card. I still could hardly believe Griffin's prediction had come through. Stunned, I went over to Ollie and asked him if he was okay.

'I'm grand, Liam, not a bother on me,' he smiled, and I smiled back. In fairness that sort of stuff happens in hurling matches everyday of the year.

That was it. After that I knew they couldn't have much else in their armoury. If that was their plan A, I knew we were one step ahead. So now we had a bit more belief, but all the same it took a Paul Codd goal just before the break to keep the scoreboard healthy.

The small band of Wexford fans present stood to clap us into the dressing-room, where Tony Dempsey was waiting to stoke the adrenalin. He had an easy job to get me going.

'We're doing this to show that there's a future for Wexford hurling,' he bellowed. 'We're doing this for the young lads all over the county who need new heroes today, lads the likes of young Billy Dunne.'

Always a great man for asking the players their opinion during games, Tony looked at me and said: 'Well, Dunner, what have you to say?'

I let rip. I had never lost it in a dressing-room before then but there was a first time for everything. People say that frenzied speeches will only get you so far and I agree, but on that day words were exactly what we needed, and so with Billy's disappointment over the Bob O'Keeffe Cup fresh in my mind, I stepped forward.

'I'd die for young Billy,' I bellowed. 'And I'd die for the Wexford fans who bothered to come up here today. But there are 14 men alongside me that I'd die for as well.'

I grabbed my jersey and reminded the lads of what we were fighting for.

'It's for the fucking county, lads! It's for this jersey that we all put so much in. To get the smiles back on people's faces at home. For our families and friends.

'This is our day, lads! Limerick are going to drive us all the way. Let us be the ones standing when it's all over!'

The message got through. I could see the astonishment on the faces of young lads like Rory Mallon and Nicky Lambert. This was a rude awakening for them but I had to show them there was something good and worthwhile about being a Wexford hurler because some had forgotten what it felt like and the new guys didn't really know what it should feel like at all.

As for myself, after a depressing four years, finally there was a sense that we could get out of the hole and I wasn't missing the lift. This was the day to put the spring back into my hurling.

The door nearly went off the hinges as we burst back out onto the field but this time we could hear our own fans. There was no game-plan but to win. If Limerick wanted to test this vulnerable Wexford team one more time, we were going to fight them all the way.

The second half never once slowed down. In all there were six goals and 25 points scored. Near the end, I started to feel my words had been in vain as we trailed by two points.

Our tongues hung out of our mouths and we looked dead and buried. But then Clem Smith took down Rory McCarthy around 21 yards from the Limerick goal and we were awarded a free. I looked around to call for Fitzy but leaders do not need to be beckoned and our goalkeeper was already sprinting up the field, ready to take the responsibility of firing us into an All-Ireland semi-final. We needed a goal and Fitzy had the most powerful shot of the lot of us.

There may have been nerves but it didn't show as he absolutely buried the ball to the back of the net. Seconds later the Limerickmen collapsed to their knees as the final whistle blew. I just wanted to run, anywhere. I needed to celebrate; it hadn't felt this good in years. Christ! I had nearly forgotten why I loved the game.

Several of the lads were on the same high. Some of them mentioned my half-time rant to reporters, who asked me what exactly I had said. But by now the dreaded migraine had kicked in and, there in the dressing-room with what felt like a spear going through my head, I couldn't concentrate enough to recall my words. I suspect some journalists thought I was being thick when I replied that I couldn't actually remember what I'd said. The game had taken a lot out of me and my main concern was to take a painkiller to get rid of the pressure building up between my ears.

It didn't take the people of Wexford long to realise the significance of what had happened: we were in an All-Ireland semi-final against Tipperary. I just gave myself a day or two to celebrate and unwind and it was back to the grindstone.

A few days later I was going about my business with C&C when I got a phone call from Griffin asking me to meet him for a chat. We duly met and discussed the challenge ahead. The purpose of the meeting soon emerged: he was touting the idea of bringing Martin Storey back into the panel.

Storey had retired a year earlier but Griffin felt his introduction as a sub could unhinge the Tipp defence and also unsettle Nicky English, who was relatively new to management.

One of our selectors, Davy Morris, disagreed, but Griffin prevailed and I was delighted to see my old buddy returning; we had great craic travelling to training together just like in the old days.

And so the big man came back. And to this day, Griffin will tell you he made a mistake. That was, he didn't bring Tom Dempsey back as well. But that is another story.

We felt we had prepared well and had a fair chance of beating Tipp. But they came out of the blocks at 90 miles an hour and we were eight or nine points down at the break. I felt we could still salvage the game but inside in the dressing-room it was general doom and gloom.

Doc O'Connor, a guy not long on the scene, came over and hit me a dig.

'Jesus, say something, will you? Get it going!' he said through gritted teeth.

Now, I had never really spoken before the Limerick outburst, but I gathered my thoughts, took a drink of water and started talking. There was no point in coming out with more bravado stuff because it won't work every time. Instead I asked the lads to raise their game and, quite calmly, told them I wasn't waiting for any Tipperary man to come out in front of us. Nicky's boys could take the hind tit. I opened the door, and as we filed out I just reminded them we had 35 minutes to save our season.

Enter Larry O'Gorman. How he managed to score those two incredible goals from midfield is still beyond me but he rattled the net twice and, almost singlehandedly, had Tipp on the ropes.

As the game went on, we brought Martin Storey on and he completely unsettled the Tipp full-back line, causing so much chaos and confusion they fumbled ball after ball.

That's where a guy like Tom Dempsey, who was still playing brilliant stuff at club level, could really have made them pay. As it was, and despite Storey's heroics, we were wasteful and our shooting was erratic, and we still trailed until Rory McCarthy grabbed a late goal.

The ding dong battle continued until, near the end, we were awarded a free 45 metres out when Paul Codd was fouled. The ball sailed wide and I had a sickening feeling that with it had gone our 2001 All-Ireland hopes.

With 45 seconds left on the clock, the scores level, and Tipp on the rack, Pat O'Connor, the best referee I have encountered, blew the game up. I was angry because there was still time on the clock, and maybe deep in my heart I knew we had lost our chance.

Again, the county came alive and there was huge spirit and enthusiasm around the place as we looked forward to the replay, which was played the following Saturday evening in a drizzle and a downpour. I started at centre back on John Carroll, who got in behind me, soloed through and kicked a goal to the back of the net. Then I was dispatched onto Brian O'Meara and we all know what happened from there. The two of us were sent off.

Mitch Jordan joined me a moment or two afterwards and in a farcical game, Tipp ran out easy winners by 3-12 to 0-10.

As I have said, the fact Brian got a straight red card and missed the All-Ireland final is something I regret but there wasn't a whole lot going on between us and although I spoke on his behalf at the GAC meeting, from time to time I have had to remind people it wasn't all one-way traffic. I was sent off as well.

For the second time in a year, I sat in the dressing-room as my team got destroyed out on the field. I had let the lads down but really felt sick at what had been one of the worst refereeing decisions of all time. Even now, taking Brian and I out of the equation, it's universally agreed that Pat Horan's job on that All-Ireland semi-final was nothing short of a vaudeville act. He was a joke and I have been living ever since with the consequences of his disastrous decision-making.

Sure, I might have deserved it but Brian O'Meara missed an All-Ireland final because the referee was so poor. Of course we had started it and ultimately had ourselves to blame, but in games all over Ireland, from under-eight to junior B to intercounty senior, that sort of handbags stuff goes on. Pat decided to be a hero and went with the ill-advised counsel of his linesman Pat Aherne, who has also proved a disaster on occasions over the years. Technically, they applied the letter of the law, but if you applied that in every game you wouldn't have six men left on the field at the end of the 70 minutes.

I had tapped Brian and he had hit me back. It was so on and so forth, but to have officials like those two making decisions in an All-

Ireland semi-final, well it just shows what the GAA know sometimes.

The Star newspaper ran a 'Let Brian play' campaign and underneath the logo was a 'Men not wimps' catch-line. They were right but Croke Park's top brass didn't get it and despite all the hype that surrounded the case afterwards, Horan had his report submitted within a few hours of the final whistle.

Nothing anyone could say or do was going to change minds, if any, in Croke Park. I was reported for striking and was back hurling a month later, while Brian missed out on playing in an All-Ireland final. But if people think I got off lightly, they need not worry. That red card and that incident meant I had walked two years on the trot in the Guinness Hurling Championship and by now referees were making extra special efforts to keep an eye on me. I was a marked man. You could have sworn I had killed someone; there was kind of a 'leper factor' about me as far as some people outside Wexford were concerned.

I got many phone calls. Some offered consolation and support; others were less complimentary to say the least. Sometimes it was a case of just putting down the phone to cut off the stream of abuse. Some letters arrived and sometimes I regret I didn't keep them – they might have made colourful material for this book – but really, the bin was the only place for them.

I stood up and took it on the chin and I have to say that those around the village, my neighbours and those close to me, never made an issue of the sending-off. When my mother got over the disappointment, she never blamed me at all but everyone else got a blast alright.

I met Brian at a League match in Nenagh the following year and I walked back 15 yards to shake hands with him but he looked away as he shook and maybe I couldn't blame him. But we met in Wexford Park after that again and he walked by me so I knew that was it. Again, I don't know if I could blame him.

It was the end of an eventful year but I had consolation in the fact that we had at least put the pride back into Wexford hurling. We were rewarded with a holiday to Lanzarote and did a fair bit of fundraising to generate spending money, which was no bother because the goodwill factor was high in the county again.

We raised £20,000 with a race night alone. We put pressure on the county board to get a donation from Croke Park to help the students on the team enjoy their holiday a little better. We were aware the GAA had raked in £535,000 from the replay with Tipperary alone, and while we didn't win the All-Ireland we contributed enormously to the excitement and shape of the season in our games with Laois, Kilkenny, Limerick and Tipperary. And so we wanted just £10,000 to divide among the lads still at college and asked the GAA president, Seán McCague, and his top table, but they refused and we never got a penny from them.

Whether he was directly involved or not, I felt the president should have made a name for himself on this issue, and though I've often been told McCague was a players' man, I don't believe for a moment he was.

On a trip to Amsterdam with C&C, I met a work colleague, Gene Sherry, who was from Scotstown, McCague's stamping ground. Gene sang his praises but I had my own theory.

Darragh Ó Sé could get out of a suspension incurred in a club game and be back to play with Kerry in the All-Ireland series but John Boland, a minor hurler from Tipperary, had to take the GAA to court to play the biggest game of his life.

Although John took the case, the GAA tried to stop him from playing in an All-Ireland final after he had been sent off in the North Tipp minor championship with his club, Toomevara. They wanted to deprive a young chap of playing in an All-Ireland final, a massive opportunity for him, yet the president and his colleagues allowed Ó Sé to return to the fold when, according to the rules, he was suspended and should have missed the final.

It disgusted me.

I met Seán on an All Stars trip early in 2004 and briefly spoke to him. My own feeling is he was not the players' man he was cracked up to be, and I know plenty of the Wexford lads would share my view after our plan to raise a few quid for the students was scuppered. My own opinion is that the current office holder, Seán Kelly, is twice the president, and thank God, we have moved a little in terms of player welfare.

Players don't ask for much. I mean the holiday to Lanzarote was a great break, but apart from that, some mileage expenses for travelling to training and a bit of gear, we pretty much get on with it.

Anyway we had our little break, which was very much male-dominated – about 95 percent of the players decided they wanted to travel without wives or partners.

When we got back some of the lads were wondering if I would call it a day but I had no such intentions. I was hurling well and greatly enjoying the game again after my slump in 1999 and 2000, so I earmarked 2002 as a season of further progress.

Our first Championship game that year was against Dublin, and in a welter of scores we beat them 3-15 to 2-12 in Thurles to qualify for another date with our old pals Kilkenny in the Leinster final at Croke Park. Unfortunately, the script here was pretty much the same as the previous two years. Though they beat us by only two points this time, I became the first ever intercounty senior hurler to be sent off in three Championships in a row.

We were pipped 0-19 to 0-17 but I wasn't on the pitch to witness the end, and to be brutally honest, the referee, Ger Harrington, had to send me off.

It was a wild pull on Martin Comerford. Harrington did very well in that game and leaving me on the field would have been a black mark on his copybook.

This wasn't the way I wanted to make history and while Wexford got ready for the qualifier match against Clare, I resigned myself to the fact that my season was over and there was no escape. I duly received a two-month ban from the game.

And so, unsure of how to cope, I hit the drink and carried the piss-up over for five months. I had been in the media spotlight in the past but this was the worst ever. I believe I got a small taste of how Vinny Jones or Alan Smith or one of those Premiership bad boys must feel when he turns on the TV or picks up the tabloids. There were snide remarks on television, the odd stab in the newspapers and a nasty focus on my mother and family.

Apart from letting my own people down, I had let myself down. It had taken me so long to make my name as a hurler but I had gone from people telling me I was the county's best player in 25 years to just being a dirty little bastard who didn't have the sense to quit when he was losing it. Thing was, deep down I knew I wasn't losing my hurling and had faith that there was a little bit more in the tank.

But after almost six months of drinking, it took an innocent but piercing look from my own two children at around seven o'clock on a November morning to make me see sense. Their Dad coming into the house, rotten drunk, in the half-light of dawn. Was this something they were going to have to put up with for the rest of their childhood?

On many occasions over the year, and I know this might sound melodramatic, I felt my situation resembled that of Roy Keane, who had just walked out on the World Cup. The Saipan incident is history now and the Cork genius is back playing with Ireland, but for 18 months or so he had to live with the tag of letting people down.

Of course Roy's situation split a nation. Mine was far less newsworthy, but it was no less important to me and my family and I was always wondering how the constant controversy was damaging them. The fact I always admired Keane so much, I suppose, created a few parallels in my mind between the two of us. We both had our problems with the drink; neither of us was a stranger to the early shower; and though we played different sports, we would both have built up reputations as loose cannons prone to the red mist followed smartly by the dreaded red card. On top of that, the two of us had suffered bad leg injuries.

I suppose a failed drugs test was about the only thing I didn't get landed with during my career. Roy had also sampled many of the downsides to his sport, though the stakes, at least the financial ones, are obviously higher as captain of Manchester United.

Maybe drawing a little strength from what he went through to get back playing with club and country, I finally decided there was still a little willpower left in my alcohol-soaked brain, and so I arranged the meeting with Griffin.

We spoke for hours. He agreed that maybe there was a last chance at bowing out on a high, one last hope of salvation.

At Vinegar Hill, o'er the pleasant Slaney
Our heroes vainly stood back to back;
And the Yeos at Tullow took Father Murphy
And burned his body upon the rack
Boolavogue

– CHAPTER SIXTEEN –
Vinegar Hill, the farewell

Vinegar Hill holds lots of history for Wexford but I never really saw its beauty for a long time. When Ray Keogh and I were sprinting up and down it, I certainly didn't appreciate its view or historical significance.

Running on Morriscastle beach was not enough for me; I had to push myself to the extreme limit if I was going to make it back with Wexford for one last time and get a chance to redeem myself by hurling my way out of the game. That's what Griffin had told me anyway.

This time it was about Liam Dunne. That may seem selfish to anyone else in the county but it had to be that way. It was time to do my own thing. I took the social element out of my game and almost turned into a hermit.

Jim Bolger the racehorse trainer, who loves Wexford hurling, sent me a cheque for €250 and with it a little note asking me not to retire.

'Don't worry, Jim, I have other things on my mind,' I thought.

To be in the best physical shape of my life, to get back to the level I had achieved in 1996, I had to be in the best mental state of my career as well.

That's where the real battle started because I felt under heavy pressure. Before Christmas, I made up my mind to go at it hell for leather, persuading myself each time I went for a run on Vinegar Hill or the beach. It was a time for keeping your mouth shut and getting on with the job. The beach each morning and evening – such was the plan anyway.

Ray was also keen to lose a bit of weight so he said he would join me on a few runs to The Hill as well. As the two of us were by now associated closely with the bar stool, no-one really believed we were doing the runs together, but we were and it was serious stuff.

It suited me. I had a bit of company now, someone who wouldn't be streets ahead of me and put me off the job before I had even started. The first day I went with Ray, I confessed to him that I had never been to The Hill before and deadly in earnest, he turned around and told me that as a Wexford man I should be ashamed of myself with all that had happened there so many years before.

I was a little embarrassed by Ray's rebuke, but there was no time to wallow anymore and I set about conquering the killer peaks and slopes. The punishment was unreal. For my runs on the beach, I would throw on layers of clothing to sweat out all the toxins and alcohol. But after a few sprints, I would throw off a few layers at the foot of the hill to give me some chance of making it to the top.

Although a friend, Declan O'Connor, and I had put in some groundwork by running four miles every so often, I was coming under brutal pressure on The Hill, which was dominated by a deadly incline so steep I wouldn't even send John Troy up it.

I seized up several times and threw up many more, wondering what the hell I was doing. But I persevered. Some people thought I had lost the plot but I knew what I was doing.

One day, Declan Ruth came out with me and, without intending, he demonstrated the fitness I needed to reach to hurl my way back onto the Wexford team. He was way ahead of me. But later I went back on my own and managed to negotiate the huge sandbags five times in one session.

That was it for me. Every limb and muscle had tightened near the end of my third run and I felt like giving in but stamina was my biggest problem and if I was going to play against the likes of Kilkenny again, I needed to be able to keep up and compete.

One night, with the wind howling and the rain pouring down, I was about 10 seconds away from jacking my session in. I had 'conquered' The Hill three times and felt I hadn't the strength to raise the flag a fourth time. But just as I was about to throw in the towel, Pat Delaney came into my head and I remembered the way he'd roared at me when I lay on the ground in Belfield with my leg smashed.

Pat doesn't know this but he got me up Vinegar Hill a fourth time and gave me all the motivation I needed to make it up a fifth. With tears of pain welling, I ground out the fourth ascent, jogged slowly back down, thought of Delaney with every step and, though almost reduced to walking pace, got back up a fifth time.

I sat down at the top. The wind was howling and it was lonely. I thought of what I had put those closest to me through and what a selfish prick I had been. There, on top of that historic hill, I recalled the way I had neglected my wife and children and what an absolute waste of space I had been for the 16 months I had spent moping in the absence of hurling.

I also wondered what encouragement Griffin might offer if he could see me here now, on top of The Hill, exhausted but with no badness or drink in my system. And fuck it, for a few minutes I was proud of myself again. I got up and stumbled back down, the legs like jelly, going from under me.

The following night I was there again and undertook the same regime. In a perverse sort of a way, I grew to love that hill; it reminded me of who I was and who I needed to be. But while The Hill was a test, the beaches were just as challenging. I wouldn't let a day go by without doing two runs at either Morriscastle or Kilmuckridge and, would you believe, by now I was enjoying it.

Morriscastle at 7 am frightened the shit out of me just as it did at 7 pm – you couldn't see your hand in front of you. But I was ready for it. Togs and socks, wet-suit and plastic bag, jersey and tracksuit bottoms, a cap: they were all I needed. The rest I would do myself.

After two weeks, I decided to cut out the little breaks I'd been giving myself during the training runs and instead chalked out a little circuit, where I would stop and do stomach exercises instead of waiting to get the breath back. My circuit was a 20-minute run, sit-ups and press-ups until my stomach looked like a six-pack, another run against the wind and then three shuttle runs and 10 hill runs. I spent an hour there in the morning and an hour each evening for well over two months.

The windy nights were miserable and I was often afraid of my life that, like my uncle Seán Woulfe, I would be swept out to the raging sea by the howling gales. I sometimes imagined there was someone behind me, someone not too friendly. I was a bit like the man in the poem we learnt at school, *The Ancient Mariner*, 'Like one that on a lonesome road doth walk in fear and dread, and having once turned round walks on and turns no more his head, because he knows a frightful fiend doth close behind him tread.'

I adopted a friendly street light in the distance as comfort, a light I never let out of my sight for long. It was the one bit of assurance I had.

I trained from the first week in November until Christmas and managed to stay out of the pub. Eithne thought the holiday season had come early. The only time I stirred out it would be to have a game of cards with the lads. I had gone from one extreme to the other: from drinking heavily every night to not touching the stuff. People couldn't really believe it but I kept my head down, already thinking ahead to the following summer.

I took a little break from training on Christmas Day and New Year's Day but nearly felt guilty about it when chatting to Doc O'Connor soon after. Doc informed me he had even trained on Christmas Day so I knew the bar had been raised higher again. Even though I was bursting my hole, someone was doing more than me; it only motivated me even more.

As weird and masochistic as it sounds, I grew to love the training regime. It allowed me time on my own and gave me the discipline I needed if I was to go back hurling with the county team again. But the runs, climbs and sprints – I knew in my heart and soul this would be the final such extreme effort. I would never be able to go through such a purgatory again. Never.

My mother in law, May Sinnott would see me running, the rain pissing down and the wind almost driving me back into the sand. She never said anything but I swear she thought I had lost the plot.

When we went away on holidays to Lanzarote with the Wexford team in the new year. I decided to let my limbs and muscles settle in the sea, relax and take the week off training. I had a few drinks every day as well but there was no danger of slipping back into the hole; this was my therapy and I spent a happy week with Ray Keogh, Chris 'Hopper' McGrath and Mitch Jordan.

I didn't feel one bit bad about having a few pints, not even after what I had put people through. This time I felt in control of my life and felt I could stop if I wanted to. This suggested to me I was not after all 'the one' Griffin had referred to.

Sure I had gone overboard on the drink and people might say, with some justification, I had a problem. But as for being an alcoholic? Well, the fact I took a few drinks for a week and then gave it up again reassured me my problem was not full-blown.

So I tried to enjoy the holiday and although it was great craic, there were plenty of times when I was the subject of the team's wit and wisecracks. The lads used to conduct little quizzes in the bar. One day as I walked in some smartass called out: 'And who was the first intercounty hurler to be sent off in three Championships in a row?'

'LIAM DUNNE,' they all roared in unison and fell around laughing. All very well. I can take a slagging from the best of them. But this was not the way I wanted to be remembered after giving 16 years with the team. Instead I stored it. Any motivation was welcome. I just kept repeating the goals I had set for myself. Metaphorically, even though we were away, I had pinned the words 'Honour' and 'Respect' on the walls of my hotel room.

I revealed very little to any of the lads about what I was doing but I knew that when it came to pre-season training and those long runs I used to dread, I would be ready and better than any of the lads at them. And if I could manage those bloody runs so early in the year, there was every chance my hurling would speak for itself later in the season.

The new Wexford manager, John Conran, had been onto me about going back and had assured me I was a big part of his plans but even though I was training my arse off and awaiting the chance to meet Offaly and their selector Pat Delaney, I didn't let onto John that my mind was fully made up. I told him I needed time to think about it.

He was stern: 'People tell me I'm stone mad to be even thinking about you,' he warned. 'But as I said, you're a big part of my plans, Liam, and although some people don't want you involved, I do.'

He called a fitness test for the Tuesday night after we returned from our team holiday. The night before the test, I rang him and told him I was coming back 100 percent.

'That's all I wanted to hear,' he said before hanging up. It was a short conversation and in fairness, there was nothing much to be said. When the fitness test was held, most of the lads had faces on them like they had to hand over a winning lottery ticket but this time I was up at the front, for the first time in ages.

As Sod's Law would have it, they decided to abolish those lung-wrenching and mind-numbing long runs I used to dread. I was looking forward to a chance to show what I could do, but the training had changed completely. We had shuttle runs and heart monitors, sprints and strides. All around me, lads were stretched out on the ground, suffering with their lungs and thighs. But I got through it okay and the lads started to twig I had been doing extra training.

I had let it be known I meant business, and though I was only a sub for the first League game against Derry, I was on the Club Lemon the night before. Most players are off the beer at that stage of the season anyway but this was a big deal for me.

Before that game, Dickie Murphy, a top senior referee and a former Wexford selector, took me by surprise by asking me would I now feel under pressure with referees after all the sendings-off.

'No, I wouldn't think so, Dickie,' I replied without thinking. But he had hit the nail on the head, and later that evening I mentioned our conversation to John Conran and Martin Quigley.

'Well, do you feel under pressure?' came the question.

'Yeah, I'll be bricking it every day I go out, to be honest,' I replied.

And it was true. One wild pull from Liam Dunne and I was off again and the reputation was totally gone this time. So I made a few decisions before the start of the season. My main task was to get to the ball first; I had never been the fastest thing on two legs so, now more than ever, I would have to fall back on experience and an ability to read the game. Secondly, I would no longer pull on the ball. That might sound crazy for an intercounty hurler but I couldn't afford to get sent off again and I knew I was a marked man in every match I played. No, instead I would bat or block.

And I would do it my own way. I even decided to go over to Parkhead and watch Celtic play Hearts just before the start of the League. Nowadays a manager would laugh at you if you asked for time off to go and get married, never mind tear away with the lads for a few days. But I knew what I was doing and had a feeling the break back to reality would do me no harm at all. I had trained my guts out for several months, a little respite would do me the world of good.

John Conran agreed and so a few of us went over to watch the Celts, and in particular my hero Henrik Larsson. It was a great crew that included my brother Seán and some old friends. It was a brilliant experience, capped by the fact the Bhoys won 3-0. I spent much of the game observing Martin O'Neill on the sideline; it would have been nice to meet him.

When I returned to the county team, my focus was on writing more history and not wallowing in the past. And do you know what?

Playing Derry in my first game back was a grand way to begin a season of redemption. There was no glare or spotlight, no expectations and few supporters.

As the game went on, however, the team almost collapsed and I came on. I had just arrived when a Derry player stared at me like I'd just been released from jail.

'Are you the lad who was sent off last year?' he nervously enquired.

'Yep,' I replied, 'and the year before and before that again.'

He was supposed to be my marker but after that he kept his distance, maybe half afraid I'd hit him a tip.

Anyway, we were five points down when I came in at centrefield, got a point and set Mitch Jordan up for another one. First game over. We won by two.

The Wexford papers, who had been good to me during my troublesome three years, wrote that I changed the game, but that was rubbish; I had hit only about four balls. And so I was again named as a sub for the game against Tipperary at Nenagh.

Once again, we were being destroyed. My clubmate Keith Rossiter was taken off, which I felt was a disgrace because Mark O'Leary had scored only a point off him. I came on and O'Leary said to me: 'What are they doing taking him off?'

I agreed with the Tipp man and let the selectors know what I felt at the half-time break. But we were well beaten again and had to beat Offaly at Wexford Park by at least 12 points, just to make the second stage of the League.

This was the first time I'd been in the same stadium with my pal Pat Delaney since the broken-leg episode in 1997 and I really revelled in beating them by 14, though we had been six points down at one stage.

It was nice to get a chance to hurl on young Brian Carroll that day, though. I had remembered Brian's late father, Pat, very well and recalled Pat Fleury's great speech when Offaly won the 1985 All-Ireland final. I would later play Railway Cup with Brian in Rome; he could be as good as his Dad.

I was selected at centre back for the Offaly game and scored a point from 100 yards to a huge roar from the stands. That put us eight up and a Paul Codd goal left us on our way to the big win we needed. I ran towards the tunnel, raised my fist to the crowd and suddenly saw Delaney in front of me.

He turned away.

'That's the first part of the job,' I thought to myself. 'The next will be at Nowlan Park in the Championship.'

Galway ended our League hopes after that and we prepared to face Offaly on the June Bank Holiday Monday. I remember saying to Eithne before that game that it was the first time in my career I thought I wouldn't make the first 15 for a Championship game. I don't know what it was but I had a premonition I wouldn't make it.

And the next thing we heard, Rory Mallon, who was flying it at corner-back, just left us and headed off to America. They moved Keith Rossiter back to cover for him and, to my huge relief, I was named at wing-back.

It would have been a dire feeling to have started from the bench for the first time in my Championship career and I later mentioned my pre-match jitters to Conran. He said he couldn't understand where I was getting this from because I was the first name on his team-sheet.

I was still concerned about my status, however. In the past, I had always used a heavy hurl, but in latter years, wary I would get roasted by some guy 10 years younger, I decided to lighten my hurls. Albert Randall, my hurley-maker and old friend, knew what I was about and though the sticks were now lighter, he still managed to make ones that fitted me like a glove.

We knew the game was speeding up. Albert left out three or four sticks and asked me to pick my favourite. He then pointed out those he considered best for me, and 10 times out of 10 over the years he would be right and I would bow to his superior wisdom.

Of course, in the Offaly game Rory Hanniffy and I clashed on the first pull of a ball and my hurley broke. But I had my spares well broken in and ready to play a high-speed Championship match.

I have never understood how lads play with just the one stick every year and then when it comes to the Championship they break their number-one hurl and have to use a replacement they have no connection with.

And this Offaly game was a typical Championship match. I needed my stick to be light so I could swing it fast and under pressure. I had to use my head and experience to compensate for my lack of pace. Still, all the experience in the world cannot legislate for playing with Wexford. And this was a typical display; we went from eight points down to winning by one, 0-16 to 1-12.

Near the end, Brian Carroll missed a free for them from 40 yards out and I screamed at Pat O'Connor that he owed us 45 seconds from the Tipperary game two years earlier. I'm not sure he understood what I was on about but in the end we hung on for dear life to get through to meet Kilkenny yet again, our fourth Leinster final meeting in six years.

After the Offaly game, I was introduced to official GAA drug-testing for the first time. It was like a scene straight from *Fr Ted*. The former Kilkenny hurler Richie Power was a steward that day and part of his job was to haul four players, two from each team, into the dressing-room for the tests.

Of course, my name was called, and as I ran into the tunnel, waving and pumping my fists at the crowd, Richie nabbed me and almost cringed with the embarrassment of having to tell me what lay ahead.

In a newspaper interview with the journalist Christy O'Connor earlier that day, I had joked that I'd been caught for everything else so it would be no surprise if I was done for failing a drugs test. But to tell the truth, I wasn't laughing as I was led into a tiny room just away from the dressing-rooms.

My team-mate MJ Furlong was dragged in with me and we were

handed little tubs by an official of the Irish Sports Council and told to piddle 75 milligrams of our best.

It was one hell of a farce. MJ was grand. He had been on the pitch for only the last two minutes and could fill the River Slaney at the driest of times anyway. He was done and dusted after a minute or two.

But I was in trouble. Forgive the graphic description, but I was so dehydrated I couldn't even force out a dribble.

'I'll turn on the taps for you, that might help,' the guy from the Sports Council ventured.

'What in the name of Jaysus difference will that make?' I asked in disbelief, as MJ roared laughing on his way out of the room.

Looking around, I saw the two Offaly lads, Damien Murray and one of the subs, had done the sensible thing and brought their gear into the room with them. They were showered and changed by the time they had their business complete.

Anyway, with all the water I consumed, things finally started to happen and as I went about my business I was horrified to notice the guy from the Sports Council staring at my family jewels while I filled his tub.

'What in the name of Christ are you looking at?' I roared.

'Oh sorry, we have to keep an eye on things in case anyone tries to slip a foreign substance into the tub.'

'Oh sweet Jesus!'

I nearly cried but managed to produce 70 milligrams and, embarrassed as hell, handed it to him.

'You're still five mills short,' he pointed out.

I burst out laughing, tilted the tub to one side so the precious liquid reached the 75-milligram line and said: 'Don't spill any of it and you'll be alright.' Then I left the room.

Two weeks later, I received a letter saying I had passed the test with flying colours, so obviously your man had done a good job keeping it all in the tub.

And so it was all set up for another tilt with Kilkenny in the Leinster final. You would get so sick of playing these lads after all the beatings they dished out since 1997. That's why the 2004 team enjoyed so much beating them, because it was totally unexpected and out of the blue.

Before the game, Griffin rang to tell me I would be marking John Hoyne. All he kept saying was: 'He's a hardy bastard, a tough hoor.'

I didn't need Liam to tell me that. It was like marking John Power all over again. But Brian Cody knew who he wanted on me.

Before the throw-in, we started the parade and I broke momentarily because I saw Cody out of the corner of my eye. He had always backed me up, especially in the three years I'd been sent off. Even after the clash with Martin Comerford, he spoke in my favour. The man has a ferocious appetite to win and I think he is the driving force behind that Kilkenny team because even when their hunger dips, Cody keeps the ship on course.

I don't really know why but I went over to Brian and shook hands with him as we headed up along the Hogan Stand. People asked me afterwards why I did it and I just replied that it was something I wanted to do.

I still wanted to take his crown. We had run Kilkenny close in 2002 but, to be frank, they could have ended this game at half-time and Eddie Brennan and DJ Carey could have had six goals between them.

We absolutely caved in after the break, though I was reasonably happy with the firefighting job I had done on my own patch and was mildly surprised when one newspaper, the *Irish Mirror*, gave me a rating of five the following morning and predicted I had graced Croke Park for the last time.

Players do read papers but I smiled when I read this, knowing I had marked four Kilkenny lads, including Hoyne, Martin Comerford and Henry Shefflin, and held them all scoreless.

Like I said, I had changed my whole game so I didn't stand out anymore. I don't remember one incident in that match where I pulled on the ball. I just blocked, and when my opponent went to shoot, I tried to shoo him away from the posts, keeping him at bay. And while I succeeded, Kilkenny were awesome and the result went against us.

In the end, and believe me, the end couldn't come quick enough, they beat us 2-23 to 2-12. It was my sixth time losing a Leinster final. I had been beaten in 92, 93, 94, 2001, 2002 and now in 2003, which I have to say was one of the worst thrashings of the lot.

To be truthful, I had expected a few smart comments or jibes from the Kilkenny lads during that game about my three red cards in a row but to be fair, there wasn't a word out of any of them, and no other player from any team I faced in the 2003 Championship offered an opinion on the matter, which just shows the character of the players.

The Wexford team needed to show some character now. We had an unmerciful row at our first training session back after the final. John Conran had a go at us because some lads on the team didn't have their socks pulled up for the parade. Management also tore strips off us for throwing water bottles around the field, expecting them to come in like lackeys and gather them up. The county board had been fined €750 or something because only Darren Stamp had his socks pulled up for the parade, but I thought this focus on the pre-match hullabaloo was the greatest load of horse manure and I walked off the field in disgust.

Dave Guiney came over to me and put his arm around me.

'Take your hands off me, Dave,' I snapped.

He had a go back and then Adrian Fenlon had a go at him. Most of the boys got involved in one way or another but I kept going into the dressing-room, where John Conran followed me.

'This is a load of shite, John. We're after getting hammered in a Leinster final and all we're worried about is who had their socks pulled up and who didn't and who was throwing water bottles around the pitch. It's a load of bollocks.'

But John was only a scapegoat for my anger. We had been rolled over by Kilkenny and I was furious because there is no county I hate losing to more than them. John had his own problems and I shouldn't have had a go at him. He found it difficult to get instructions to our players that day; anytime he stepped onto the pitch, he knew the county board would be hammered with another fine, the victims of another idiotic GAA rule.

It also didn't help matters that Niamh Fitzpatrick, someone all the players knew and trusted, had left the camp. She and John didn't see eye to eye on a number of issues and we were without her services for the Leinster final. I felt she was always worth having around but it was the manager's call.

For me, Niamh had been an absolute star; it was no surprise to me that she was snapped up by the Irish Olympic team straightaway. Many times I had poured my heart out to her and she had greatly assisted my mental preparation before games.

It was my own fault that I felt I needed her more than most in the 2003 season but I couldn't blame John Conran for deciding she was surplus to requirements. I had put my hands into the fire in 2000, 2001 and 2002 and had come out burned but the manager had the whole team to look after, not just me.

But as the year went on we missed her. And the year did go on, despite the fact we were annihilated by Kilkenny and drew Waterford in the qualifiers.

Waterford are the biggest enigma in the GAA; they had just been beaten by Cork in the Munster final, and on their day, well, they were likely to blow us away.

We travelled down to Nowlan Park to play them on a Saturday evening in July and as we walked out onto the pitch, we could see it was like a billiard table, it was so smooth. The Wexford fans had made the journey in force as did the Waterford supporters and the atmosphere was unreal.

Of course, true to the great tradition of the Irish weather, by the time we changed and emerged from the dressing-room, there was a gale and a monsoon to greet us. In fact the rain was so strong you could hardly see in front of you.

Well, we couldn't, but the Waterford lads certainly had no problem and within 10 minutes they went ahead by eight points to three and it looked like we were about to get creamed, something that looked even more likely when we lost Adrian Fenlon through injury.

But sometimes fate intervenes, and though Adrian is one of our best ever players, his substitution allowed Larry Murphy in from the bench. Larry had been injured earlier in the year and frustrated because he couldn't get his place but, by Jesus, he turned the game around that day.

He started to create havoc in the Waterford defence and each time the ball went his way, he either scored or broke it to the likes of Rory Jacob, meaning that although we were played off the field for most of the first half, they led by only a point and you could already tell the pressure of being overwhelming favourites was getting to them. I would go as far as saying they got a mental block in the second half. We tore out of the traps and hit two or three quick points and it seemed as if Larry was involved in all of them. We dictated the game from there on and Waterford started their usual trick of switching forwards all over the place.

Dan Shanahan was moved away from me and out came Paul Flynn.

'Jaysus,' he groaned. 'I didn't think I'd have to face you today.'

And while I chuckled back at him, he had the ball over the bar, which wiped the smile off my face.

Near the end, big Dan came by me again and I tugged his jersey and asked him if I could have it afterwards.

'It would be an honour to have yours as well, Liam boy,' he said, with a sort of a smile that made it look like he had half his front teeth missing.

Dan had the year of his life in 2004 but I had felt for years that he must have been the victim of local politics because Dave Bennett and he, both Lismore men, were the first to be taken off whenever the team went bad. Both of them can hurl and, from what I hear, are dedicated trainers, so it must have been local stuff that kept them down – the politics isn't just confined to Wexford after all.

We clung on in one of the most tension-filled endings to a game and came out on top 1-20 to 18 points, and they were just devastated. As the final whistle blew, I ran to the sideline, where young Billy was thrust in front of a steward, who lifted him out to me. The young lad knew it had been a great day at the office and just smiled and looked around the field, taking everything in.

I think Billy will be a great little hurler. It's only better he's getting and he can strike cleanly with both sides already even though he's only seven. Griffin asked me about him one day and I said all he needed to be a fine player was the heart, to which our former manager responded: 'Ah, would you leave him alone, his little heart is only growing.'

Suddenly, people recognised the Wexford hurlers again. They didn't shy away as you walked by them in the street or pretend not to see as you slumped out of Croke Park, destroyed by another sending-off. No, we were heroes again. It's so fickle. The county went berserk but in fairness to the fans there has always been a core support around.

Just after we had beaten Offaly and qualified for the provincial final, we held a barbecue and race night and raised an amazing €45,000 for the Supporters' Club. It showed what was out there for us if we could get back to winning ways. It felt like we were on our way back when the All-Ireland quarter-final draw pitted us against Antrim. The excitement only increased. No offence to the lads up north – they're fighting an uphill battle all the time – but we were expected to win this one easily and the supporters could smell an All-Ireland semi-final.

At the back of our heads, we couldn't help but look forward to an All-Ireland semi-final. We never really knuckled down to the prospect of playing Antrim; the challenge just didn't really faze us. But it should have.

Dinny Cahill had them fine-tuned when we met them in Croke Park, ahead of the semi-final between Tipperary and Offaly. They got two goals in the first half and another that was disallowed for no reason at all. That score would surely have put them out of sight.

The year before, they had tested Tipp, but in all fairness, they couldn't beat us, could they? Well, they had us on the ropes until late in the second half, when Paul Codd stepped up and buried a 21-yard free. We got another straightaway and that left them on the ropes.

But they weren't finished yet and brought on Aidan Delargy at corner forward, who scored some lovely points. If he'd been brought on earlier, we were finished. We got them by three points in the end, 2-15 to 2-12, but we can thank Rory McCarthy for that win because he really saved us. Like several others I had fallen into the complacency trap and had a stinker, but at least we survived.

At the end of the game, the referee, my old friend Pat Horan, ran 50-odd yards in my direction. Pat had sent me off in 2001, and as he approached me the Wexford lads must have wondered what reception he would get. He stuck out his hand.

'I wish you the very best of luck in the All-Ireland semi-final,' he said.

'Thanks, Pat.'

He wasn't finished: 'I sincerely mean that.'

'I know you do.'

He didn't have to do that but our relationship didn't just go back to the Brian O'Meara incident. I had known him from a shinty trip in 1988 and while it's hard, sometimes it's better to just leave stuff on the field. Besides, we had a semi-final with Cork to look forward to. I played the best hurling of my career against them in those epic 1993 League final games.

This time one or two of that Wexford team were still intact, while they had an entire line-up of new faces.

It was a huge task for us to stand up to them. Around 10 years previously, I peaked against them and received an All Star for my efforts, but it would be asking a lot to reproduce that form in a different era, especially at the ripe old age of 35 and marking possibly the fastest hurler in the land, Ben O'Connor.

We had two weeks to prepare, though, so I was going to give it everything. Wexford went Boom! Kids on the streets wore our jersey; the feel-good factor was back and everyone wanted to hurl the game as you went about your work.

Our build-up was intense and on the ball. Mick Kinsella started to do a lot of coaching work with us and Griffin was around again to help out. We knew one area of great concern to us was the half-forward line. Cork had dominated that sector all year long and had snuffed out teams by winning the battles on that line. So we devised a game-plan to disrupt their lethal half-forwards. The entire defence, midfield and goalkeepers met for video analysis one evening and we drew up a blueprint that would stop the likes of O'Connor and the McCarthys, Timmy and Niall, from running amok.

My bit was simple. Their goalkeeper, Donal Óg Cusack, hit 95 percent of his puck-outs down on top of their big corner forward Alan Browne, which didn't make sense to me when you had the speedster Ben O'Connor on the far side of the field.

Before the game, I rang Griffin to ask him his opinion on stopping Ben the Bullet. 'Get to the ball first,' was his curt reply.

And so our instructions were that each time the Cork half-forward line retreated inside their own half for our puck-outs we should go back with them and either win the break or prevent them from flying down into our half. We had to take risks, take a chance, try and get to the sliotar first and then hope like hell it would break in your favour.

It was potentially my last game for the county, something I dreaded. And in the past, under such pressure, I would have retreated home and got all wrapped up in the tension. But this year, I was taking a different path. I was happy that my fitness would ensure that discipline would not be a problem and while I lived most of the year like a hermit, if I wanted to go and relax, I would do so.

Armed with the security that I was in great shape and had plenty of tactical knowledge of both the Wexford and Cork teams, I decided to kick the heels up one Friday night, just 12 days before the big match. Eithne and I had arranged to take a trip to Wexford town to see the film *Veronica Guerin*. Martin Storey and Rosaleen decided they would come along and so we agreed to meet up outside the cinema a few minutes before the film started.

Storey went to pay but was told all the seats had been sold. I could see he was disappointed as we had been looking forward to a night's company so I suggested we go to Charlie Kavanagh's pub for a quick pint.

'Jesus, you're not supposed to be drinking,' he said.

'One won't kill me,' I replied.

And up we went. I was immediately aware people were looking at me so I sent Storey to the bar and we sipped away for a while. Again, eyes turned in my direction but I was my own man and didn't need some fellow in a bar to tell me what I should and shouldn't be doing.

So we ordered a few more and it turned out to be a great night between the four of us, and while I hoped and prayed Adrian Fenlon and the lads wouldn't hear about it, I knew it was just the relaxation I needed in the lead-up to that Cork game.

Of course when I woke up the next morning I didn't exactly feel like a primed athlete. But I dragged myself out of the bed and went to work. I had to lacquer a stairs for someone and the smell of that didn't help me either.

I arrived back home at 5 pm and even though Liam Griffin was taking a training session at 6.30 in Wexford Park, I knew I wouldn't be able to make it. So dialling John Conran's number, I came clean – well mostly clean.

'John, I have a sick stomach. I won't be able to make training and I'm actually in bed right now.'

Not a word of a lie and John was fine about the whole thing. Of course, I didn't tell him fully why I had a sick stomach.

If you ask me, that little bit of craic with Martin Storey and the two wives was the best fun I had in ages. Like the visit to Parkhead, it crowned me. My preparation had been intense but you can't maintain that all day, every day, and in order to be fresh for the All-Ireland semi-final, I knew those few pints were as good as any sprint or stamina run. And when match day came along, I felt like a million dollars: refreshed, confident and ready to restore my reputation. I knew how important it was for Wexford to win that game but it was equally important that if I was going to retire, people would remember me as a hurler.

And in the dressing-room, I reminded myself once more that it could be my last game for Wexford, and as I went through my normal pre-match routine, I did it more solemnly than ever before. Thinking of Mam one last time, I burst out of the dressing-room like Carl Lewis and out into the light.

After the game, Larry O'Gorman asked me what was that sprint out of the blocks all about.

'You made me look bad,' he said, deadly serious. 'I had to make a break after you and it nearly killed me!'

Jesus, Croke Park never looked as well. I looked around and made sure to take in everything. There were over 50,000 people cheering or jeering. It was a daunting arena to be in. I knew I might never get back there again so I made a mental recording of everything I saw.

The glare. It seems everyone is staring at you with a big bright lens.

The colour. Sprinting out in front of the purple and gold rainbow in front of Hill 16, all of us hoping to find the gold at the end of it.

The concentration. From Fitzy to the referee, everyone is focused, and even in the pre-match puck-around, no-one wants to drop a ball.

The goons or match-day stewards. The gents on the sideline who walk around Croke Park with the puffed-up air of a US President about to hit the red button but serve little purpose.

The opponents. Sometimes, though not always, I can tell if a guy really wants to be out here. It's written on his face.

There were a lot more Cork fans than Wexford fans in the stadium, which was strange because they don't usually bother turning up in droves for semi-finals down there. Maybe they were expecting something special. Or else they just wanted this win as much as we did. Like ourselves, Cork hadn't exactly set the world alight with All-Ireland titles in recent years.

The whole day went by me like a rocket but something I do remember was the stupid warm-up we undertook in front of Hill 16. These bloody drills are all the rave now, but in my book they are a load of baloney and are used on match days mainly to justify the trainer's existence.

Anyway, within a few minutes, I heard the unmistakable voice of Marty Morrissey calling out the names of the Cork team.

'Would you please welcome the Rock of Cloyne, the one and only Diarmuid O'Sullivan' and 'One of Ireland's top forwards, Joe Deane.'

The Cork crowd lapped it up and cheered in delight as their heroes were announced in glowing terms, but it really got up my nose.

'Would you listen to those arrogant bastards?' I roared at our lads. 'Who the fuck do they think they are?'

I kept drilling the message into the team, trying to hammer home the message that this Cork team were way ahead of themselves. Next thing, just as my words were sinking in, I heard, 'And now, the marvellous Damien Fitzhenry.'

'Waaahhheeeyyy!'

The roar from our lot was almost as deafening as Cork's. It was a circus, and the lads started laughing. To tell the truth, by the time Marty called out, 'The ageless wonder, Liam Dunne,' I was half looking forward to the cheer I would get.

With my main motivational tool out the window, I shrugged my shoulders and smirked as the rest of the names were called out and the

Wexford supporters went berserk. Now for my battle with Ben the Bullet.

We actually played the game-plan to a T, but to be frank, I was very lucky all during that game, because when Ben and I retreated for a break from the Wexford puck-out, the ball just seemed to hop in my path. If I took two steps to the left, it came with me, and if I hopped to the right, well, it was there as well. I motored along pretty impressively on the wing before John Conran opted to move me into the centre-back spot in a switch with Declan Ruth. Our men followed and Ben O'Connor zipped in after me towards the centre-forward spot.

'Jaysus, Ben,' I thought. 'Would you ever feck off and give an old man a bit of peace.'

We could have been a little bit sharper in the full-back line, however. Setanta Ó hAilpín was on Doc O'Connor, leaving Dave Guiney to look after Alan Browne, who was winning most of their puck-outs. I would have swapped our corner-backs and let Dave plague Setanta for the 70 minutes. But with me being back in the centre, the whole thing had gone full circle and it was a fine feeling to be there again in an All-Ireland semi-final, 10 years after playing the best stuff of my life there. Against Cork as well.

I really enjoyed the game, especially when we went five points up and looked like we were on our way to an All-Ireland final.

'Oh Christ,' I whispered, 'we're nearly there.'

Maybe after all the shit that had gone on for the past three years, I wasn't too far away from the summit once more. As the sun shone down, I appreciated why I had been in tears climbing Vinegar Hill and running in Kilmuckridge and Morriscastle on all those early mornings. This was the feeling I lived for every day of my life.

But Wexford hurlers are famous for snatching defeat from the jaws of victory, and while I knew we wouldn't cruise into the final, I didn't think we would cave in like we did either.

In the space of 11 lousy and agonising minutes, our five-point lead turned into a six-point deficit. Cork nabbed two goals. I'm not sure if either of them was legal but the ref, Aodhán Mac Suibhne, decreed they were. Alan Browne shot over a great point with time just up. It left them three ahead.

My lungs stopped pumping air and, desperately looking into the vast blue sky above Croke Park, I pleaded with God to lend us a hand. I'm not a religious man and the last time I had chatted with the Man Upstairs was during the last few minutes of the 1996 All-Ireland final, when I begged Him not to let Mike Houlihan's late free hit the back of the net.

God must have felt sorry for me because He listened to my prayers back then and He did it again in 2003. For whatever reason, He came up trumps once more and I will never as long as I live forget the sequence that followed.

Fitzy took a long puck-out and the ball broke to Tom Kenny, who was brilliantly hooked by Mick Jacob, who robbed him and sent a pass towards Mitch Jordan, who didn't hang around long and instead sent a pass to Rory McCarthy, who was on the run and heading away from the Cork goal. Still, it didn't seem to matter to Rory where he was heading because he almost ripped open Donal Óg Cusack's net with a rasping shot.

'Oh God, thank you!' I cried, with my face to the heavens.

Ben O'Connor was also staring at the sky but for a different reason, I would guess.

The final whistle blew straightaway and I tapped Ben on the chest and as we swopped jerseys I started to babble about, of all things, the Celtic soccer team. Earlier in the week, I had read that Donal Óg was a huge Celtic fan and was organising a trip to Parkhead and so I started waffling to Ben, who probably hadn't a clue what I was on about.

But this was a great feeling, one I had forgotten existed. Excited and drained at the same time, I went to the sideline to look for Billy and approached a member of the Garda to ask for his help.

'Where's the child?' the garda enquired.

'Somewhere in the Cusack Stand,' I panted.

'You may find him yourself,' the garda laughed and walked off, leaving me to pace the sideline up and down like a weary donkey, looking for the young lad.

As the crowd cheered I spotted my great pal Martin Dempsey in the crowd and went over and gave him Ben's jersey. The crowd cheered louder as, barechested, I shook a defiant fist in their direction before tearing back into the dressing-room. I cringed later that night when I saw TV footage of it because I looked like William Wallace from *Braveheart* rallying his troops but I suppose it was one of those days.

The replay proved to be my last game in Croke Park. We gave it everything in the drawn game and even though we hit two early goals in the rematch, I knew deep down we were never going to play as well again. I was moved to centre-back. And despite the fact we started brightly, and a big crowd turned up to support us, we mostly huffed and puffed around the place while Cork did all the hurling.

I hurled my own patch pretty well even though The Bullet did nab two points off me. Again there were one or two doubts over some of Cork's goals but they were by far the better team and deserved to make it through. They came at us in droves and we had no answer in the second half.

It was funny. Looking around with the game over and still 10 minutes to play, I had an eerie feeling and turned around to talk to Ben in between a break of play.

'Win, lose or draw, at least you have some chance of being here many more days,' I told him.

'Not at all,' he replied. 'There's plenty of hurling left in you.'

But I knew that time was up, and when the final whistle blew, we shook hands and I dropped my head in disappointment. Walking off the field, I looked around at the four corners of the great field of dreams and knew I would never be back as a player again.

Before I had time to think, Diarmuid O'Sullivan, the Cork full-back, came over to shake my hand. Billy was with me this time and

Diarmuid took off his jersey and gave it to him. The young lad was delighted because while Sully had a tough time in the first game, he was absolutely awesome in the replay and Billy was fascinated as he burst out of the square and drove the sliotar down the field.

I was last into the dressing-room, where Mick Kinsella grabbed me and sort of pinned me against the wall.

'This is not a time to make any rash decisions,' he said. 'You're after having the year of your life – you've hurled as well as ever.'

At the start, Mick and I hadn't been the best of buddies. As an officer of the county board, he went mad one year and demanded our shirts back after we swapped jerseys with Laois. I lost the plot with him and threw a jersey in his face. But we had mellowed since then and got on a lot better in recent years. And I think both of us had the same interest at heart and that was Wexford hurling.

And here I was at the end of my particular role for Wexford hurling, finished. Dejected, I sat there in the dressing-room, saying nothing and taking everything in. This was my last time in a Wexford dressing-room. I looked over at Fitzy, one of the best of them. Sometimes it was his way or the highway, but he was a friend, an old reliable.

Darren Stamp was in one of his trances; he often goes into them after losing games. He dropped off the Wexford panel in 2004 but maybe he can come back a better man and carry on Oulart's tradition of supplying defenders for Wexford.

Beside Darren was Darragh Ryan. The man is just awesome, an inspiration on and off the field. I wished we had more years on the field together.

Skippy Ruth was there as well, one of the lads. His standards went so high there at one stage that they would inevitably slip for a little time. And now they are back up there again.

I looked over at Rory Mac. He was baby-faced when all this started for him in 1996 but the innocence of it all is gone now. He grew up a lot after that All-Ireland final win.

Adrian Fenlon, the iron-man of the team, was close by.

Larry O was drying himself, absolutely gutted. He was the best hurler I ever shared a field with and that includes Brian Whelahan, Willie O'Connor, any of them you care to mention. He would have been Hurler of the Year two or three times if he was with Kilkenny.

There was Paul Codd beside me. There's only one Paul Codd. You couldn't possibly make another.

I didn't want to take my jersey off just then. It didn't feel right. Instead, I put my head down and thought of older team-mates with whom I used to sit all those years ago. The ghosts of Wexford past.

Ger Cushe: I would trust him with my life. Martin Storey: one of my closest friends – the craic we had. The O'Connors: they would go through a wall for you. Billy Byrne: respect.

All the old names and faces came back to me and, more than ever before, I took in the atmosphere and just sat back to look at the lads. John Conran came over and shook hands with me.

'Good luck, Liam. I'll be talking to you. Don't make any decisions yet.'

But there was no need to even respond to John. I nodded at him and thought about something I had dreaded for several years. For what I took to be the last time, I pulled my purple and gold jersey over my head. It felt like a piece of me went with it.

Did you ever really doubt when you set out at the start?
Did you hope that you'd achieve the goals on which you set your heart?
At times it must have been so hard to keep your focus true;
At last you're past the post and congratulations due
Card from Anne Woulfe to Liam Dunne

– CHAPTER SEVENTEEN –
Respect in the heel of the hunt

Rome, November 8, 2003. Hurling had left me in a mess a year ago but it got me to within an inch of the Pope as well. Since I retired, I have learned never to underestimate the power of hurling. A lot of my work contacts are made through the game. The little perks and bonuses that come with the sport have set me up nicely and even though you are gone, you are not forgotten.

Just a year ago, I was getting out of my bed in Kilmuckridge and drinking cans of beer at two o clock in the morning. Now I'm in the foyer of a hotel in Rome, getting ready to meet Il Papa with seven or eight lads from the Kilkenny hurling team, each one of them a superstar. And although I put the work into getting here, it's because of hurling that I have got my life back in order in such a short space of time.

Henry Shefflin, John Hoyne, Brian Whelahan, Brian Carroll, young Tommy Walsh, and the Hanniffys were all in the hotel lobby, waiting to play against Connacht in the Railway Cup final and then visit the Vatican. They treated me as though I was their team–mate and, for that weekend only, I was. I loved every minute of it.

The Railway Cup may have become the laughing stock of the GAA world but it had been 10 years since I won my last medal in that competition and it was time for another. We were in Rome to do the job. Not long after Cork knocked us out of the Championship, Mick Jacob rang my house, told me he was a selector and wondered if I was interested in playing in the competition.

'Jaysus, Mick, I've forgotten about the Railway Cup a long time ago. It's the other direction I'm heading in. Forget about me.'

But Mick wasn't done: 'We have Ulster in the semi-final and the final is in Rome.'

'Count me in, Mick,' I interrupted. 'Jaysus, do your best for me now.'

I nodded like a headbanger at a rock concert as he told me the plan. The prospect of playing in this competition had suddenly become strangely attractive.

Rome. What a great and unique way to say goodbye to top-flight hurling! If I could just get on the panel, there would be a seat on the plane with my name on it. When we travelled to Casement Park to play Ulster, the pre-match training session turned into a booze-up for some of the Wexford lads on the team, myself included. Darragh Ryan was off to Boston and Skippy Ruth were heading to Lanzarote so both of them were going to miss the final anyway, and they weren't too bothered about playing Ulster.

But Noel Skehan, the manager, was and he had words with Skippy after we eventually made the team hotel at 2 am. I said nothing and headed off to bed.

When I awoke, I was amazed to hear I had been picked to play at left-wing back. To be honest, I felt I was just making up the numbers and that Skehan had never been a fan of mine, but fair dues to him, he picked me and we beat Ulster.

Some friends and I had a trip to Parkhead organised for the same weekend as the Railway Cup final in Rome so that had to be cancelled. And so I headed off to Italy to play the men from the west in the final.

I took it seriously, trained hard on my own for it. And when we arrived over there I was glad I did, because it turned out to be one of the best weekends of my life.

Not only did I maintain my fitness and form at maximum but once the game was out of the way we absolutely tore the arse out of the trip. I got to know the likes of John Hoyne, with whom I'd had many battles, and Brendan Murphy, all those lads I had played against but didn't really know.

In the final itself, Connacht were well up at half-time, but even in a much-maligned competition like the Railway Cup, which people said was on its knees, I noticed how much the Kilkenny men wanted to win.

First up for the half-time pep talk was Henry Shefflin, who said we were a disgrace, and he wasn't far wrong. Then Michael Kavanagh had a few words about what winning another Railway Cup medal would mean to everyone, especially the likes of me, who had won one a decade earlier.

Brian Whelahan wanted it too and said so, and we were a different team in the second half. Hoyne started the ball rolling with a goal. Gary Hanniffy made a huge difference when he came on as a sub. At the end of the match, which we won by two points, 3-9 to 2-10, Tommy Walsh ran over to me and we started hugging; it meant a lot to the Leinster team and that just made the weekend.

Afterwards, Tom O'Riordan of the *Irish Independent* wrote a report headed 'Dunne's Railway Cup of honour', in which he referred to me holding my medal 'like a boy clutching a toy'.

It did feel that way but the fact I got to know so many lads I had hurled against was another really enjoyable aspect of the tour. Shefflin and I became great old friends over there and he kept asking if I was going to call it a day. I told him the Railway Cup had been my last game.

At the banquet that night, the Leinster Council organised a free bar for us, but by the time we reached the hotel most of us were well hydrated anyway. Manchester United were playing Liverpool on the box so a crowd of us gathered around to watch that before heading back for the dinner. Derek Lyng, Don Hyland from Wicklow and about six other lads came back late for the official meal so we were put sitting in a room of our own.

Seán Kelly didn't forget us, though, and came in for a chat.

'I hear this is your last year, Liam. You'd be mad to go now and you going so well,' he said.

Liam Mulvihill, the Director-General, arrived over.

'Well done, you had a great year,' he told me, 'I hear you're retiring but why don't you keep going?'

Nice words and great to hear them. It just added to the trip, as did the next morning, when I went down to the hotel lobby to meet Hoyne, as we had arranged to visit the Vatican. We missed the Pope by a few minutes; he had been out on the balcony but left just as we arrived in St. Peter's Square. It would have been great to see him but we contented ourselves with a tour of the area and bought some souvenirs for the folks at home.

When I got back home, all the talk was that I was set for a fourth All Star. Noel Skehan had told us the All Star selectors would have noticed who played well in the Railway Cup, and while I didn't believe him for a minute because he just used it as motivation for the team, I still felt I was in the shake-up.

My hopes were raised even higher when I was voted Wexford Hurler of the Year for the first time. Hughie Byrne from the Supporters Club contacted me with the news.

'We must have got 600 votes and your name was on all of them,' he said.

The brilliant Matty Forde got the Footballer of the Year award. It can be only a matter of time before Matty gets his first All Star – the man is phenomenal.

And so expectations rose. But experience taught me not to get too carried away and despite the local papers and fans launching a campaign on my behalf, I decided to keep my feet on the ground.

Mick Kinsella told me he felt I was a certainty but again I reminded him of my 1991 experience, when I really deserved an award but didn't get it. That contrasted with the season before, when, incredibly, I got my first award and didn't deserve it at all. But Mick told me after the season I'd had and the level I'd reached, they'd get it hard to ignore me.

Still, one piercing phone call from Damien Fitzhenry, the day before the All Stars were announced, dashed all hopes.

'We're only going up for the spin,' Fitzy said, referring to the Wexford players' hopes of walking up those famous steps. 'They didn't even give us one.'

Well, he didn't put it as politely as that. Around Wexford, people went nuts. Martin felt very aggrieved but at this stage I was well comfortable handling the rollercoaster ride that is hurling.

Sure it would have been nice to end my career with an award but others were more disappointed than me. John Conran called for a Wexford boycott of the ceremony, which I'm glad we didn't operate, because as I said earlier, I had the pleasure of sitting with Cormac McAnallen that evening.

The week after the All Stars, my itinerary for their trip to Arizona arrived. Brian Cody had ensured I was picked as a replacement. With such a fuss over the fact no Wexfordman had made the team, I knew there was a chance a few of us could make the trip and sure enough, I got the nod. It was a real bonus; we had another great trip and here I met lads like Eoin and Paul Kelly for the first time.

I had really enjoyed the past season. It's not often that trips to Rome and Arizona come out of the blue. During the Arizona trip, four or five reporters were trying to establish if I had made any decision about hanging up the camán but though I spoke away, I wasn't going to officially announce anything over there.

Only one man knew my plan and that was Liam Griffin. My Mam and Eithne had encouraged me to go back for another year but I knew I would be doing it for all the wrong reasons. There was no point going back to Wexford hurling just to keep your contacts in place, help your job prospects or get some free gear. Too many players had done that and it didn't work.

People started pointing out that I would make a grand little corner forward but as far as I was concerned, if I couldn't get my place on the half-back line, then it was all over.

On my return, I got a text message from Offaly's Brendan Murphy, who was with me on both trips: 'Well, Dunner, will I get Santa Claus to get me an Ashguard glove for my hand or what are you doing?'

I had to laugh out loud when I read it. But Brendan didn't have to go and buy that protective glove after all; I was definitely gone. I delayed the decision until we came back from our Wexford team holiday in San Francisco. By now I could have got a job with RTÉ's *No Frontiers* because there were more stamps on my passport in a month than many people have in a lifetime.

For the third year in a row, the Wexford hurlers voted to go on holidays without wives, partners or girlfriends, and while that may seem selfish, the fact is only three of the team were married. The decision was almost unanimous: 27 out of 28 opted for the solo run.

Dave Guiney from Rathnure wanted to bring his wife, Brenda, and in fairness, he was perfectly entitled to. But on our arrival at Dublin Airport, the members of the Players' Committee, Darragh Ryan, Adrian Fenlon, Damien Fitzhenry and I, received a letter from Dave. He took us to task for voting against taking partners along and pointed out that Brenda and he had given huge commitment to Wexford hurling over the years. Dave wasn't coming on the holiday.

The first thing I said to the lads was does this fellow think the rest of us have done shag all for Wexford over the years. We were disappointed with his attitude, and even more so when we heard Dave had gone public with his views.

It was that time of the year when the GAA columns are short of material and this story was as juicy as you would hope to get. It spread like wildfire all over the national media, and the local papers and radio stations went to town on it.

Beyond in Frisco, in a fit of exasperation, I told a few of the Rathnure boys it would take one of their own to stir things up. But they retorted that Dave originally came from Rosslare, which shows what they were thinking as well.

Jesus, at the back of it I could see where he was coming from. All of us gave huge commitment over the years and Dave had been around a long time. We knew our partners made all the sacrifices as well. No holidays, no social life. Christ, no-one knew better than Eithne, who watched me almost fall apart because of Wexford hurling.

Dave didn't have to go public on the issue. It was a squad decision. The year before, Ger Cushe declined to go to Lanzarote. Ger wouldn't go because his wife, Mag, wasn't invited, but you didn't see him in the newspapers. He just rowed in with the decision.

Anyway, on behalf of the team, I was asked when I returned to respond to Dave's comments and did so. We could have done without the whole controversy, though he probably still feels he was right to speak up.

Soon after, I phoned John Conran and told him I was finished. There were no dramatic statements or behind-the-scenes manoeuvres. John just said he would do the same thing if he were in my shoes.

After that I rang county secretary Mick Kinsella and he alerted the local media, who had always been fair to me over the years. When the local press got hold of the story, word wasn't long in spreading to the national media but nothing prepared me for the response the announcement received. It was absolutely overwhelming. The kind wishes and words of hundreds of people really helped me cope. It was a tough decision, a really complex one, when you have known little else for 16 years.

I still feel the GAA world must have been itching for news on the week in March 2004 when I retired, because it dominated newspapers for almost seven days. The lads in TV3 would hardly be renowned for their hurling coverage but even they sent cameras down, and RTÉ TV and radio did interviews as well. The whole affair blew up once more at the weekend when the Sunday papers came out and I got an even bigger farewell.

Overall, the coverage of my departure blew me away as did the response from the people of Wexford, who I like to think appreciated the effort I had put into wearing the jersey.

I got a lovely parcel from the Clare hurler Seánie McMahon, with one of his famous number-six shirts enclosed. Seánie had been the only intercounty player from outside Wexford to send me a card when I broke my leg in 1997. The man is a real class act.

But now there were so many goodwill cards I didn't know what to do with them, from the likes of the former Wexford and Dublin manager Michael O'Grady to the Laois hurler Niall Rigney. People and clubs presented me with gift tokens, crystal and vouchers.

Some of the more memorable functions included the one hosted by the Wexford Association in Carlow, where Tom Neville, Jim English and Ned Wheeler greeted me and led a standing ovation. The same thing happened at the Bunclody Dinner Dance and on each occasion, though naturally delighted, I wanted the ground to open and swallow me. On my first League game with Oulart after my intercounty retirement, the captain of Oylegate-Glenbrien made a presentation to me in front of the stands before the match. He gave me a lovely piece of crystal but afterwards, their chairman, Séamus Walsh, came into our dressing-room and apologised to me because he was after having a smashing time! Séamus had let the precious crystal fall. Fair dues to them, within a fortnight they had a replacement piece up to me, another lovely touch.

Perhaps the biggest compliment ever paid was a throwaway comment by a former Wexford goalkeeper, Pat Nolan. Pat was just chatting to Tomás and I one evening when he asserted that of all the Wexford players of the modern era, only one would have made the famous team of the 50s and 60s, and I was the man.

That meant an awful lot coming from him, because retirement

had left a big gap in my life, and such positive feedback helped me ease into life after Wexford hurling. Albert Randall, who used to make hurleys for us in 1996, presented me with a lamp carved out of ash, with two little hurls on its sides. It was and is a beautiful piece. Underneath, it has 'Liam Dunne, Oulart-The-Ballagh, 1994, 1995 & 1997' in honour of the three county titles we won. Below that it has the years I won the three All Stars inscribed, a lovely job. In return I handed Albert the last intercounty hurley I wielded and one of my last Wexford jerseys.

Albert has sticks from all sorts of past players, including legends like Billy Rackard and Mick Mackey, but he was reluctant to take mine because he said there was more hurling left in it. It wasn't as if I felt my legs were going to go. As I've admitted many a time, pace was never my big asset anyway. The harsh reality was that I couldn't face doing the training programme I had set out for myself a year earlier. To keep up with the Tommy Walshes of this world, that was what a guy my age would have had to do. And probably even more. Even the great DJ Carey went into training at Nowlan Park an hour earlier than everyone else to retain his sharpness.

In my own mind, I was full sure I could have retained my place on the Wexford team, but that wasn't sufficient reason to go back. Again, you must really want to go back, and not just because you will get your game and your free gear and your holidays.

My old friend Larry O also went soon after and even though I was up in the stands in the summer of 2004 to see Wexford, without my input, pull off the biggest hurling shock in a decade by running the Cody gang out of town (unfortunately, they snuck back in a while later), I knew I had made the right decision.

I stuck to my guns in the close season but kept ticking over in training, just in case something clicked and changed my mind. I suppose if Adrian Fenlon, Darragh Ryan or Damien Fitzhenry had arrived at my door, I just might have done a U-turn. Now the boys are always welcome at my door but this was one time when I was glad they didn't ring the bell.

My family had enjoyed all the fuss of 2003 and probably wanted more but I had set out to prove a point and achieved the three aims I set: Honour; Respect; Wexford Hurler of the Year. The only way was down. One bad belt or one roasting and I was back to square one all over again.

In the heel of the hunt, I felt that in some way I had restored my reputation and my name. And maybe now when people spoke of Liam Dunne, 'Dirty little fucker' might not be the first words out of their mouths. The critics might even remember I played fairly well in my last year, almost as good as I had ever done. Maybe they would say: 'Hardy little bastard but he was a good hurler.' That would be more like it.

I also got to move back home in 2003. No wonder I look back on the year with affection and real peace of mind. There is no doubt the switch had a settling effect on me. In five years we had lived in five different houses but I always knew I wanted to go back home to Kyle Cross, and when my mother moved out and into a house beside Tomás, I moved back in. We had just built a house in Kilnamanagh but when the opportunity to move home came up, I couldn't ignore it. To be frank, I always felt that if the old homestead were sold to someone else I would never be able to pass by and would regret it for the rest of my life.

Things had come together nicely. Closure at last.

Win together, lose together, play together, stay together.
Debra Mancuso

– CHAPTER EIGHTEEN –
The hurler on the ditch

Expectations were hardly ever lower in Wexford than in 2004 but typically we delivered a Leinster title out of the blue. During the League, the writing was on the wall. Players left the panel quicker than the sun deserted our summer and we got some woeful drubbings in the League. We had to face Kilkenny in the Leinster Championship on June 13 and that would be the beginning and end of the team, many felt.

When Darren Stamp decided he didn't want any more, Robbie Codd, Anthony O'Leary and Barry Goff all jumped ship as well. And with Larry O and myself out of the equation, it didn't look great for the team.

We seemed to fall lower and lower during the early part of the season. Cork destroyed us under lights at Páirc Uí Rinn at the end of February. Tipperary gave us another hiding, 4-18 to 1-13. Kilkenny hammered us as well.

John Conran came under huge pressure and all sorts of rumours and stories hit the national press, having been leaked from Wexford. Many of them were untrue but there was some substance at the back of it. The harsh reality is that some of the players were unhappy with the manager and wanted a change.

Behind the scenes, people worked frantically to keep him in the job because they were afraid of who might take over and I bet they are glad now they didn't decide to act on that impulse because 'Wexford:

Leinster Champions 2004' has a nice ring to it.

At the end of the League, the popular theory was that the team had overtrained, but I think we were just looking for excuses, and after about six weeks of being slated, the lads finally decided enough was enough. After a lock-in meeting one night, they all rowed in together.

Jim Kilty, the athletics coach and former Tipperary trainer who specialises in what is now known as SAQ – speed, agility and quickness – started to spread his gospel, and John Conran let his defence go to work on tactics for the Kilkenny match.

Paul Carley decided he had suffered a pain in his ass long enough being sub keeper to Fitzy and so made the wing-forward slot his own. The Jacob brothers picked up their form. Eoin Quigley, who had joined the panel out of nowhere after leaving a soccer career at Bohemians in Dublin, looked the part.

No-one gave us a hope in hell of beating Kilkenny in the Leinster semi-final and they were right. Why should they? In the eyes of most people, Wexford were on the way out. But they hadn't bargained for the new leaders who emerged in the team when Larry O and I left.

The Friday before the Kilkenny match, I rang five players: Adrian Fenlon, Darragh Ryan, Declan Ruth, Damien Fitzhenry and Rory McCarthy. Each one told me we would win and I felt I had no choice but to believe them. They told me the preparation had been good. There were no overblown expectations but they had a game-plan and were sticking to it.

In the past few years, Kilkenny have dominated the half-back department and players like Peter Barry, JJ Delaney and now Tommy Walsh have routinely chewed up and spit out opposing forwards for fun. This time, Wexford decided to avoid these key players as much as possible.

Fitzy played short puck-outs to a good stick man like Rory Mac and what balls arrived in the half-forward line were low into a guy who had made a crossfield run, hungrily looking for it.

On my way into Croke Park, I was swallowed up by Wexford

supporters wanting to ask about my retirement. But there was no danger of getting lost in the crowd, because only 27,000 turned up for the game. Not even our own supporters believed and that itself was rare. And yet by half-time, the Cats were only a point ahead, 0-11 to 0-10, and the onlookers in purple and gold knew we were in with a shout.

I didn't find it too hard to look on at first but it was torture as the game reached a dramatic conclusion. With time up, we were two points down and when Adrian Fenlon cut a brilliant sideline into Peter Barry's hands, I groaned with despair, thinking we had blown our chance.

Suddenly, Mick Jacob hooked him, turned around and goaled in the same breath and you just can't defend against play like that. We won the game in the last second, 2-15 to 1-16.

In the stand, I went nuts. Billy looked at me as though I had two heads but it was one of the greatest feelings I ever experienced. Charging onto the field, I jumped on any of the lads I could find and shared a few hugs with some old team-mates.

A despondent looking Brian Cody walked into the tunnel and I went over to him and said: 'Brian, you can't begrudge us this.' He looked back at me and simply replied: 'Well done, well done.'

Eddie Brennan came over and shook hands, but in the Wexford dressing-room I was pleasantly shocked to hear Declan Ruth and Darragh Ryan talking about how this win would be no use unless the team won the Leinster final. I really admired that attitude. My lot would have gone haywire, but this is a different Wexford team than in the past. We failed to build on our 1996 success but maybe this time it will be different; there are five pioneers on this present side and everyone else eats, drinks and sleeps hurling. Now is the time to bring the younger lads on, when we have inspirational players like Ruth, Fenlon, McCarthy, Ryan and Fitzhenry still involved.

We played Offaly in the Leinster final on July 4 but I dreaded that as well because I felt they were waiting in the long grass for us. We had done the hard work knocking Kilkenny out and it was nicely teed up for them to throw us out now and leave us with egg on our face.

Maybe it was the fact I had soldiered with the team for the three years before that and each time we had lost Leinster finals that I was kind of glad to be in the stands again for that match. Of course I have to admit there was a pang of sadness when the lads came out onto the field for the warm-up but that didn't last too long because Offaly hopped out onto Croke Park like toned sprinters and played like demons for the first 15 minutes.

Folding my arms and looking on as they dogged us in the opening quarter, I just sat back and prayed.

'That pitch is not made for old lads anymore,' I thought.

And as Eithne, Billy, Aoife and I looked on as a family, I knew this was the way it had to be from now on.

At half-time, I was asked by RTÉ to go down to the sideline and do an interview with Jim Carney. I offered an honest view of Wexford's display, pointing out that only for four great saves from Damien Fitzhenry we were history.

The second half was just as edgy, and it wasn't until the last few moments that we pulled away. A great goal from Paul Carley and two late points from Rory Jacob made it 2-12 to 1-11. We were through to the All-Ireland semi-final.

It was bedlam after that. I grabbed Billy. To go into the dressing-room, shake the lads' hands and share the joy after that game meant a lot to me. I got a thump on the back and a hug from the happiest man in Croke Park, John Conran.

'It's an awful pity you weren't with us,' he smiled.

'Jesus, John, I was with ye,' I said.

Only a liar would say he wouldn't have loved to be out there. Of course I would, but that wasn't the case when we got hammered in the League by the likes of Cork, Tipperary and Kilkenny. You can't have it both ways.

I mean, I wasn't sad I had retired when in the semi-final we got walloped by Cork, 1-27 to 0-12. Jesus, Cork were good but who could have seen that one coming?

Doing an interview with RTÉ at the break, I could see the lads' heads were down as they trooped off the field 11 points in arrears. Again, only for Fitzy it would have been several times worse.

I would think after that drubbing a couple of the lads are wondering if they can go on any longer and it goes back to what I said; the Leinster title win was great to get but it only papered over the cracks. We needed guys steaming through the ranks to replace the fellows who left and give the squad strength in depth, but Cork had a much stronger bench than we had and they were on fire. It was disappointing for us to lose like that. I privately thought we had a great chance of winning and felt we could take Kilkenny in the final. How wrong was I?

If some of the lads do quit, then their wishes should be respected. I had my time, made my mistakes and moved on. I did my best for the cause of Wexford but no-one is irreplaceable. Generations evolve and now we have Metal Mickey and Razor Rory Jacob and the boys leading the charge, waiting to take over from Adrian Fenlon and company as the new leaders.

That's the way it should be. Michael is getting his chance now. He hurled with a bit of mettle this year and apart from the Cork game, his brother was razor sharp in the corner.

I'm still waiting for my clubmate Keith Rossiter to really get over his injuries and become the player I know he can be. Maybe Darren Stamp will also come back next year and show us what a man he is as well.

Just as Martin Storey and Tom Dempsey once made their names in Croke Park, we had a young lad, Eoin Quigley, coming in and hitting 0-3 in a Leinster final out of the blue. Eoin didn't get going against Cork either but it was his first season and Ronan Curran was All Star material.

John O'Connor had a bad day at the office against the Rebels too. Few outside the county even knew who he was before the provincial final, but the Rathnure man is now captain of the side and will gain in confidence.

We're still waiting to get the best out of Paul Codd. He can do it if he wants to do it, when he wants to do it. But that's not good enough; we need him all the time. It's as simple as that. He is crucial to Wexford.

And if this time we learn our lessons from the success and failure of the 2004 season, which we didn't from the 1996 success, and get the production line at underage level going, we can do even better.

The harsh reality, though, is that juvenile structures in Wexford are a shambles. There are too many people with too many private agendas and not all of them about trying to get Wexford hurling back to where it should be. And if this situation persists we're in big trouble regardless of the relative successes of 2004.

Take the 2004 minors for example. We were beaten in the provincial semi-final by Dublin and it's common knowledge around the county that some of the backroom team weren't even on speaking terms. That would be funny if it weren't so tragic, and to make it worse you still have clubs trying to get the sons and nephews of cronies on the team. It has happened with all county teams over the years and until we can get shot of it and play the best players we will struggle.

I witnessed these backroom shenanigans so many times from my progression from underage to senior. Only I had the opposite experience – lads in my club were pushing for me not to be played. But it's a silly situation. Our 2004 minors had to bring in Tom Dempsey and George O'Connor to help them, and while both did a job, Dublin beat us and Kilkenny hammered them, which is worrying to say the least.

It's time for the Kilkenny dominance to be stopped. I respect them for what they've achieved, but it's time for the rest of us to stand up now. Two years ago, they lost one Leinster minor final in 10 years and had a crisis meeting. We could have one of them every week in Wexford and it still wouldn't make a difference.

Liam Griffin is finally getting somewhere, though. It was heartening to see so many people from different clubs at the recent launch of the development squads. These squads will be an enormous help because they will keep the groups together the whole time. Players should have thundered through since we won the All-Ireland title but they didn't.

I'm not saying we have a divine right to win the All-Ireland every year, and I don't set a whole lot of store by tradition. But the brutal reality is that we haven't moved forward since 96 and I would go as far as saying we have actually gone backward; the structures have weakened and some of those running our underage teams should be ashamed of themselves.

It's sad and sickening to see the direction we have gone and in case you think I'm talking sentimental shite just for the sake of it, here are the facts. Just say we don't win another All-Ireland title by the time 2008 comes around, and that is quite likely. That will mean Wexford have won the Liam MacCarthy Cup just once in 40 years. You would see a better strike rate with Emile Heskey in front of goal. If that statistic comes to pass, it's a bloody serious problem in anyone's language.

We are in deep trouble. I mean, it took us 19 years to end the Leinster final hoodoo and 28 years to end the All-Ireland drought and even though we brought success to the county, nothing has been done since to ensure the next generation get a chance to emulate us.

The last time we won a Leinster minor title was in 1985 and although we won under-21 provincial titles in 86 and 87, it was 10 years before we did the trick again in 96 and 97. That's inconsistency. And while I was lucky enough to be there on that team that ended the famine, it gives me no great pleasure to sit back and watch another start all over again.

Tradition is gone out the window in Wexford hurling. If we keep harping back to the men of the 50s and 60s, we are only fooling ourselves. We have not moved on and I'm going to put my money where my mouth is and sink my teeth into this deficiency that is killing hurling in the county.

I want to put a stop to all the talk and get the right personnel in place to bring future hurlers along. Just look at Mick Kinsella, one of the best hurling coaches in the county, who is stuck behind a desk doing administration work when he is most needed out on the field. The likes of Jim English and Ned Wheeler put Wexford hurling at a certain level and really it hasn't moved on a whole lot.

To progress, we have to change the framework of the county senior hurling Championship, which at the time of writing is farcical. A team could be out in the first round of the Championship at the end of May and might not play again for seven weeks. There are no midweek games of any value and so players, finding they are not getting enough action, have turned to rugby or soccer. Can you blame them? At least they get a chance to raise a bit of sweat.

I have noticed how bad the situation is only since I retired from the county scene. Unless a guy is actually on the first 15 for Wexford, he has no hope of getting a game. The club Championship is put on hold until the county team are well into their campaign, and even if you are a sub on that county side you cannot get a game for your club. The county board won't allow you to play. So the lads at club level are stuck with 12 or 13 senior players at training while others go off and train with the county minor, under-21, intermediate or senior teams.

I know damn well we all have to get along and I'm only too well aware how important the county scene is to everyone, but we are only shooting ourselves in the foot at grassroots level. Lads only have Mickey Mouse games to contend with during the summer, when they should be playing serious Championship affairs.

But there are more problems. Some are now starting to use the emergence of the county footballers as an excuse for the lack of progress we are making on the hurling fields. And it's just stupid to blame them. The reality is that players have always tried to get along by playing both codes. If you go back through the early years of the GAA, you will find that Wexford were always very strong at football, people forget we were the first county to do the football four-in-a-row, from 1915 to 1918. There are still certain people in the county that would have little interest in hurling and fair play to them, they are looking after their own patch.

But the finger is pointed in their direction and that's just a load of baloney. And when you have a lad like Matty Forde setting the world alight and pushing for an All Star, well I think everyone should row in behind him and support the footballers as well.

There is plenty of room for two successful intercounty codes in Wexford. We are surely not so flush with success in hurling that we have to begrudge the footballers their days in the sun.

Why not consider midweek games for both county League and Championship? And if a county under-21 player does not have a game with Wexford for two weeks let him play for his club.

I would also recommend we cut the number of senior hurling teams in the county from 16 average sides to 12 decent outfits. Give the Wexford League a makeover. The board are running this competition for the sake of it and if I was the sponsor I would be upset – they put little or no effort into it.

And now to something more uplifting. For the record, here are the best 15 Wexford players I have hurled with:

Damien Fitzhenry in goal; he was one of the greatest of them all.

The full-back line has to be Niall McDonald, Ger Cushe and John O'Connor. McDonald was one of the most underrated hurlers in the county.

My half-back line is Seán Flood, Darragh Ryan, whose father, Tossie, always argued he was better there than at full-back, and Larry O'Gorman on the other wing.

I include my brother Tomás at number eight and for once in Wexford that's not a case of jobs for the family. And partnering him is John Conran.

My half-forward line is Martin Storey, Georgie O'Connor and Adrian Fenlon. Martin I would pick at number 10. Georgie would be my centre-forward and Adrian would line out at number 12.

Tom Dempsey has to be in the corner. Billy Byrne is a shoo-in at full forward. And for his sheer goalscoring opportunism, I put Rory

McCarthy in the other corner.

The likes of David 'Doc' O'Connor, Colm Kehoe and Larry Murphy will be justifiably disappointed, but these are the guys I would like beside me if I were in the trenches tomorrow.

As for the future, I feel now is the time that Griffin must call most of his 1996 troops together to decide what is the best way forward for Wexford. That is what happened in Kilkenny; they called anyone who won an All-Ireland with the county back to help out at underage level. And if you can't beat them, join them. We are a proud county but in this instance there is no shame in learning from Kilkenny.

Georgie and Tom were involved with the county minors in 2004. Storey is heavily involved with Oulart-The-Ballagh. But you also need the likes of Billy Byrne and Ger Cushe coming back into the scene some time soon.

This is the best way forward. Learn from Kilkenny. We were all great men when we won the All-Ireland but you have your time as a player and if you can put something back into it as a coach it's all the better. As a group we must try to come up with different ideas on how to progress, but hurling is a simple game and the fault is that we are inclined to make it complicated.

Maybe we are also suffering from the changes in Irish society, like the drinking culture and the counterattractions of other social activities that leave people with less time for sport and fitness.

Initially, I was opposed to the 'back door' but how wrong I was. We really need it now for the game to survive. You have to change with the times and Croke Park officials have to do the same. And if we are to save the game, it's time for an open draw.

If you came from rural Ireland in the past, you played either hurling or Gaelic football. Now there's soccer, rugby, basketball, squash, golf, cars, music, television, women, men, whatever turns you on, and the reality is that what happened 15 years ago will not do.

Jesus, the GAA won't even entertain a debate on Rule 42 or the potential opening of Croke Park to either soccer or rugby. They are almost €100 million in debt and still won't even discuss the matter. It's no wonder tickets cost €35 for a replay like the Clare and Kilkenny game in Thurles in the summer of 2004.

I think a debate will happen sooner or later but the fact they didn't even table a discussion of the affair was the biggest PR disaster in the history of the Association. And believe me, I'm an expert in PR disasters.

There was no great wringing of hands when we played the Railway Cup final on a rugby pitch in Rome, and yet they won't entertain the prospect of gaining a few million euro from the rent of the ground to the Government, FAI or IRFU.

As for the game in general, well I look at the likes of Laois and just don't know what can be done to save them. I don't know what's going to happen to them. During all our battles, we rarely used to beat them by more than three or four points and now they're hurling at a tempo slower than you would see in many a third-tier county. Their manager, Paudie Butler, knows his hurling and is doing all he can, but I just think they need to focus on the age groups from eight to 16, try and get a few good minors coming through at the one time and take it from there.

Just look at what happened their footballers when they won a couple of minor All-Irelands in the late 90s. It took them a while to come through but they are getting there.

It was the same with the Westmeath football team. All of a sudden the team wins a Leinster title in 2004 after threatening for the past four years.

The Laois and Wexford hurlers need to start winning minor titles, bring them to under-21 straightaway and then see how they do at the top. But they are not getting much support because the ruling classes in the GAA are ignoring hurling. You can even see it with small things like TV coverage; you have football games on TV most of the time. Yet there was huge scope with this year's hurling qualifier draw to televise more games and they failed to do so.

The Sunday Game is dominated by football and even if there is more unpredictability in that code, they are not giving hurling a sufficient profile at all; I would say the show is 70 percent football.

I suppose the GAA can do a lot more with the footballers, who at least go off to Australia and play in a high-profile international series, while the hurlers are stuck with a domestic Championship that only three or four teams can really win at present.

County boards who choose not to promote the game and focus on Gaelic football instead, and there are many, should also be called to heel. Maybe the GAA could decrease grant allocation and other funding until boards begin serious development programmes.

And county boards who forbid hurlers to play both codes should be penalised, because that is a personal decision and no player should be deprived of the chance to wear a county jersey.

Seeing Laois play hurling like Longford is not good for anyone. We need them motoring through trying to carve out a breakthrough in the Leinster Championship, but they simply won't get there playing at walking speed.

The same applies to Wexford. Just because we won a provincial title this year doesn't mean we can take the foot off the pedal. We have only realised in the past few years how bad we were when Kilkenny hammered us by playing at 100 miles an hour. After those defeats we at least went into the qualifiers knowing we had to up the pace to get anywhere.

With the safety net taken away from us and a do-or-die qualifier ahead, the mantra was always speed, speed and more speed. Speed is why Kilkenny are that bit ahead all the time. They consistently use it – just look at how they demolished Galway in the 2004 Championship.

But other counties have failed to get to that level and I suppose I shouldn't single out Laois because others are more culpable and, for example, I just don't know for the life of me what goes on in Galway either. Take a look at the hurlers they've had over the years and ask how in the name of God they've won so little. Even the team of 1987 and 1988 should have won more than the two All-Irelands they managed. They won the 2004 National League and instead of growing in confidence went on to get murdered by Kilkenny in the Qualifiers with players like Eugene Cloonan, Damien Hayes, Alan Kerins and Kevin Broderick.

Of course, they should have taken their move into the Leinster Championship. It would have brightened up our competition and at the same time given them a much better chance in the All-Ireland series.

There is so much to do and so little time but I intend to do more than just bellyache about it. Now that I've stopped playing, I want to earn my spurs as a coach and put something back in.

It's not just hurling that's in crisis. The Association has many problems waiting to explode. When you see the Circuit Court and High Court cropping up in the GAA pages of our newspapers, you know there's something seriously wrong.

Take the Gerry Quinn and Henry Shefflin incident in July 2004. I was no angel over the years, but I felt that Gerry had to go for that offence and yet he wasn't even booked. Pat Horan, the referee, didn't see the incident so nothing happened.

The same Pat is an amazing character. He didn't see the incident between Brian O'Meara and me in 2001 and yet he sent the two of us off.

When I see the 'fouls' I got red cards for and compare them with incidents that have gone unpunished since, my transgressions look petty. Look again at the video of the 2004 game between Tipp and Cork. There was a brawl on the sideline and hurls driven into ribs and Pat Horan was there again, and again nothing happened. The inconsistency is crazy and that is leading us to court cases.

When Brian O'Meara and I were banned a few years back we could have produced a watertight defence by showing videotapes of our little bout of handbags and the following day's mayhem between

Kilkenny and Galway and comparing the two, but of course that didn't happen.

This is going to be a serious obstacle for the GAA. If players are going to miss big games, they will see an opportunity to go to court. And in Quinn's case, if he is 'done' by video evidence, then he is entitled to go to court to fight the action. After all, he wasn't even booked in the match.

The whole area is a minefield. If a guy who isn't booked or sent off gets caught on video evidence and misses a big game, the Four Goldmines is going to be his next port of call.

I picked my all-time great Wexford hurling team and would like to do the same for those I played against over my 16 years. I think picking a Team of the Millennium or a Team of the Century is a waste of time. How can you possibly make worthwhile judgements over that length of time? Instead, I'm going for men I played against.

Offaly's Jim Troy was the best keeper I ever faced.

Willie O'Connor broke my heart several times at corner-back; Brian Lohan was the best full-back in that era; and Martin Hanamy was just as good in the other corner.

Brian Whelahan is a shoo-in on the half-back line; Seánie McMahon was the greatest centre-back in my time; and Niall Rigney from Laois takes the other half-back role.

My midfield pairing is Teddy McCarthy and Ciarán Carey. Johnny Dooley, John Power and Joe Cooney form my star-studded half-forward line.

I opt for Henry Shefflin at corner-forward; Declan Ryan is an automatic choice at full-forward; and DJ has to go in at number 15.

That's a team I would love to manage and would love to pit them against anyone. There is not a position I would change.

I wish hurling had as many genuine superstars on the way through the ranks but I suspect that's not the case. And there are many other problems facing the GAA apart from the decline of hurling.

Apart from on-the-field problems, they also have a problem with the field of dreams. They need to rip up that Croke Park pitch as quickly as possible. After sinking €2.5 million into it, they produce the worst playing surface you will ever see. It's an abomination. You can't stand up on it. It's terrible watching lads slipping and sliding chasing after the ball and when you have guys trying to twist and turn on such a surface there are going to be huge problems with knees and ankles. What genius thought artificial grass was going to work?

They tried for 30 years to promote an artificial hurley and had to go back to ash. The sooner the Croke Park brass go back to grass, or get put out to grass, the better. Thurles is the best pitch in Ireland by far and they should try to replicate that. Players deserve the best and a good pitch is the least they could ask for. Their welfare should be the number-one item on the agenda.

As for pay for play, I don't expect players will go professional, but there are already a number who are doing well out of their image and reputation and getting by without having to do full-time day jobs. Fair play to them. I think company endorsements and private deals are the way forward. For the €1,500 involved, the Paddy Power deal with Paul Codd unsettled the Wexford team in 2003, but if the business is conducted properly, then that's fine.

If I was starting out again, I would go straight to DJ Carey and chat with him on this issue. He is the one player who has used his image to the maximum. When a guy has nine All Stars in the bag he would be foolish not to.

I can see DJ going into that end of looking after players when he retires. He would be an ideal agent for players, someone they could trust, a man who has done it all.

Tom Dempsey would be my choice in Wexford. He has the intelligence, diplomacy, personality and contacts to broker deals to look after players. It's already happening. Hurlers and footballers pull up with their names on cars, and while not all of them want to turn professional, they want to get money out of it. The perks are few and far between for players; even the hurlers were stopped going to the US to play a year or two back.

The rugby player Gordon Darcy got a few quid for endorsing Wexford Creamery this year. Some of us have worn their jersey for 14 years but if we individually endorsed their products there would be a big fuss over it and we probably would be discouraged for fear of upsetting the applecart.

In this context, the GPA is a disaster. Certain players have done well out of it. The top five, the likes of DJ, Henry Shefflin, Jason Sherlock, Peter Canavan and Kieran McGeeney.

Wexford played their third All-Ireland semi-final in four years this season and the GPA has not even organised a boot deal for any of our players. When we joined the association we were supposed to get a fleece top and a mobile phone from the Carphone Warehouse. Rod and Dave Guiney went up to collect them and the warehouse was closed.

I am a member of the GPA but think it is fading big time. It didn't help that the GAA had their own players' union, headed by Jarlath Burns, two years ago. You need one voice, an official one, but the GAA won't merge with the GPA. They wouldn't like the players dictating on any policy matters.

The most annoying thing for players is that it's common knowledge that big-name managers and even managers at local level are getting well paid under the counter for their efforts.

Lots of people can manage a club team and get a good few quid for it. In fact, the only way you won't get a few bob is if you train your local team, because insiders generally get nothing.

But some of the amounts big-name managers receive are just crazy. If there are thousands of euro going to club managers, you can imagine what the high-profile county managers are pulling in. That's something the GAA has shied away from.

Another is of course the above-mentioned Rule 42. I would totally open up Croke Park. Maybe it would be hard to listen to *God*

Save the Queen there, but surely you could come to some arrangement. Why would you deprive the likes of Brian O'Driscoll and Gordon Darcy the chance to play in the finest stadium in the land?

As with everything in the GAA, we will be a long time waiting for an answer.

Yes, there were times, I'm sure you knew
When I bit off more than I could chew;
But through it all, when there was doubt,
I ate it up and spit it out.
I faced it all and I stood tall;
And did it my way.

Frank Sinatra

— CHAPTER NINETEEN —
Passing the camán

It still feels strange to take my wife and children to Croke Park and watch Wexford play. Part of me is still on that team bus listening to Tom Dempsey and Larry O having the craic, or putting the headphones on and letting the music take my mind away.

Those tapes Griffin gave us, *Search for a Hero* and *Simply the Best*, did the job. The lyrics may have been simple and straightforward but they were honest and helped us focus.

These days I listen to *Sunday Sport* on Radio One on the way to Dublin and keep an eye in the mirror to check that the youngsters are okay in the back seat. And now I have Billy blowing those bloody hooters in my ear. Mind you, I took it off him and blew it myself when we won the Leinster final this year. He's the one now. Only a child, but he can hit the ball just as good off his left as he can off the right and for a child seven years of age, well let's just say the signs are good.

I started bringing him into the Wexford dressing-room in 2001 when I felt he was old enough to realise what was going on around him, and somehow we always managed to get to him after games. He would hop out over the wire and walk into the dressing-room to share some minerals and biscuits with the lads.

At the beginning, he would shy behind me and you couldn't get a word out of him. When I was suspended for the Clare game, I brought him into the dressing-room before the game and that was a major mistake; he was afraid of his life at the noise, and I said I would never do it again. But he persisted and progressed to sitting on Declan Ruth's knee while I was drug-tested after the Offaly game in 2003. Now, you can't stop him.

I was sitting in the players' lounge hours after we won the Leinster final and, realising I hadn't seen him in a while, went searching. I found Rory McCarthy and himself sitting back on a couch, chatting away like old buddies.

'He's telling me some stories about you,' Rory Mac laughed.

It was grand for Billy to see me playing at Croke Park for the couple of years although he probably saw the worst times. He loves watching hurling videos too. When we moved into our new house we never brought them down from the attic because Eithne was sick to the teeth of watching them. She was right – there were a few I wouldn't want to see as well. But Billy loves them all.

He's hurling with the six-to-10-year-olds at the moment and is handy enough but if I let him go up through the ranks too quick, he could get a bad belt and be finished with the game.

As for his club loyalties, there was a bit of confusion in the early days, through no fault of his own. If Eithne and I had been away for a few days, he could come home from the Sinnott house with a Buffers Alley jersey, a terrible-looking geansaí altogether. That was soon nipped in the bud, I can promise you.

There are times he just leaves me in stitches. Like last Christmas, when the Sinnotts brought him the present he wanted, a set of goalposts, and we started taking shots on one another. He was pretending to be Rory Jacob, Roy Keane and Setanta Ó hAilpín because he got a sliotar, a football and an Aussie Rules ball as well.

I took a fairly hard shot and he never even saw the ball go by him, but, quick as a flash, he turned around and roared: 'Jesus Christ, Daddy!

I'm only a kid!' He went to fetch the ball but I was gone into the house in howls of laughter.

Aoife has the same effect on us. She's five now and it's gas watching her grow up. She adapted a lot quicker to being an Oulart girl than Billy did to being an Oulart boy and is starting to get stuck in on the camogie end of things now, just like her mother.

I will never forget the day Aoife hugged me after I was sent off in the 2001 All-Ireland semi-final. She is a sweet child and I don't think she can yet believe her Dad is coming in from work and not flying straight back out the door with a gear-bag every night of the week.

She will soon have me around the house most of the time. In the next year or two, I will hang up my boots for Oulart. For some reason, I feel the 2006 season will be the final chapter in Liam Dunne's hurling career.

I look at Martin Storey, who at 40 is still as fit as a fiddle and loves the game. I see him training like a demon for Oulart and still making the senior team. I don't think I'll still be playing for the club when I'm that age and I'm near enough to it now. Maybe it will be hard for me to retire when the day comes; maybe I will want to hang on a bit more. But the feeling right now is just one more year.

As I write this, I'm still adjusting to intercounty retirement. I've had a few offers to go coaching here and there but I'm quite content to help look after the Oulart juniors and seniors. In the future, I would love to help out with the underage structure in Wexford and maybe take charge of the minor team.

Will I ever manage the Wexford senior team? To be honest, I don't know. It's the road I want to go down but you have to take these things step by step.

It's the end of 2004 now. Another year has flown by and instead of getting ready for another gruelling pre-season training campaign, I'm quite happy to look out the window at Billy and Aoife playing together.

Breda Jacob was my first teacher and she was Billy's as well. It's funny how things go. Now Billy wants to get Rory Jacob's name and number on the back of my old jersey. He's already looking for new heroes.

The days when I went to matches in Dublin with my Mam and Dad don't seem that long ago but my time has come and gone. While Oulart and Wexford will always be a huge part of my life, I have a new home and a family to look after.

It's just a pity the old man never got to see the house. It's a fine job: a dormer bungalow that Eithne and I put our own stamp on.

Shortly after Christmas 2003, we found out he was dying of leukaemia and for a while my mind was far away from hurling. My father was in hospital in Southampton all during the summer of 2004 and received bone-marrow treatment. But we knew it would make no difference so the brothers and sisters went over to see him.

It took a while for me to go over and when I did, it wasn't exactly a moment I was looking forward to. Dad asked about retirement and then asked about the house at Kyle Cross, enquiring what it was like and looking for a description. I couldn't really describe it to him; I just said it was a nice dormer bungalow and it was different. I felt like joking: 'Yeah, and I finished it, not like the way you left it.' A few years back, I had told him of my intention to buy and renovate it and had made the same crack about actually finishing the job, so this time I just left it alone.

He asked me about the 2004 Wexford team but though the boys had reached the Leinster final at this stage, my father was dying and I knew that once I walked out the door I would never see him again, so hurling was way down my agenda.

My mind was all over the place, angry with him for going away and yet at the end of the day knowing he was my father. I know Dad had done his own thing and that was his decision and so I tried just to chat away. We spoke of different things but inevitably it returned to hurling again and I told him I intended going into the hurley-making business. He recalled how he used to make and splice them for me when I was a small child.

When I got up to go, I shook hands with him.

'I was always a proud man at Croke Park,' I told him,

And he just looked at me and replied: 'Yeah, the spliced hurls got to Croke Park.'

'They'll be there again,' I said and left the hospital.

And that was it. I came back home glad I had seen him.

He passed away in England on July 23 2004 at 71 years of age but, thank God, his body came back to Oulart, after such a long time away. When news of his death came, we didn't know if he was staying in England or coming home to be buried. The good thing was that my eldest brother, Kieran, had a foot in both camps – he had stayed in contact with Dad through the years – and he made sure things were right from Mam's point of view before looking after the details.

The crowds that turned out on Friday and Saturday were overwhelming. And our parish priest, Fr Jordan, handled the funeral, and the whole weekend, with great sensitivity, knowing it was a complex situation.

When Dad left home we found it hard to deal with and at the same time we all got on with our own lives. But Mam was left there to cope and I think she coped brilliantly. And it had been difficult all through the years when people were afraid to mention my father in case they would overstep the mark.

Years ago, Dad had remarked the number of Buffers Alley people that turned up to my grandmother's funeral and it was funny that they also came in their droves to Dad's funeral. We and the Buffers Alley crowd had half-killed each other over the years and it usually took a wedding or a funeral to get us together. But when all is said and done they are decent people. Tony Doran probably got the biggest reception from us; I think I shook his hand three or four times.

With his coming home, Dad was at peace and so were we. The

locals had found it difficult over the years but the fact of bringing him back and having so many turn up at his funeral, it was a bit of honour and respect restored to him in the end.

There was a huge crowd; he had 28 grandchildren alone; and I could even smile at the sight of a Buffers Alley hurl, something that under different circumstances would get my dander up big-time, being brought up to the altar as one of the symbols of his life.

All the older guys who had started the Oulart club wore jerseys over their shoulders as a mark of respect, and for the removal, the current players formed a guard of honour. My brothers played their tin whistles at the altar; Dad loved traditional Irish music and the boys played their hearts out.

We got great comfort, my mother and sisters especially, that he came home. It was a chapter that was finally closed. Dad would have been shocked and humbled at the numbers who turned up in his memory. And under the circumstances, it was a weekend that went very well.

A couple of days after the funeral, I looked out the back garden and saw Billy getting ready for the All-Ireland semi-final with Cork. He was buzzing around with his mop of blond hair shouting 'Razor Rory hits the ball to the back of the net!' and dreaming a million different dreams, all of them played out at Croke Park.

Maybe Billy will wear the Purple and Gold some day. If he doesn't, other young lads will. They can draw confidence and inspiration from the memory of the days the county beat Kilkenny and Offaly to win the 2004 Leinster final, just as new heroes emerged when our 1996 team did the job.

Life passes by all too easily. It's sometimes hard to believe I'm finished my intercounty career after 16 frustrating and unpredictable but downright brilliant years.

But the wheel keeps turning for Wexford hurling. I hope I gave it a right good spin.

I like to think I did.

LIAM DUNNE'S ROLL OF HONOUR

Played 126 competitive games for Wexford.

1 All-Ireland SHC 1996

2 Leinster SHC 1996 and 1997

3 All Stars, 1990, 1993 and 1996

2 Railway Cups, 1993 and 2003

6 Walsh Cups

2 Leinster Under 21 HC medals 1986 and 1987

Wexford Sportstar of the Year 1997

Wexford Hurler of the Year 2003

The *Star* newspaper/Waterford Crystal Hurler of the Year 1997

Shinty Under 21 International 1986 and 1987 and senior 1993

4 Wexford SHC medals

(captained Oulart-the-Ballagh 2004 team to success).